D0121562

The Oratory School
* 0 0 0 0 9 7 1 9 *

Crossing the Shadow Line

Crossing the Shadow Line

Travels in South-East Asia

Andrew Eames

HODDER AND STOUGHTON
LONDON SYDNEY AUCKLAND TORONTO

British Library Cataloguing in Publication Data
Eames, Andrew
Crossing the Shadow Line : travels in
south-east Asia.
1. Asia, Southeastern—Description and
travel
I. Title
915.9'0453 DS522.6

ISBN 0 340 39862 0

 Printed in Great Britain for Hodder and Stoughton Limited, Mill Road, Dunton Green, Sevenoaks, Kent by St Edmundsbury Press Ltd, Bury St Edmunds, Suffolk. Typeset by Hewer Text Composition Services, Edinburgh.

Hodder and Stoughton Editorial Office: 47 Bedford Square, London WC1B 3DP.

For Oliver and Soh Chin

The sole cause of man's unhappiness is that he does not know how to stay quietly in his own room.

Blaise Pascal, *Pensées*

Travel broadens the mind.

Anon

Everybody in the world is a little mad.

Joseph Conrad, *The Shadow Line*

Contents

Maps

Crossing the Shadow Line

1 *Bangkok*

Two whistles meant forwards, one whistle meant backwards, and a long sustained blast meant hold it right there.

The conductor on the stern blew the last with a note of urgency, and up in the bows of the 60-foot launch the driver's eyes flickered up into his mirror. The stern of the Chao Phya Express thumped into the rickety piling of the last of its stops in the north of the city. A pity, I thought, that an otherwise impeccable performance from jetty to jetty along the length of the river should be spoilt by an ungraceful bump at the last moment.

The conductor went ashore with the stern painter, and the queue of saffron-robed novices followed him. As the last passenger off I tried to match their dignity, but the driver was impatient to be away and the stern was already moving: I had to make a last-minute and ungainly jump on to the untidy planking.

Ashore, I took my bearings. The vista of the city had slowly unfurled throughout the journey upriver, with the arrogant red and gold roofs of the temples standing high above the dirty greys of the rest. Downstream, clanking old rust-buckets forged up through the current, but here empty barges stood high out of the water showing their bellies to the sun, crew and children sheltering under tarpaulins on the stern. In the murky river water that slopped around the jetty two girls in sarongs washed themselves and each other, and giggled at the foreigner. It was hard not to stand and stare.

I tore myself away and headed inland, aiming for the point where yet another arched temple roof curved above the corrugated iron.

But the streets were narrow, and the roofs of the houses almost met overhead. Within minutes I had lost sight of my target. The cool rush of air of the river-boat ride was forgotten, and my feet began to slide around on that already familiar slick of sweat and dust between foot and thong. I tried tailing the saffron robes of the novices, hoping that they might be going my way, but once they became aware that I was following them they stopped to grin and let me pass.

Eventually, tired and frustrated, I sat down beside a mobile fruit stall. From the stall – a glass case mounted on the front wheels of a tricycle and packed with ice – I ordered saparot, pineapple. Sitting down brought a feeling of security: and I felt less visible and thus less lost.

When the pineapple came, chopped on a plate with a pile of salt for dipping into and a toothpick to spear the pieces, a girl came too. For a while she watched me silently, but when she spoke it was in English. She asked me all the usual questions, and I gave all the usual replies. She told me that she had learned her English at school in America, and that she was studying in the humanities faculty in Ramkhamhaeng University, near-by. I wondered whether she was the daughter of a GI, but I couldn't see any Caucasian characteristics in her face, and I thought that it might have been rude of me to ask.

After a long pause, whilst the melting ice of the fruit stall dripped steadily on to the spokes of the front wheel of the tricycle, I admitted that I wasn't too sure where I was in relation to the river-jetty, and she volunteered to guide me back.

We walked for some while. I didn't recognise any of the streets, and she seemed increasingly nervous, unsure of where she was taking me. We reached a bridge over one of the klongs (canals), and I stopped. She said she would go and fetch one of her friends from his house just around the corner, and he would lead me to the landing stage.

I waited on the bridge until she had gone out of sight and then set off in the other direction, not believing that she would come back. At the end of the street I turned left in what I considered to be the general direction of the river.

As I passed a couple of parked pick-up trucks I heard a man call from behind me in Thai. Instantly two girls rose from a doorstep and approached me, smiling. "*Pai nai, falang, pai nai kha?*" – "Where are you going, foreigner?" They held my arms and stroked them. But my nerves were already on edge and I appreciated instantly what was happening. I turned in time to grab the wrists of the man behind as he reached into the camera bag hanging by my side. The girls vanished, and I was left holding on to a suddenly very frightened man. I was furious; we were both trembling. I had no idea what to do next.

I pushed the pick-pocket against the side of one of the pick-ups and stared hard into his eyes, to give myself time to think. By this time most of the street was aware that a foreigner was attacking a local; a cyclist stopped to watch and a dog started to bark. I backed away and kicked the man twice on the shin. In my thongs I did no great damage, and the blows must have hurt my toes as much as they hurt his shins, if not more. Then, with all the dignity I could muster, I turned once again the way that I had come, completely unconscious of where I was headed and expecting to hear the sound of running feet as the rest of the street came to lynch the foreigner who had dared to assault a local. The dog barked incessantly at my back until I turned the corner, but no feet followed me.

I found myself on a main road. There was a bus-stop, with a bus drawing up. I climbed aboard. As I turned to look back up the street I found myself looking straight into the eyes of the same girl.

For a moment we looked at each other with the naked, unguarded stares of people who did not quite know what to make of what had passed between them – or if indeed anything had. I don't know fully what expression there was in my eyes, and I could not decipher in that split second whether she looked guilty or disappointed. I looked away, but as the bus drew away I remained conscious of her presence at the bus-stop, and hers was a Bangkok face that I remembered for a long time.

"In the first half of 1982 5,700 murders were recorded in Thailand. Police seized 481 weapons, including 135 automatic rifles and 206 hand grenades. In 1983 a total of twenty-one newspaper reporters were murdered – an average year. Bangkok accounts for the vast majority of all criminal activity in the nation, just as it accounts for most of the nation's industry. Every year the Bangkok police arrest an average of 20,000 prostitutes in the capital, only to release them again: the state cannot afford to feed them any more than their families in the provinces . . ." I culled these facts from the *Bangkok Post* during my first days in Thailand. I wrote them down in my diary; I was fresh, eager, fascinated, and twenty-one. I had arrived at Don Muang airport, Bangkok, on a grey and muggy afternoon of wet heat. The city sprawled out along the Phahon Yothin highway, great standing pools of water lying between the pitted road and the shacks of the suburbs. The airport was jammed with travellers and soldiers sitting on their kit. The humidity made the pages of my guide-book as soggy as flannels. I found myself queuing for immigration behind a huge and muscular Middle-Eastern woman, a pair of polythene bags crammed with duty free goods dangling from each heavy arm. She wore dark glasses, and had it not been for her clothing I would have found it hard to distinguish her sex.

The rainy season had just ended, but many parts of Bangkok are permanently under water. The city is sinking in the Chao Phya river plain faster than Venice, but no preservationist thinks it worth saving. In places in the city the single step between pavement and road turns into a three-foot drop, despite the constant re-tarring of the edges of the road to paper over the cracks. The pavements are blotched with patches of water that drip down from overhead air-conditioning units.

In those first days in Asia I leaned heavily on my Lonely Planet guide, *South-East Asia on a Shoestring*. It was an appropriate name for a travel book publishing house: travellers are amongst the loneliest people on the planet, and every word in that yellow book was a comfort.

The guide told me that one of the best value hotels was confusingly called the Malaysia, and that there I could find a whole community of the new breed of traveller that I had just joined. The Malaysia proved to be more than just a community; it was a subculture of a certain sort of white man, and it attracted a certain sort of Thai. Only the video in the bar is new since the days of the Vietnam-scarred GIs, who thronged Bangkok in search of the two Rs, rest and recreation. I could see no GIs, but the euphemistic rest and recreation was still in the downstairs bar in plenty.

The hotel notice-board was covered with messages from traveller to traveller, scrawled on scraps of paper, sometimes cries of anguish, sometimes enigmatic. "Watch out for samlor driver called Han – I've lost everything." Or, "Jan and Eric – see you in the Cameron Highlands on the 27th." "Anyone want to buy a Lonely Planet?" "Danger. Don't do your deals in the bar." Travellers quoted the Malaysia notice-board as far apart as Burma and Indonesia.

I had been warned about the samlor drivers. Samlors are three-wheeled taxis, better described as three-wheeled scooters with a roof and bench above the back wheels. Selling their driving services was just the beginning as far as those who worked the Malaysia patch were concerned. These drivers offered cheap student cards for cheap flights, cheap blue shows and cheap teenage girls, cheap Thai sticks and cheap smack. According to them everything was 'cheap' – they had a clear perception of the priorities of their customers.

Avoiding the clutches of the drivers I sat down in the bar and ordered a Singha beer, acutely conscious that as the only unaccompanied man in the place at that time in the afternoon I was attracting quite a lot of silent interest from the girls at the bar. I concentrated hard on the *Bangkok Post*, and straightaway found myself reading a story about the Malaysia Hotel. An Australian tourist and his Danish girlfriend had been surprised in their room in the hotel by the entry of three policemen, who then arrested them for smoking marijuana. Although the tourists later stated that they had not been smoking, and that the drug was planted on them by the officers, they were frightened enough – perhaps even by the notice-board warnings – to co-operate. The policemen held them in another hotel, and demanded their total savings in return for their release. Once the money (£3,890 at the going exchange rate, according to my maths in the paper's margin) was in their hands they let the frightened pair go. Fortunately the couple found a sympathetic English-speaking Thai who believed their story, and he in turn convinced the courts. By the time the verdict was announced, however, only one of the three policemen could be found. I tore the story out and abandoned the *Bangkok Post*, to dig my head into my Lonely Planet and see what it suggested I did next in my life.

In the meanderings of those first few days I visited most of the sights that didn't cost money to get into; I saw the emerald Buddha in the Grand Palace, the solid gold Buddha in Wat Traimitr – where I also read how the gold had been hidden from the plundering Burmese in a plaster-cast and forgotten until a crane operator dropped the god and shattered the cast. I visited the Poste Restante every day in the vain hope that someone might just have written me a letter within a couple of days of my leaving England, and I parcelled up my sturdy black policeman's shoes and sent them home – they were useless in that heat. From the Chao Phya Express on the river of the same name that bisected the city I saw what I could of the klong life that is widely promoted as the city's tourist attraction, and from the boat I could see what Joseph Conrad had meant when he described the river approaches to the city: "above the crowded mob of low, brown roof ridges, towered great piles of masonry, King's Palaces, temples, gorgeous and dilapidated, crumbling under the vertical sunlight."

The travellers' evenings were more of a problem. I walked up and down Pat Pong road a couple of nights running, reading from the proffered pieces of paper of the amazing feats that the show-girls could achieve with pieces of string, cigarettes, bananas, and ping-pong balls. With three others I braved one of the bars. The tout whose graphically illustrated paper had caught our attention pressed a buzzer on the door that activated the girls as we entered. We were the only customers, and we shied off staying longer than was necessary to pay for a drink.

After a couple of visits to the Blue Fox – a pick-up bar near the Malaysia which catered for those travellers who wanted a girl to take to the beaches in the South – I concluded that I was not yet ripe for the picking of the girls there either, and thereafter occupied myself in the evening by going to Western movies and watching the Thai dubbing turn Hollywood epics into farce. What I did not experience of the more lurid side of Bangkok life I made up for in the *Bangkok Post* and the *Nation*. Two policemen assaulted robbery suspects so violently under questioning that their testicles had to be amputated; another pair was 'told off' for accepting a bribe and allowing a heroin trafficker to walk free from his cell just a day after a huge hunt had netted him; then there was the eccentric case of Police Lieutenant General Suwan, who marched into the local police station and demanded that he be fined 400 baht for driving through a red traffic light.

I read the story of Lamduam, a prostitute and servant in the city. At the age of fourteen she had come into Bangkok from the provinces to stay with an 'uncle' who had then sold her as a slave. Her owners had vented their perversions on her; they had forced her to drink boiling water, stabbed her with kitchen knives and locked her in a wardrobe for days on end. When the police rescued her and hunted down her parents in the province of Udon Thani, her mother freely admitted, "When I read about her in the newspaper I couldn't remember her."

One day there was a massive student demonstration, confusingly in protest against rather than for the opening of a spanking new university campus. The papers revealed that the Ramkhamhaeng students objected to being told to move for many reasons; they had not been forewarned that a new campus was being built; they were in the middle of their exams; there was nothing wrong with the old campus, and the buildings in the new area had been finished so quickly that they had developed lethal structural cracks. In short they suspected shady dealings behind the affair, and rumour swiftly spread that government officials had benefited from handing out construction contracts to the builders and new leases to the shop-owners attracted to the area. The shop-owners then supposedly wanted to see a quick return on their investment, and had pressured the contractors to finish the buildings as soon as possible, hence the cracks. Counter-rumour then claimed that the whole student rally was staged by the shopkeepers in the old campus area, who wanted to stir up trouble in the hope that it might prevent the loss of business that the move would involve.

It wasn't long before I got fed up with reading about the world around me. I had come to Asia, after all, to experience things. What these nebulous things were to be I had no real idea, but I did know that assimilating events reported in the papers or on the Hotel Malaysia notice-board did not constitute experience, no matter what impression my literature course at Cambridge had left me with.

I noted with some satisfaction after my third day of self-conscious diary writing that I had covered a whole lot of paper, although with less satisfaction I had to admit that half of it had been contributed by Lonely Planet and the news and features writers of the *Bangkok Post.* The paper rate was to dwindle rapidly and, as time and destinations passed, the written side of my life lagged further and further behind what I felt. Even at that early stage times of both physical and emotional stress were going unrecorded. If I had kept a more honest diary I would probably have gone home sooner.

That arbitrary period of two years I had allowed myself for travel assumed a psychological significance, even if I was rarely conscious of it. At the lower points of the first few months it was like a jailor, and I had to serve my time. Later it made life unreal – something to be tolerated for a short period and not to be taken seriously. But if my deus ex machina had pointed down at me after eighteen months and said, "You down there, yes you, stop it. Stay still. You are hereby sentenced to remain in South-East Asia for the rest of your life," I have no doubt that my attitude would have been quite different.

In those early days in the Malaysia the seeds of discontent were sown. Such a concentration of travellers, each with a story to tell – and each determined to tell it at the earliest opportunity – was both intoxicating and frustrating. There was some great pretence about the whole thing that I couldn't quite fathom. As a newcomer to the Asian scene I was a ripe target for everyone's stories, and although I welcomed the words of those more experienced than I, after the third time of hearing the same thing I made no further attempt to take notes. I had read my guide-book well, and consequently I knew the phrases they would use about a place almost before they uttered them. The kudos of months on the road was important; the kudos of numbers of places visited equally so. One former traveller who had become an English teacher used to appear every night in the Malaysia bar, solely for the gratification of being able to tell the migrant travellers that he actually lived in Bangkok.

Two years later I too sat smug in that same bar, smug with the knowledge of Asia that I had gathered, and doubly smug in my self-promise not to tell anyone of my history unless they specifically asked; but a week was enough on my first arrival. After a week of gathering the addresses of people I never really warmed to I quit the Malaysia and humped my bag along to a hotel in Chinatown, in the heart of the city.

The hotel I chose was Chinese, and very matter-of-fact. The reception desk stood in the middle of a car park at the bottom of the hotel lift, and not until the money for a night's stay was safely in the hand of the receptionist did the room key come to rest in the guest's hand. A young floorman, wearing only shorts, regarded me carefully as I stepped out of the lift, assessing my needs. As he showed me the way to my room, his bare feet padding like wet fish across the cold stone floors, he asked whether a girl or girls were needed straightaway, or later.

In my room the traffic noise was intense whilst the windows were open, and the room became unbearably hot when they were not. The ceiling fan rotated slowly and unevenly, on the point of wobbling itself off its spindle and slicing down on to my perspiring body lying below. The plain white walls were smeared with the sweaty hand-prints of previous guests. In the evenings the floor-man had his shirt on, and sat close to the lift with a couple of plain girls, waiting for business. In the mornings the same girls came round to clean the rooms, bringing their children with them.

I had traded the bar of the Malaysia, the videos, the newspaper stories, the girls in the Blue Fox and the Western menus for a far more captivating environment. Bangkok's Chinatown still bears the mark of the Chinese, even though integration here is more complete than that in Indonesia or Malaysia, and the Chinese Thais all have Thai names. Thai temples are soaring, spacious, and austere Buddhas preside over cool, marbled halls within. By contrast the Chinese temple next to my hotel was small, dusty and full of ash. Shafts of sunlight filtered through the incense smoke to pick out the grin of the fat Buddha, who seemed to mock my presence in his temple and my absence from my own culture. A single shaft of light lit the gold on his ring-laden hand; around him worshippers mumbled thanks for wealth and health.

In Chinatown one row of shops deals in car spares, another in spices. One sells textiles, another garlic. In one street a row of shops hatching and selling chickens is bizarrely interspersed with undertakers. Eggs lie in shallow boxes in the first shop; in the second, flat baskets contain a mass of yellow chicks, cheeping and stumbling; by the third the chicks are incarcerated in ventilated boxes to prevent them escaping. The boxes in shop number four have a similar purpose – coffins, gleaming and ornamental. An old Chinese gent in a grubby white vest and baggy shorts sits reading the day's newspaper in the sunlight in front of his coffins, whilst behind him in the shadows his wife bends over the desk, adding up columns of figures on an abacus. The loose change is kept in a bucket and suspended in mid-air by a Heath Robinson pulley arrangement. A bell jangles when the bucket is pulled down, and thus alerts the proprietor against being raided.

In the later afternoons the streets fill with Hino trucks, their original Japanese bodywork covered in wooden panels decorated with paintings of film-stars and brightly coloured Thai landscapes. The young Chinese who load these trucks stab evil-looking metal hooks into the sacks for a secure grip before walking the plank into the rear of the lorry with a piratical grimace; a torn strip of towel prevents the sweat from stinging their eyes.

At night the lorries are replaced by portable food stalls, and the pavements are jammed with trestle-tables laden with cheap wallets, T-shirts and lottery tickets. Most people wander; few buy. Many just squat on the roadside and watch. The noise is so intense that even the cassette-selling stalls are inaudible beyond a few feet. Through the gaps in the shuttering that closes off most of the shops I could see families gathered around their evening meal beneath incense-wreathed red and gold altars, mounted on the rear walls. Sometimes the shop-owners, seemingly so lethargic in the heat of the day, emerge into the street dressed immaculately in the latest sparkling-white tennis gear and disappear down the dank alley where the full-grown chickens reach the end of the line. White is the colour of death for the Chinese; the alley's floor is dark with blood. In the midst of all this noise stand lorry-loads of yet more chickens, stacked high in rough bamboo baskets. In amongst all the noise they are apprehensively silent.

It was hard not to feel more in touch with Thai life in Chinatown, although I missed the security of white skin. The girls who worked my floor did not seem to mind my lack of interest. They were simply a facility that the hotel provided, and they were not to know of my Victorian horror of anything labelled 'prostitute' – a horror that did not stop me being fascinated by them and desperately trying not to show it. They worked hard on my prudishness, and every time I went for the lift I had to fight to keep my shorts on. I giggled as much as they did on these occasions, and by the time I left I had come to think of them as fun.

But I never quite got to grips with the transport system. Bangkok's buses are an experience in themselves. Their drivers sit jammed into the corner of their vehicles, sitting sideways on to the wheel. This is to allow Buddha a better view of the road and thereby to ensure a safe journey. Most of the buses have a massively long gear stick which clears a considerable space on the crowded deck as the driver crashes through the gears. In the rush hours (unpredictable, and most of the time) buses list dangerously to one side as passengers who cannot worm their way aboard cling to the sides like barnacles.

The through current of wind from the open windows is all that makes every trip possible, and bus travel is unbearable when it rains: the windows slam shut, and the bus becomes a sealed oven. In normal conditions I could feel the perspiration beginning to gather into streams down my back, but in that suffocating and drumming canister I lathered with sweat, and staggered out into the drowning rain at my destination gasping like a fish.

I discovered after that nightmare that for a few extra baht you can enjoy a more temperate air-conditioned bus, and buy your ticket from a conductress in uniform. The only problem with the air-cons is that unlike the others, where one-and-a-half baht buys a ticket to anywhere, the uniformed conductresses need to know your destination, and this means both planning and pronunciation. Names such as Phlapphlachai and Prachathipatai sound completely different when pronounced by Thais, and I began to get used to that look of embarrassment tinged with panic that clouded the conductresses' faces when I fumbled with their language. Sometimes I feared that they were about to burst into tears.

On the cheaper and sweatier buses the conductors are tough and agile. They have to be, in order to penetrate the crush and collect the fares. Most of them are teenagers, and some not more than eleven or twelve years old. They are armed with a simple metal canister that has tickets at either end and coins in the middle. This they operate with one hand, steadying themselves with the other against the bucking and rolling of the bus. The progress of the conductor amongst the mass of bodies is marked by the clattering of the jaws of his canister as it doles out pieces of paper and change, and by a constant code of whistles for the driver. On the late buses the back seats are often occupied by the same conductors returning home, curled up like dormice asleep in the corners, still clutching their canisters.

Buses are dangerous for Europeans. Pick-pockets travel the most popular routes, working with razor-sharp knives. Whilst their victims concentrate hard on remaining on their own two feet and follow the route of the bus on a map (a nightmare to unfurl in those conditions) the knives flick beneath their shoulder bags, emptying the valuable guts into a quick hand. Only when the victim steps out at his destination does his relief at having survived the journey evaporate with the discovery of the empty bag, hanging like a deflated balloon by his side.

I was impressed by the way I handled Bangkok. I was stern-faced on the buses and avoided people's eyes on the streets. I had not caught any guilty diseases, and a mysterious rash on my white skin had proved to be no more than bed bugs' bites. After just ten days in Asia I felt sure I could handle it. It was time to try myself out on the countryside.

On the eve of my departure from Bangkok I returned to a place that had impressed me three days before. Whilst the tourist destinations of Wat Po and the Grand Palace close at the end of the day, the Golden Mount is always there to be climbed and provides the best and only overall view of the city – unless you happen to be an expensive hotel dweller. It was late in the day when I started up that first flight of steps. The telegraph wires that circled the base of the Mount were laden with birds, although by morning only the mosaic of their droppings would remain. Birds are a rare sight in daytime Bangkok.

The Golden Mount is in the middle of the carpenters' quarter, and the bird song mixed with the whine of electric saws as workshops churned out doors and tables, but as I stepped higher the noise began to mingle with the hum of a city going home. The steps were not spaced to encourage speed, and the small gradient allowed plenty of time for meditation on the way up. I passed pairs of novices gazing out over their city in the directions of the provincial homes that they had not seen for so long. Although the Mount may not be high the city is flat, so the view is commanding – and it is the only one accessible to the locals.

Three flights from the top I caught up with an old monk. He was moving laboriously, stopping every few steps to cool himself with his fan and survey every bit of city that revealed itself with the extra height he had gained. I followed his steps, watching the material of his saffron robes catching between his buttocks, reminding me of the body that lay beneath the loose cotton. Somehow the delineation of his buttocks did not ruin the dignity of his progress. At the top he first surveyed the city with a grunt of satisfaction, as if it matched his expectations, and then turned to me. He asked if I spoke Thai, and I had to apologise that I only spoke a little. For a moment he seemed to be trying to remember something, and then he quoted quite clearly and slowly, "Come up and see me some time." Then he turned away and started with equal dignity down the other side, towards a pattern of roofs that marked the nearest monastery and dormitory.

The greyness of the heavy day turned slowly a little rosier, but before it achieved any real beauty or even decided what colour it should be, the light had gone. The lights of the hotels and nightclubs dominated the city, with their more lurid, neon, glow.

2 *People in High Places*

I did not leave Bangkok alone. I left with Alison. Alison was wonderful, beautiful, desirable, clever . . . and I missed my girlfriend back in England. I threw myself at Alison. After all, travelling was all about the facility to have sexual relations as often as possible with as many as possible, starting with other travellers and moving on to locals once acclimatised – at least, that was the impression I had got in the bar of the Malaysia.

Alison exuded sex appeal, but she was too intelligent to be easy. In fact she was too intelligent, full-stop. Her looks and thoughts had made her much in demand for her thirty-odd years, and she had thrown up university and career in favour of a good time, which had then run out on her. Her friends had started pairing off, leaving her to get fed up with her working life to the extent that she did something about it, and left England. But travelling was not – and is not – an effective cure for that kind of depression. Nevertheless, I was glad to be able to worship the ground she walked on and to share her bed; she was glad to have a companion who valued her, but in the end I was never quite good enough. I was too young for her to take me seriously.

Together we left for the north, for Thailand's second town of Chiang Mai, but to make our journey more original we stopped off first at Ayutthya to see the ruined ancient Thai capital, and then later at Nakhorn Sawan, further off the beaten track.

Off the beaten track in this latter case meant descending from the train at a station that was some miles from the town (Lonely Planet said nothing of that) to a reception of a large number of Thai soldiers, who were obviously delighted to have their long, dull day on the platform relieved by the vision of a blonde and shapely westerner. Their hungry eyes followed Alison's every move, hardly seeing me. Behind us dogs converged on the rails in the wake of the departing train, and tore hunks of fur off each other in their struggle to share in the human debris left behind – a banana-skin, a rotting papaya skin, or even a pile of excrement – in their attempts to

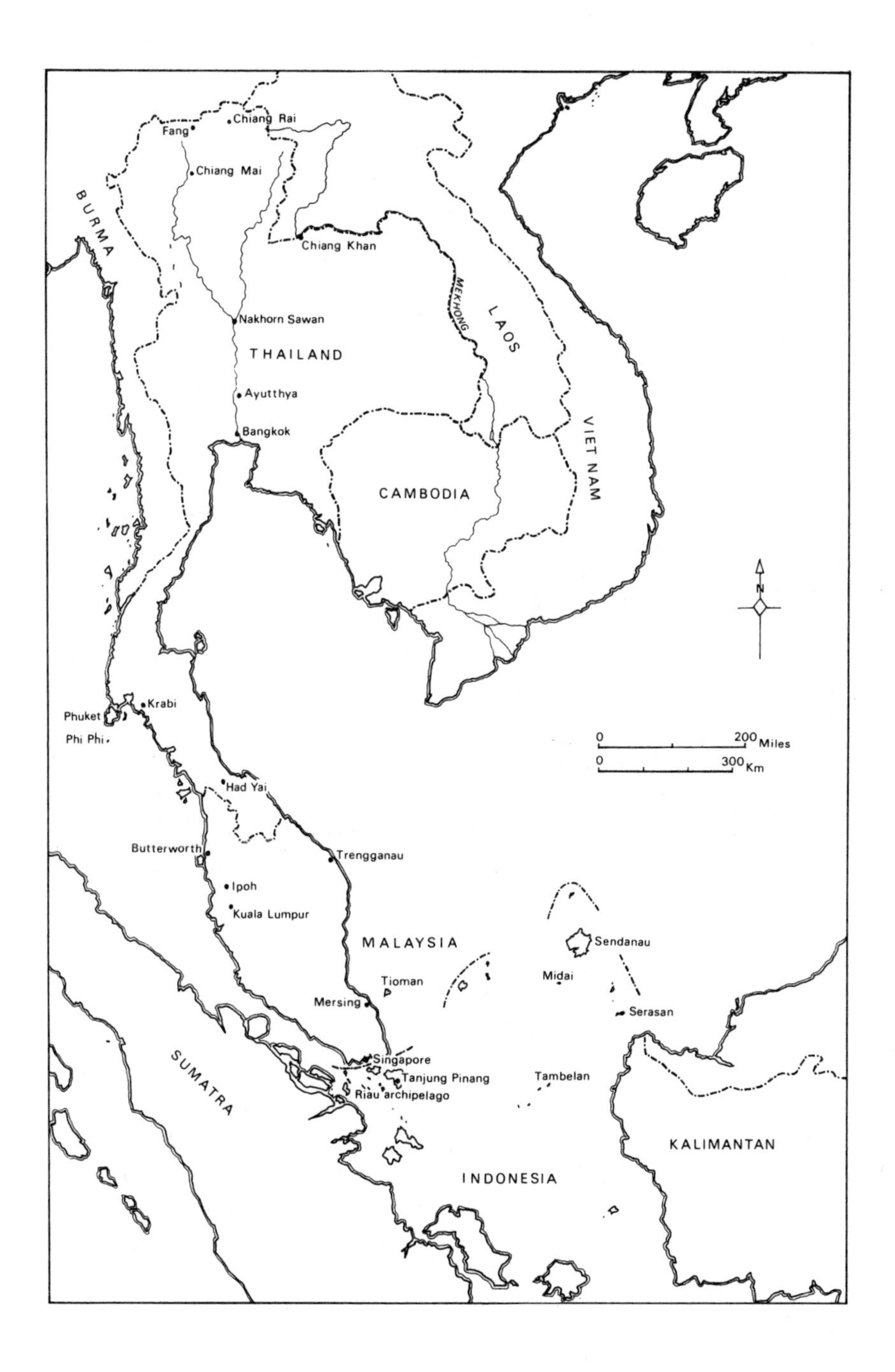
Chiang Rai
Fang
Chiang Mai
BURMA
Chiang Khan
MEKHONG
LAOS
Nakhorn Sawan
THAILAND
Ayutthya
Bangkok
VIET NAM
CAMBODIA
N
Krabi
Phuket
Phi Phi
0
200 Miles
0
300 Km
Had Yai
Butterworth
Trengganau
Ipoh
Kuala Lumpur
MALAYSIA
Sendanau
Tioman
Midai
Mersing
Serasan
SUMATRA
Singapore
Tanjung Pinang
Tambelan
Riau archipelago
KALIMANTAN
INDONESIA

survive. Few of them had a whole coat of fur, and the bare patches of blotched skin of the older dogs were horribly scarred by the lifelong fight for food. Another of the useful facts I had culled from the *Bangkok Post* was that 350 Thais die every year as a result of dog-bites, and the people of Nakhorn Sawan seemed only too well aware of the statistics, keeping the dogs at bay with volleys of stones when necessary.

First impressions of the station did not bode well. Alone on a station platform surrounded by dogs and soldiers, all hungry in different ways, we were at a loss what to do next and the focus of an intense amount of silent interest. One of the soldiers nudged another and whispered something, and many around laughed. Alison was accusing. She had wanted to go straight to Chiang Mai, but I had persuaded her to stop off in this awful place, so what was I going to do about it? All my initiative deserted me. I scanned the already-grubby page of the guide-book for a word or words which would solve the problem, but found nothing. We had stepped out of the book for the first time and the world outside it appeared to be hostile – if this was the station what would the town be like and how were we to get there? I blamed myself for everything and admitted to her that my idea had been bad, but the real cause of my anguish was not the place itself – there is nothing wrong with Nakhorn Sawan – but my own inability to take the situation in hand and make something of it. I had lost some of my favour in Alison's eyes and even more of my own self-respect. However, I was acute enough, even at that time, to make a mental note of the fact that travelling as a couple would never permit the kind of travelling I wanted, whatever that may be.

In a matter of minutes we had decided to catch the very next train away from that platform, and we elbowed our way through a passage of khaki-covered bellies and revolver-handles into the station office, to try to find out when the next was due.

Beneath the drunken circling of the ceiling-fan the deputy station-master sat with his hands clasped on a wooden desk, staring hard at the only paper in front of him. Every now and then the fan would summon up a huge effort and manage to levitate the piece of paper and move it to one side or the other, but Pinit – for this was the officer's name – would reach out and swat it to the desk before it slipped over the edge.

There was no time-table on the walls of the office, and the words in my Thai phrase book seemed so unpronounceable that I did not dare make myself a laughing-stock by trying them. Eventually I steeled myself to address Pinit in English, just as he reached out yet again to retrieve the wayward paper, and at the same time became aware of our presence.

"I am very pleased to meeting you," he said, rising from the desk quickly. "Are you coming to seeing our town? Pleased to sit down." He spoke English surprisingly well, and we instantly felt less alone. But there was no question as far as he was concerned of us going on to Chiang Mai that night. Yes, there were trains, but there would be no places on those trains – or at least no places that people from America (we assured him that we were English, but he forgot it as soon as it was said) would be able to put up with. There was a festival in Chiang Mai, he explained, and the trains would all be very full. Would we like to stay in his place, and he would show us the town? We murmured that perhaps we would like to eat something and have a wash – beginning to think that perhaps we had not made such a mistake in stepping off into the unknown – but we did not commit ourselves to staying the night with him.

So Pinit took us to his house, next to the station. It was the Thai equivalent of a railwayman's cottage, although in Thailand the managers get the cottages whilst the porters sleep in and around the station buildings. Pinit offered us water, then Thai whisky, and he sent a boy for a couple of polythene bags full of Coca-Cola. (Soft drinks always come in bags in Thailand. Bottles are in short supply and no drinks vendor will let a customer take one away.) He nipped back periodically to the station to check that everything was running smoothly, and brought us back a meal of fried rice wrapped carefully in plantain leaf.

When he came off duty he began to talk at length about himself. He told us about his life, his family, his hopes and his depressions, he told us how he had been disfigured in a road-traffic accident – he had what looked like a harelip, together with burn scars – and how that had affected the rest of his life. He showed us a letter from his 'friend', a German traveller who had stayed with Pinit for some days. The letter was full of depression. Pinit pressed us repeatedly to stay with him as his German friend had done.

There was something desperate in the way he begged our

company that we could not ascribe to simple non-comprehension of Thai formalities on our part. He was very intelligent but very lonely, and he felt the blow of his disfigurement far more acutely than he needed to. He could not unburden his heart to his colleagues, he said, or to his family, who were a long way away. On our side, we did not want to make the mistake of refusing the first real offer of Thai hospitality that we had received. We did not want to seem to refuse either because of his face or because we were European, and therefore above staying in bamboo huts. So we dithered, proposing to wait until the end of the day for a decision.

But Pinit's principal problem was women, as he confided in me once we were sitting shoulder to shoulder on the floor of his front room, the bottle of whisky half-finished. Alison had gone for a sleep in the back room, which had pleased him immensely; I think it implied trust, a feeling he did not often get from women. Pinit was so dismayed by his looks that he assumed he had no chance of getting married, and marriage is a major symbol of security and happiness in Thai society. He could not even sleep with a prostitute, he said. I could see his eyes begin to glisten with a combination of tears and the effect of the whisky, and I tried to talk him out of what I knew could be an embarrassing scene.

"In the West people are not like that. We try to judge people on character and not on looks. It wouldn't matter one bit what you looked like – Western women would treat you the same as anyone else." I prattled on, conscious that I was getting into deep water, but needing a way out of the uncomfortable scene. Pinit nodded a couple of times, sat, sipped his whisky, and remained silent. My naïve attempt seemed to have worked, and I quickly pretended a need to go to sleep before I said anything that he would recognise as ridiculous.

The next thing I knew was that Alison was standing above me, glaring, and demanding that we leave. Pinit hovered in the background, as if he had a whole lot on his mind that he wanted to say, if only we allowed him to say it. He had taken my words literally, and after I had fallen asleep he had drained the whisky, entered the back room, woken Alison, proposed marriage and tried immediate consummation. This was what my talk of the objective Western society and our 'lack of prejudice' had led to.

Needless to say we were sitting on our luggage on the platform, once again under the beady stare of the soldiers, when the night-train arrived shortly after midnight. Now that we were leaving the soldiers seemed on the hostile side of disinterested; Pinit was just confused. He saw us on to the train, and we parted as friends. I don't think he quite understood why we were leaving, and we were glad not to have to spell it out. A great burden of guilt was lifted from my shoulders as the train started to move, and we left behind the lonely figure of the stationmaster on the platform.

The whole episode was the fault of inexperience. Only once I had learned enough Thai to make myself understood did I start getting off trains and buses at unknown places again. By that time I had learned enough to realise that Asians were not all noble savages, and that their hang-ups were no different from ours, however differently we tried to treat them.

Our relief at finally getting away from Nakhorn Sawan was soon countered by the overcrowding on the train. Pinit had been right, and the festival in Chiang Mai seemed to be drawing half the country. There was barely room to stand in the corridors, so in the end we set up camp in the toilet, much to the amazement of the Thais who pushed open the door to find a couple of foreigners in residence just where they were least wanted. The toilet was not too pungent, fortunately, and we took it in turns to poke our heads out of the small window and enjoy the hot and damp night air rushing past.

Chiang Mai has little in common with Bangkok. Despite being the nation's second city, the northern town is a fraction of Bangkok's size, and the freshness of the mountain air that blows through it gives it an animation that eclipses the Bangkok frenzy.

The town was first put on the map by missionaries, who made their way northwards on the Chao Phya river. Today it is difficult to get upriver of Ayutthya, little more than fifty miles from Bangkok, let alone cover the 460 miles to the watershed at Lamphung. Chiang Mai and the provinces of the north only became regarded as the property of Thailand by default: no one else had a better claim. Even now the northern Thais have their own dialect and regard themselves as a race apart. Further up the hillsides behind the northern Thai villages live seven major distinct hill-tribes, even further removed from control at Bangkok. In fact, laying aside the troubles on the Kampuchean border and the communists in the south, the hill-tribes are the government's main security worry. Ironically it is the government that created that risk, aided and abetted by the interference of America. Nevertheless tribal trekking pulls thousands of travellers to the north every year.

I had heard of this trekking phenomenon before leaving the UK. Someone I had met had enthused about the thrill of walking up into the hills and staying with primitive people, sharing their living conditions. I imagined the tribespeople as being rather like the noble savages that I had come across in my literature course at university, which so well equipped me for the world. I imagined them as Conrad depicts them – servants who slip noiselessly through the forests, and have amazing powers of perception. I even saw myself as becoming, for a few days, something of the noble savage myself. I was more interested in the boy-scoutish nature of the trekking and in the life-stories of my fellow trekkers than in the tribespeople. In this I was aided by the lack of information on the tribes to feed the appetite of awakened interest, and it is only since returning to the libraries of England that I have been able to get a clearer picture of what is going on in the hills.

Although the tribesmen are now incorporated into the body of Thailand they are not Thai. Most of them originate from the province of Yunnan, in southern China. They are wandering farmers by tradition, because their slash-and-burn type agriculture destroys the forest land. When the tribes first settled in the area it was then all contested land. Burma, China, Laos and Thailand all laid claim to ownership, and now that the borders are fixed there are tribes in all four countries. The principle of a national frontier makes no sense to the people up above 1,600 feet in the rain forests; they only understand the need to plant at the end of the rains and shift when the soil is exhausted. They owe no allegiance to any country, and no country has ever done much for them – which is as they would wish. They are hardly conscious even of today's borders, which follow no natural barriers. The 1,100 miles of Burmese/Thai border is particularly hard to police.

The rise to notoriety of the Golden Triangle has put the tribes on the map, and has caused them to be trampled on by both tourists and politicians. The Triangle is largely the creation of a force outside the tribes themselves – the Kuomintang. After the revolution in China the Kuomintang, the Chinese nationalist army, fled southwards from the red-dominated central provinces. At that time there were 44,000 GIs in Thailand to protect the world from communism and the CIA, rightly considering the nationalists a useful buffer against any invading force, encouraged them to stay in the northern Thai hills, where they lived largely uncontrolled by Thai law.

In the 1950s the UN put pressure on Thailand to outlaw official drug production, and in 1959 the official government monopoly ceased and drug production became illegal. However, 40,000 addicts do not give up their habit easily, and the Kuomintang saw the opportunity to do good business. Prior to their arrival the hill-tribes grew a little opium for their own use, but now in a good year the Golden Triangle exports about 240 tons of the drug. The CIA well knew what the Kuomintang were developing with typical Chinese business acumen up in the hills, and even exploited the business to encourage support from guerillas in Vietnam. CIA planes used to take loads of opium from northern Thailand into Vietnam to keep those guerillas loyal.

At one stage in their attempts to suppress the industry the government went so far as to bomb villages and fields, but this only caused the tribes to fight back. In one of the Lisu villages that I stayed in – a village that was within a day's march of the Burmese border – I watched a group of sixteen-year-old boys strip down and clean their guns for the next day's expedition. An opium caravan was due to set off for the border, and they were to be its escort.

Now that the tribes have become such an attraction the government has to be careful what impression the tourists take away with them. There are hill-tribe centres and projects, and the Thai king and queen take an interest in the integration of the tribes with the Thais, but still there is little or no willingness from the tribes themselves to be other than they have been and are, and they would rather be left alone.

As for the Kuomintang, the government has at last faced up to the reality that the bosses of the KMT are more often than not opium warlords, and it is they, not the hill-tribes, who are a threat to national security. The warlords lead very sophisticated lives: when the Thai rangers stormed the village of Ban Hin Taek, the stronghold and refining centre of warlord Khun Sa, who is still at large in the hills, they found air-conditioned houses, a swimming-pool, and glossy Western magazines.

But there can be no discrete wars allowed in the hills where there are people like me wandering around and staying in the villagers' huts. Many of the new wave of westerners are directly interested in what the CIA accidentally initiated: the drugs. As for me, at that time I was more interested in trekking – and of course Alison. But in the event I was forced to make a choice between the two.

Our first night in Chiang Mai was superbly romantic. It was the night of the Loy Kratong festival, and together we leaned over the parapet of the river bridge and watched the Kratongs (burning candles and incense sticks on a floating base of lotus leaves) glide in a path of light through the arches beneath us. A feeling of liberation from the heat and hassle of Bangkok, and the enthusiasm of the Thais around us for their festival, spiced what affection there was between us. But thereafter the relationship quickly lost what little steam it had.

We followed the same route as many others, heading north from Chiang Mai up to Fang, where we took the boat down the Kok river to Chiang Rai. The ride was fast and frightening, in a long-boat that was too full and shipped water in the more violent rapids. The steersman was a teenager, and he had not yet learned to mask his own feelings of anxiety as he pivoted the massive outboard to manoeuvre the boat into the right position for the rapids, so he gave us no confidence. In the end the only mishap was going aground in the quiet shallows approaching Chiang Rai.

Chiang Rai itself was incredibly soporific. The town was full of cheap accommodation and long-staying freaks (the affectionate label used by the tribe of travelling hippies to describe themselves). It was as if the smoke that crept out between the closed shutters of their rooms covered the whole town in a kind of Golden Triangle smog. We headed north still and hired two bicycles on the banks of the Mekhong river to 'cycle around the Golden Triangle' as the cycle shop billed it. The day was hot, the tracks heavy going, and there was no sign of any drug-running. Whichever way we peered as we cycled we couldn't even spot an opium poppy. It was hard to muster up any enthusiasm for the meeting point of three countries, Thailand, Laos and Burma (thus the Triangle), where the Mekhong splits. The scrub looked the same on all three shores, and there was no activity on any of them, nor on the rivers.

These jaunts failed singularly to halt the decline in any relationship that we had built up. She didn't mind me being around, she said, but sleeping together meant nothing. She always talked of somewhere else and someone else, and as I did not want to seem over-keen and put her off I affected indifference. Between us we managed to effectively diminish our mutual enjoyment of the place. Nothing I suggested or did seemed to appeal to her. In the evenings, when we could think of nothing more to say and she tired of beating me at backgammon we buried ourselves in our Lonely Planets, chewing over the words again and again to see if there was any more sustenance to be gained from them.

When she finally voted to go south to lie on the beaches I voted to go trekking. Disappointed I certainly was – and I think she was too – but I was determined not to follow her like a dog. We would meet on the beaches, we said.

The trek guide was Ka-Moon, or Moon for short. In Chiang Mai he seemed the ideal man for the job, speaking English fluently but atrociously, and moving with boundless energy. He also looked the part in his flak jacket, with a knife stuck in his belt, bare feet, and a piece of cloth around his forehead, even though he was Bangkok-born. He reminded me of a Khmer Rouge guerilla – and in the event I was not far wrong.

Moon assured us that it was the best season for trekking. The monsoon rains had ended and the opium poppies were in full bloom, he said. During the rains the paths apparently turned to mud-slides and leeches hung from overhanging branches ready to drop down the necks of unsuspecting bodies they sensed passing below. Leeches can worm their way through layers of clothing in search of the softest and most delicate areas of flesh. Once their heads are firmly buried into the white citified skin – fat trekking westerners must be seasonal lamb to the leeches of northern Thailand – only a burning cigarette-end (or piece of sticky tape in the case of the groin) will dislodge them.

But the rains had not ended, at least not quite. We stopped after only half-an-hour's walking to strip a papaya tree of its fruit, elated to be living off the land already, and ignoring the fact that the fruit was far from ripe. As we shared the papaya beneath a palm-thatched shelter the rain began. At first it and the sun tolerated each other, and the heavy drops looked like steel strips as they slanted gleaming into the ground. The grasses began to jump with beads of water accumulating on the fringes of the roof. Assuming that it was only a passing shower some of us went for a swim in the stream below, kicking spurts of gravel into the rapids at the tail of the pool.

But the rain did not stop, and we remained wet from the swim. The sky got heavier, and so did our rucksacks. After ten minutes of silent slogging, a pick-up bounced up the track behind us. We could put our rucksacks in and ride to the village which was to be our first stop, said Moon. The driver was a friend of his. After a short exchange of views it soon became clear that there were two factions in the party. I joined the faction which maintained we had not come trekking to get lifts with pick-up trucks, we had come to walk; the very presence of the vehicle was an insult. So four of us slogged on whilst the others rode.

It wasn't worth the fuss. Twenty minutes later we reached the Lahu-Na village, disappointed that we had hardly stretched our legs at all. Our unspoken question on what we were to do for the rest of the day was answered by the scene in the chief's visitor hut, where we were to stay. The faction that had accepted the lift were already grouped around a bong, and the best quality opium was reportedly on its way. Some of us were delighted with the news, and some were less impressed.

Two years later my attitude was to be quite different, but on this occasion I was one of the dissenters. Fleming, an eccentric management consultant in his sixtieth year who had spent the best part of the last ten on the road, Zaq, a strong and deceptively slow Australian, Bernhardt, an incredibly dull German, and myself adjourned to the neighbouring room, followed by a crowd of children.

The children in that village had seen more white men than we had seen chickens, but Fleming at least was a curiosity – they never saw older white men. For a tribesman, forty is old. They followed Fleming around, counting raucously from one to ten and singing snatches from 'Old Macdonald had a farm', breaking off to ask us for cigarettes and money.

Money was the one commodity the village was not short of,

although this was not immediately apparent from their life-styles. Moon told us that the village chief had done sufficiently well out of his opium crop to be able to buy a second-hand pick-up, which he kept at the side of the road below. The chief could not drive himself, but this did not prevent him from visiting the vehicle quite regularly, if just to sit in it. He was jealous of anyone else driving it.

All in all this first tribal village did not even come close to my ideal of noble savagery, although there was one redeeming feature in the shape of the enormous, toothless and shaven-headed (protection from lice?) chief's wife who took a shine to Fleming, and would prod him and giggle whenever he got within reach, her enormous sagging breasts rippling with amusement. In the next room the chief's assistant administered the opium. He carried a revolver in his waistband, and every time he leaned forward to replenish the stock of opium and shredded bamboo in the bong the ugly glint of that piece of metal would show between his shirt and his trousers.

Meanwhile, Fleming produced a bottle of Thai whisky, some Seven-Up, and a plastic mug. Apologising for the lack of gin, tonic or ice he proceeded to offer us an early-evening drink in mid-afternoon. It seemed the best thing to do in the circumstances, and as we passed the beaker we gazed out down the silent village through the rain that had trapped us.

Eventually Zaq produced a magnetic backgammon set, and a game started. In a few moments the children had forgotten Fleming and were crowding around. The players had to relinquish control of the board altogether as the children began to appreciate the magnetic properties of the set. More people gathered, and children brought adults. We edged into the background and looked on as the villagers gradually discovered all the properties of magnets, sticking them to every piece of metal they could find. It was as much a pleasure for us to watch the Lahu learning as it patently was for them to learn, and the exhilaration of having brought something constructive into the hills – quite by accident – made the afternoon pass quickly. Suddenly it was evening, the rain had long since stopped, and we had done nothing. In the next room the bong was still bubbling. Leaving the villagers with the backgammon, we set off up the hill at the back of the village to explore.

It was not a stunning environment. Beneath the motionless

tree-tops dead lianas trailed from bush to trunk. No birds sang in the heavy air. Only our clumsy progress broke the silence. The bark of the few poor teak trees was crumbly to the hand. Concealed in the undergrowth were spirit-altars, normally comprising two or three tall bamboos with a flutter of white cloth on pieces of string from their tips. These were planted to surround what looked like a bird-table, and on the table was placed an offering of dried orange flowers and rice. Frequently the altars were neglected, the orange flowers blown over the ground below; the pigs had had the rice. Nevertheless they still had a strange potency in that quiet and dead forest, and we only dared go within a few feet of them, lest doing so would be to risk accusations of desecration.

It was these altars which led to the undoing of much of the missionary work up in the hills. Whatever the tribesmen's nominal belief might have been, they always liked to keep their spirit-altars. The potency of the white man's god was only strong whilst the white man was present, and whenever the missionaries left to return to lowland towns for essential supplies and communication with the outside world they would inevitably return to find the altars they had destroyed according to the injunction of the Book of Exodus, erected once more in their original places. On more than one occasion the tribes attributed the failure of a harvest to the anger of their own gods at the interference of the missionaries.

Back in the Lahu-Na village that night we found more entertainment laid on for us, this time more in line with what we had come for. A pig was sacrificed and a party organised along the lines of a Lahu Shi Nyi (merit-earning) day, but these ritual celebrations had the specific purpose of appeasing G'ui sha, the overall spirit, who had made one of the village girls ill. Most of the celebrations started after dark. In a rough stockade outside the chief's hut the elders took turns to play the gourd flute whilst others danced. The flute could not be more unlike a classical flute either in appearance or sound; on the contrary, it looks like a tall bamboo imitation of the bagpipes. The sound it makes is hollow and mournful, somewhere between that of a tuba and bassoon, and the player has a choice of only two notes, which he varies very infrequently. The dance itself was also unornamental: the procession behind the musician took three heavy footsteps forward, one at right-angles, a pause, and then began again. Despite that day's rain, the ground inside the stockade was as hard as concrete after many years of such stamping.

At first only the elders danced, whilst the younger men stayed outside the ring of light, mocking the dancers and smoking. They shone torches at each other and at the girls grouped on the other side of the stockade, and made jokes at the expense of the foreigners. It reminded me of the nervous moments at the beginning of a local disco. But a couple of hours of the hypnotic dance and the monotone of the music eventually drew the sceptics in. The torches flashed less frequently, and surreptitious couples started to disappear into the rain-forest. All in all, it was not so far removed from a Saturday night in the West. Inside our hut too, the atmosphere was hypnotic, an illuminated stillness with the drone of the gourd and steady tramp of the dance as a backdrop. All eyes concentrated on the only flame that lit the hut walls, as shapes crouched over it, preparing bowls of opium. The chief's assistant was offering them at five baht a throw; lying down opposite him and watching him going through the ritual of preparation was more hypnotic than the effect of the drug itself.

The next day was tedious and tiring – the rain saw to that. The path climbed directly up a steep hill, a chute of rich, slippery mud. As the day wore on the rain stopped, but the humidity of the forest was so heavy that the leaves of the trees dripped steadily, and so did our faces. As we churned up the hill, sliding and swearing, lumpish and foolish, we met shy tribespeople on their way down, funnel-shaped wicker baskets on their backs. They were heavy betel-chewers, and their lips and teeth were stained a rusty red, as if someone had just punched them in the mouth. Many reacted to us as if afraid that we too would punch them: they backed off into the undergrowth at the side of the track whilst we struggled past, as if we were some kind of wild animal that would charge them if provoked. Some trekking agencies advertise elephants for the harder stretches of climbing: we ourselves must have looked elephantine to the tribesmen as we laboured upwards through the mud.

The top was shrouded in clouds. One of the previous night's smokers – they had all been looking rather grey all day, much to the satisfaction of the rest of us – threw up with great violence, and we called a halt until he felt fit to move again. Moon made a great show of knifing a massive orange caterpillar on the track, explaining that it could kill. When his knife flicked it into the air we all scattered, but it was safely dead. Thereafter we all made a lot more noise as we walked, in order to clear a safe path.

We stopped for a lunch of noodle soup in a village of the Red Lahu. The men were addicts, said Moon, and had been evicted from their former village for not taking their share of the village work. Opium does strange things to the body after years of addiction: these men had not an ounce of extra flesh on them, but they had not lost their muscle. From a distance their bodies looked sinewy and tough, but it was only the lack of flesh that made them look strong, like the diagrams of the inner structure of the human body in school biology laboratories. Their clouded eyes seemed glad to see us, even if they could not focus enough for any direct contact. To them we were a source of income, for we would pay for our smokes which would in turn help to pay for theirs. In that village it was the children who did the work, their eyes carrying expressions far older than their years. It would only be a matter of time before they too became addicts.

In the hut Moon prepared the soup whilst a couple of the Lahu prepared the opium. In its raw state the resin is a tacky black substance, not unlike solid black treacle, with a slightly sweet vegetable taste. The 'sky-pilot' – the man who prepares the bowls – and smoker lie on the floor with a flame between them. The sky-pilot melts some of the resin on to the glass around a small hole in the side of a small medicine bottle. The neck of the bottle is joined to a bamboo tube, and the smoker draws on this tube whilst the sky-pilot holds the hole above the flame. Smoke from the burning resin is drawn into the bottle and up the bamboo.

That lunchtime most of us were more interested in soup than opium, but there was to be no escaping the drug that day. Moon led us through opium fields until we were sick of the sight of them. Almost every path opened out into yet another field. Many were in flower, but the majority of the flowers were an unimpressive dirty white. Moon showed us how the harvester cut a slit in the fruit and collected the resin that seeped out, rather as rubber-tappers do. We were all surprised that such obvious cultivation could take place so close to the Chiang Mai–Chiang Rai highway; did not the police or army come to destroy the crop? Moon explained that the politicians themselves made good money from the trade, in backhanders from the dealers, or by diverting overseas funding that was intended to assist in the suppression of the trade, so there was no great pressure from high places to stop anything.

Moon seemed to know many of the people working in the fields, and stopped to talk to them often, indicating that we should go on ahead. Over the next couple of days it began to dawn on us that there was a dimension to him that we had not fully appreciated: he was a discreet addict, but his addiction was only part of a complex character. He obviously had a great love for the tribesmen – who he referred to as 'my people' even though he had been born in Bangkok. The tribes, too, seemed to welcome him with open arms, though whether that was through pure friendship or because in various ways he brought them money it was difficult to tell. Moon had all the makings of a revolutionary. His hatred of politicians and the south dated from the massive student riots in Bangkok in 1976, when the army opened fire on a student demonstration and killed 100 people. He had been a leader, he said, and consequently became a marked man. Like many of the other leaders he fled to Chiang Mai and went into the tourist business, and like the others he still felt that he was carefully watched even in the north.

But amongst the tribes Moon was not so much spreading revolutionary ideas as encouraging the opium business. Perhaps he saw this latter as a means to the same end. Undoubtedly the tribes had no political aggression, and the only way to force them into a political stance may have been to encourage their persecution by the government. He took care never to let us see him smoke, and whenever someone offered to buy him a bowl he refused – he had given up the habit, he said. Yet it was always he who arranged for the drug to be brought and supervised its preparation.

At first we took his assurances at face value, and admired the strength of someone who had managed to kick a heavy habit whilst still remaining in contact with the drug. But this wasn't the complete picture. At every village Moon would disappear for a while to "visit his friends". As the trek went on these disappearances became more and more lengthy. Then he began to stay behind when we were about to set off. He would indicate the path and say he would catch us up in a few minutes – he had to say goodbye to a friend. Someone then spotted an account book in his rucksack, and we began to speculate. He would never let us near his rucksack, even to remove basic supplies. Although we never had definite proof, between us we agreed that he was conducting a very tidy dealing job, every week doing the rounds of the villages, picking up the raw opium and paying off, making a note of all weights and debts in his book. Then he would return with the tourists to the town, but his pack would be a little less innocent than theirs. It was a perfect cover.

On the fourth day of our five-day trek we woke to clear skies and the ground had dried. The fresh morning air quivered with the dull beat of rice-thumpers chaffing the day's padi. The women shouted to each other as they shifted their weight from ground to thumper and back again, the hammer end of the pivoted log stabbing its head into the wooden pestle. The colours of the flowers glowed through the flimsy walls of our hut, signalling to us to make the most of the day.

The first of the village's workers to leave that morning was the rice-planting team, taking with them lemons and salt: they knew how hot the sun could get in the clear days of the rainy season, and they knew what best sustained them through a long day of that heat. One villager returned from an early-morning shooting trip, his only prize a tiny bird. He demonstrated with pride how he had shot it whilst it was sitting, singing, in a tree. The barrel of his gun was enormously long and had been made by his father, he said.

We left the village with the last of the workers: the daughters of the households, on the backs of the family buffalo, heading for a day's foraging and dreaming in the hills.

That day's walking was the most pleasant. The trend was downhill, as we were to return to Chiang Mai the following evening. Enormous yellow-winged butterflies hung over delicate orange flowers, like humming-birds. Amongst the trees the beetles set up an electric whine. We had to be wary of tree ants, which brushed off grasses on to our legs, and bit with such ferocity that their whole bodies would curl up with the effort. Fortunately the bites were only temporarily painful. On either side of the track hidden crickets made the air vibrate, and a small Golden Oriole flashed through a patch of sunlight over the path, carrying a long blade of grass in its beak. The ribbon of green catching the light made the bird look like a flying snake. I wouldn't have said that the forestscape was beautiful – it was too hot, tense and unknown for that – but it was certainly atmospheric.

The transformation in the weather transformed the spirits of the party. We became one group again, instead of two factions. Moon walked sometimes at the head, sometimes at the tail, but always singing, practising his English and talking about the tribes. It was a delight to walk, and there was little real desire for the day to end; for this was our last full day's walking in the hills. The evening and the village of that night – belonging to the Yellow Lahu – came too quickly, and with it came a sad story.

The village clearing was pyramid-shaped, with its base at the bottom of the slope. An aqueduct made of split bamboo bisected the houses, raised on poles above the reach of the animals and bringing a steady flow of clean, bright water out of the forests above. At the point where we broke out of the furiously green and lush post-monsoon undergrowth that had hindered our progress all day the aqueduct ended in a small waterfall, a pool littered with smooth stones, and a stream that wound its way down into the blackness of the rain-forest again.

Three village girls squatted in their panungs beneath the waterfall, creating and re-creating shapes with their washing on the stones, like potters at their wheels. Where the water passed through the shadows around the stones it emerged polluted with the dye and dirt of the material, but by the time it reached the trees it was clean again, as if the sandy bed had sucked up the stain. I recalled, as I splashed through the stream behind Zaq, that Moon had said the tribespeople used sand to clean their teeth with – sand was probably the only thing abrasive enough to scour away the stain left by betel-chewing.

The village dogs had started barking as soon as we emerged, blinking out of the forest and into the sunlight. One of the girls looked up, saw us, and said something to the girl by her shoulder. Together they bent over their work, but I could see that they were listening carefully to the progress of the foreigners.

"*Ahb namh mai?*" I called, knowing that it was a stupid question – obviously they were washing – but I wanted to seem a friend, not an invader. The limits of my newly learned Thai did not allow me any more perceptive remarks, and anyway it seemed to fall on uncomprehending ears. Neither of the girls looked up, but a suppressed giggle passed between them. Feeling a little foolish I turned to catch up with Zaq at the tail of the party, which was already weaving up between the first of the huts, when my eye was caught by the third girl. She was sitting a little apart from the others and staring at me with some intensity.

Her hair was smoothed back from her forehead and secured loosely into a crude pony-tail by a couple of elastic bands. The harsh tropical sunlight renders most faces cadaverous and spectre-like in their highlights and hollows, but her skin managed to look smooth and luminous, a colour half-way between the fairness of the Chinese and the dark of the southern Thais. Her face was heavy-boned, but the characteristic high-ridged cheekbones of the more mongoloid tribes gave it a grace that I had not seen before. There was something about her, the way that she knitted her eyebrows in concentration as she stared, that held my attention for a moment, and I found myself gazing at her. It was some intensity of feeling - hatred, anger, fear, hope – it could have been any. The panung she had been washing dripped red dye steadily into the stream that ran around her ankles, but she was quite motionless. Suddenly I felt ashamed and intrusive, and turned my head away. My face tingling with embarrassment.

Moon called a halt outside the last and biggest hut at the top of the village. "Chief's hut," he said. "This things" – he indicated a tall cluster of bamboos, each with a strip of white cloth tied like a flag to its top – "this for bad spirit. This mean this chief hut. We sleep here." For a moment it seemed that we had taken his words literally as we fell out of the single file that we had unconsciously adopted, and sank wearily on to the ground around the steps of the hut.

"Tired," I said as I struggled out of the straps of my rucksack.

"Question or statement?" Zaq asked as he strained to pull off a boot.

"Either."

Zaq grunted as he straightened up and pulled a packet out of his top pocket. "Smoke?" I shook my head; after three days' trekking he still didn't seem to realise that I didn't smoke. I heard the flare of a match behind me as I climbed the steps on to the flat area that formed the balcony outside the hut entrance, and carefully placed my rucksack alongside a stack of hollowed-out bamboo tubes that were used for carrying water. Apart from these, and a small stack of firewood at the far end, the balcony was clear. I lowered myself to sit cross-legged on the floor. Like the walls it was made of flattened bamboo, and was springy beneath the unaccustomed weight of a white man. Through the strands I could see an old sow rooting around in the dust below, whilst a couple of chickens followed and pecked at random at what she disturbed. Moon had explained that all but one of the tribes built their houses on stilts both to keep out of the mud during the rainy season and to provide some shelter for the animals below.

"No one here," I remarked to Moon, who had joined me on the balcony and was in the process of pulling packets of dried noodles out of his pack.

"No one here," he echoed, as he struggled with a zip. "Later they here. Now in the field," he added as he straightened up and disappeared into the hut to start a fire. He seemed suddenly abrupt; perhaps he too was tired, I thought.

Three quarters of an hour later he called us in from the balcony to eat inside the dark hut. The sun was low in the sky, and dusk was about to come and go as quickly as it always does in the tropics. As we sat around the flames of the fire I felt pleasantly loose. The flickering light made our shadows move rapidly about on the walls, as if our shadows were reliving the day's walk, but our bodies were hypnotised into stillness by the light. Nights in the hills can be surprisingly cold, and the fire's heat began to be welcome as the strength of the sun diminished.

I knew that if I remained still for too long my body would seize up like a rusty bed as the joints stiffened from the day's walk, and I would not want to move at all. To sit around a fire in the company of Europeans whilst in the middle of a tribal village was a waste, I said to myself, so I got up for a quick tour of the village before darkness descended completely.

As I emerged into the half-light I saw to my surprise that two women were squatting on their heels on the balcony. From inside the hut I had heard and seen no one moving outside except two children, who had appeared briefly at the door to stare at Fleming before their mothers called them away. The older of the women was staring out over the village, quite motionless, with a short pipe of dark wood clamped between her jaws. She took no notice of me. It was impossible to judge her age, though as she stared out at the darkening fringe of the forest against the sky she could well have been looking back over 100 years.

The younger woman was pounding away at what looked like a giant leek with a giant pestle. When the balcony floor creaked under my weight she stopped working and looked up: the rhythmic thumping that had accompanied my thoughts for the previous few minutes ceased, and I realised with a slight shock that I was looking into those same eyes that I had met before, beside the stream. In that moment I knew why I had been struck by her: she was beautiful. There was a kind of majesty about her that matched that of the old lady, and she had the same depth of experience in her eyes even though she couldn't have been more than seventeen or eighteen years old. Again she stared incautiously, almost questioningly, at me, then her eyes slipped past my shoulder into the gloom as if she were disappointed at what she had or had not found in my face. She lowered her head over her work, and the balcony floor once more vibrated with rhythmic thumping, now more deliberate than before. After a moment she paused to push a wisp of hair out of her eyes and stick it to her forehead, and she muttered something to the old woman as she did so.

I realised in that moment that I was standing stupidly in the middle of the balcony, and remembering my original purpose I moved over to the top of the steps. Through the walls of a nearby hut I could see the yellow flicker of flame as glutinous rice was steamed in a basket for the evening meal. A couple of buffalo moved like shadows over the stream at the bottom of the village, followed by a woman with a stick in one hand and a child on her hip. Two men crossed from one hut to another, talking quietly. It was so foreign to me, this evening scene, and yet so familiar. I felt out of place, awkward and clumsy, a trespasser in a land where I had no place. Suddenly I wanted intensely to return to the fireside and the company of other Europeans. I stood for a moment longer, transfixed by indecision.

"Sun's gone fast." The voice startled me, and it was a moment before I picked out Zaq's shape from the shadows at the foot of the steps.

"Yup." My voice sounded unsteady, so I didn't risk saying anything more.

"I've just been round the village," continued Zaq. "It's a deal cleaner than last night's. Must be the different tribe, I guess. Whad'he call 'em? Lamen, or something?"

"No, Karen was last night. These are the Lahu, the Yellow Lahu." The lilt in the Australian's voice was reassuring.

"I wonder why they are called yellow," mused Zaq. He came up the steps steadily, and together we sat on the top step looking out over the darkening village.

When Moon came out of the hut a few minutes later, heavy eyed from the heat of the fire, he noted the two foreigners sitting on the steps talking quietly, and then turned and greeted the old lady courteously. She deliberately and accurately squirted a jet of betel juice through a gap between the strands of bamboo flooring, then she nodded slowly, without a word. Moon seemed satisfied with this and crossed to where the girl was working. She lay down her pestle as he squatted down beside her and asked him a series of questions. He shook his head sadly, shrugging his shoulders with each monosyllabic answer.

I had become aware of the conversation as soon as the thumping of the pestle had ceased, and I felt sure that the last couple of questions were about me: as Moon stood up they were both looking at me, and both looked quickly away when they became aware of my stare. I felt simultaneously angry and intrigued: why me? As soon as Moon joined us (I'm sure he would have slipped away if he'd thought we hadn't seen him) he slotted immediately into his role of guide and informant, but to me it seemed clumsily done.

"Chief mother and chief daughter." He gestured expansively at the two women. "Chief have three daughter and one son. All my frien'."

"Everyone here seems to be your friend," said Zaq with a laugh.

"Yes, I thing so, everyone my frien'," Moon beamed. He referred to every European as 'my friend' basically because he found our names hard to remember, and even harder to pronounce. He continued in his role: "She make food for pig from banana tree. This people not eat banana like Bangkok. That banana-tree inside" – he pointed at a length of the giant leek that lay beside the girl – "she make food for pig from tree." He seemed frustrated by his inability to explain it better, and looked at us to see if we had understood. Zaq put his mind at rest. "Uh-huh, I got it. She's mashing up the trunk of a banana tree for the pigs to eat."

At that moment the girl stood up and heaped the pulped fibres on to a round, shallow, basket. She paused at the top of the steps for us to make way for her, refusing to meet any of our eyes. I wanted to look at her again, to speak to her. She was so close that I could almost have reached out and touched her skin. "*Nee kluay mai?*" I said. "This is banana?" I cursed my inadequate Thai for making me sound crass again, but it was the only thing I could think of in the circumstances. She gave no sign of having heard anything. She descended the steps without looking up once, and when she reached the bottom she began to make a harsh sound with the back of her throat. As she disappeared into the darkness I could hear the grunt of pigs answering her call.

"She very sad," said Moon finally, after we had all watched the gleam of the nape of her neck until it had vanished from sight into the darkness.

"Why's that?" asked Zaq.

Moon seemed to consider for a moment. "No good story," he said, eventually. "Very bad."

"Oh come on, Moon, for God's sake, now that you've told us there is a story you've got to tell us what it is." I had intended to speak casually, but my voice sounded petulant and impatient. It struck a harsh enough note to make Zaq look at me with some surprise, but the expression on my face was concealed by the darkness. I could hear the crackle of flames from within the hut, against the background of the hum of cicadas celebrating the coming of darkness within the forest wall. I could sense that Moon was looking at me, gauging my mood and my reactions. Then he seemed to reach a decision and cleared his throat.

"She chief's daughter, I say already," he began. "We come this village many time, maybe eight time one year, with foreigner. Always stay this hou'." He nodded towards the door, and split a splinter of bamboo away from the floor with his fingernail. "Not last time, but time before, one my frien' [one of the trekkers], my frien' he see this girl and he like her. Is pretty girl." He glanced at me as he said this, but I didn't acknowledge him. His voice was stronger when he resumed. "My frien' he says to me, 'Moon, you go. I stay here.' I say is not possible – how he know way home? He say he know way, is no problem. I say many, many time is no possible, but he make me ask chief, and chief say is OK." Moon scratched at the floor with the splinter.

"I thing maybe chief thing he can get money, or maybe he frighten to say no. This people little bit frighten' white people sometime." Moon sounded almost apologetic. "So I must say OK and we go and my frien' he stay, laughing and play with girl." Here Moon paused to consider how best to relate the remainder of the narrative.

"Next time I come here, three week ago," he resumed, "I look but I no see frien'. I see chief and I ask where my frien' go, but he look angry and not speak with me. So I ask my frien' chief son and he tell me that my frien' stay maybe three, four nights then he go back to Chiang Mai, he say he must fine letter and see other frien', but she so very sad he say he coming back later. Now she not live with her brother and sister. They say she marrit to falang and must live in different hou'. She stay with grandmother in small hut in field and she wait till her frien' come back to fine her."

I became acutely conscious of the presence of the old lady, motionless as a sentinel in the dark. I was sure that I could hear her teeth grinding the stem of her pipe as she chewed the pan. I wondered if she had any idea of what we were talking about. Moon continued.

"Today she ask me if I bring frien' with me. She not sure what he look like – to this people falang they look little bit same-same." Moon lowered his voice as he looked at me in the dark. "You look little bit like her frien'," he said. I was beginning to understand. "Today she ask me if I bring frien' with me, and when I say no, she ask me when I go bring him, and I say I not sure." Moon stopped scratching the bamboo and spoke so quietly that we had to lean towards him to catch the words. "I thing maybe he never come back."

Into the silence that followed, the sound of the cicadas welled into a deafening roar, and the walls of the forest closed in on us as we sat petrified in the darkness.

For a long time after the others had gone to bed I sat motionless on the balcony. Three metres away from me the old lady sat on too, facing the moon as it climbed the sky, seemingly oblivious of my presence. Occasionally I coughed and shifted, but she squatted on as if she were carved from granite, only moving when she inclined her head at intervals to squirt betel-juice through a now-invisible gap in the floor. I could hear the soft pat of the jet as it hit the dusty ground below. When I finally felt the cold, and went in search of my sleeping-bag, I lay in the hut feeling the ache in my bones and listening to the shifting of the animals beneath the flooring that was my bed.

In the morning it was raining steadily again, the sky an unbroken grey. Small streams ran down through the village, turning the dusty shallows that the pigs had made into baths of mud. Water spilled over the edges of the bamboo aqueduct at its joins and corners. The stream at the bottom of the slope had spread beyond its banks, and ran an ugly brown into the trees. There was a steady rattling sound from the rain-forest as the leaves of the trees wept one on to the other. Over our breakfast – sweet Thai bread that had come up in Moon's pack, and sweeter coffee – we were silent, chewing steadily and looking out into the rain. Someone asked whether we would be setting off.

Moon, who was gathering up the plates, paused for a moment and looked around the circle of faces that were all turned towards him.

"We go. It's stop soon," he said. "Raining season finish already. No problem." And he smiled.

There are few places in the world where green and immature westerners can come into direct and prolonged contact with very primitive people, but northern Thailand is one of them. As I pointed my camera at a succession of children's faces, to see as I did so a furrowed expression that mixed anxiety and fear cloud each of them, it dawned on me that here is the sharp end of travel, and the most sensitive; here is the travellers' paradox – here travellers destroy the very things that they particularly travel to see.

But the destruction in the paradox does not just end here. Eighteen months later I returned to trekking in northern Thailand. My impressions of those later treks are far from vivid; I had very little sensitivity left to give. I needed more and more to stimulate a dulled palate, as a drug-addict does. On those treks I walked with the opium-smoking faction, and I too was pale and sickly when the morning came.

3 *Fishermen Friends*

I was not in a reflective state of mind as I left northern Thailand. I was looking ahead – looking forward to my reunion with Alison. I had so much to tell her – at last we would have plenty to talk about. I made a mental note of which of my experiences since we had parted were worth relating, and I tried to find out all I could about the southern resort of Phuket, which was to be the scene of our rendezvous. I was earlier than I had anticipated in leaving the north, so I dawdled for a few days in the Chinese hotel in Bangkok, lying beneath that old familiar ceiling fan. I left the hotel on schedule for a perfect meeting, but when I saw the sea for the first time, three days later, I was forty-eight hours later than I should have been, and in agonies over the possibility that Alison might have left without me, her patience exhausted.

The delay was out of my control. Long-distance travel in Thailand is usually done overnight, either by rail or by coach. On the roads travellers have the choice of private air-conditioned coaches or government buses. Most Western travellers chose the former, but to be obtuse, authentic and cheap I chose the latter. What I saved on the price of the ticket I more than paid for in time wasted. Because non-Thais seldom travel by government bus there were no signs in roman script at Bangkok's western bus station. The headboards on the buses were all in Thai script, and I had to enquire which one went to Phuket. It was only once we had reached the fringes of the extensive Bangkok suburbs, shortly before midnight, that my ticket was checked, and the mistake discovered. The bus shuddered to a halt and deposited me and my bags on the dusty and dark roadside to make my way back into the city as best I could. This involved a lot of walking and cursing.

The following night I was not going to make the same mistake, so I asked a kind Thai bank-clerk to write a note which read – as far as I knew – "This gentleman is going to Phuket. Please make sure that he gets on the right bus." I felt a little like Paddington Bear as I showed the note, but I also felt a great deal more secure as I settled into my seat.

The express buses are not alone on the night roads. Strings of lorries move in convoy, their coloured lights flashing, stirring up the dust from the unmetalled surfaces and reducing visibility to a matter of feet. Our driver's hand was glued to the horn as he overtook, the windows of the bus rattling in their frames. There was little hope of sleep, but I consoled myself with the thought that it was cheap, and that it was moving in Alison's direction.

The road had been bad for some while when the first tyre gave way, shortly after midnight. The puncture came as no surprise – the surprise was that it hadn't happened earlier – but the peace that came with it was welcome. The co-driver was roused from where he lay fast asleep across the back row of seats, and he and the driver between them managed to change the wheel within half-an-hour.

An hour later another tyre went with a bang, and we all piled off the bus a little more tight-lipped than previously, some to disappear off into the bushes and the rest to stand in a loose circle around the flattened wheel. After a lot of swearing and jumping up and down on levers it soon became apparent that the deflated tyre did not want to leave the bus in the lurch. As we no longer had a spare, I didn't really know why they wanted to remove it anyway. Another bus stopped, the drivers consulted briefly, and the other bus left. We stood in the road and stared at the cursed thing. There was a lot of mutual commiseration on the bad luck of the same misfortune happening twice, which then turned into more general conversation about roads and travel, whilst the women began to drift back into the bus and settle down for the night. Then a passing car stopped, and one of the drivers was persuaded to go off in search of assistance. Some of us kept watch for his return for a couple of hours, squatting around the wheel but hardly a car passed and nobody else stopped.

The inside of the bus was humming quietly with the sound of sleeping Thais when I finally gave up the wait and returned to my seat. Like most Europeans I am no good at simply waiting for time to pass, and the frustration of the added delays that separated me still further from Alison kept me awake for some while. Before I eventually lapsed into sleep I heard a train rattling over the flat land in the far distance, and wished that I was on it.

Most of us were awake for the dawn. The darkness to sunrise period is very short in the tropics, just as dusk to darkness is, and I missed the long, leisured beginnings and endings to days that we know in the West. This sunrise was not glorious, but for a few moments it was peaceful, subtle and delicate. As soon as the sun had climbed a little way into the sky the day became hot, as if someone had turned on a tap of wet heat.

Then a strange little scene took place at the roadside, for by this time everyone was out of the bus and looking for private places in the undergrowth to do morning things. Into this scene cycled an old man with a large tin box mounted on the rear wheel of his bike. He was on his way from the ice-cream factory to work in the local town, and in his box was his morning's stock of ice-cream. Having had no breakfast to speak of, everyone crowded around the old man, and soon the orange bus was surrounded by bleary-eyed travellers licking ice-creams in the early-morning sun. When we had all had one, and some of us had had another, the old man stood for a moment with one foot poised on the pedal, surveying us all with the smile of a fond parent, then he swung his leg over the saddle and turned his bicycle back in the direction of the factory for a second load.

The driver then returned after spending a comfortable night in a local town; within thirty minutes the wheel was replaced and we were back on the road. The tin and chrome of the bus was already too hot to touch, and every window was open.

I soon learned why long-distance buses travelled by night, quite apart from reasons of temperature. By day Thai roads are thronged with cattle, ox-carts, cyclists, pedestrians, and bemos, the pick-up trucks that function as local buses, their tailgates scraping the road with the weight of baskets of market produce. At times we slowed to the pace of the ox-carts, and took most of the day to reach the mountains that separate Hua Hin and the northern part of the Kra peninsula from the southern island of Phuket.

I consoled myself with the thought that the journey could have been worse. One of the first bus-loads of tourists for the newly created resort of Phuket had met with a more dramatic fate. They had been travelling en masse in a luxury coach that was easy to recognise. Warned in advance of their arrival by the newspapers, a band of communist rebels had had no trouble in shredding the tyres and stopping the bus in the dead of night. Once they had unloaded the rich foreigners from the bus, and the possessions from the foreigners, they ordered everyone to strip, threw the clothes into the now-blazing and doomed vehicle, and disappeared with the loot. No doubt the gentle old ice-cream seller would have been very surprised at the sight of a strange collection of naked foreigners advancing cautiously towards him out of the undergrowth, covering what they could with plantain leaves. The boys back at the factory would have found that one hard to believe.

There were to be no more surprises for us, fortunately. I slept through the afternoon, by now thoroughly fed up with the journey but largely resigned to my fate. The sight of monkeys in the mountain tree-tops and working elephants ambling up the roads – sights which I would have missed thanks to the darkness if all had gone according to plan – did little to relieve the frustration of the time wasted. It was only once we rounded one of the worst bends on the way down from the mountains that a rain-cloud suddenly parted and we emerged into strong sunshine, and there, way, way down below in the distance was a striking expanse of bright and sparkling blue sea. In front of me a child, wedged between his parents, stopped crying at last and stared at the startling blue. I suppose that my reactions were the same – but tempered with adult restraint.

Phuket island is covered with straggly rubber plantations in a poor imitation of Malaysia. Inland it is unexciting, but the seas that lap the island shores are rich in corals and fish. At appropriate times of year the silvery-white squeaky sand of the beaches is littered with relaxing foreigners, all busily acquiring that leathery, tanned look that distinguishes travellers from the plumper and pinker tourists, who have less time to perfect their appearance. Tourist or traveller, the locals made no distinction and thought everyone mad for lying in the sun with no clothes on; for their part they tried hard to stay in the shade and keep their skin as fair as they could. Many parents cover their children's skin with powdered sandalwood, making their pale faces gleam like ghosts in the dark shade of the trees and the restaurants that fringe the beaches.

The main town is as noisy as any in Thailand, with pick-up trucks blaring the sound-tracks of the latest movies as they slowly circle the centre. In front of the cinema itself – a breast complete with nipple on the lurid poster shows that this is a far cry from neighbouring Malaysia – a cigarette and magazine seller sits behind her table. On the cover of one of her magazines a very revered abbot is frozen in mid-speech by the crude light of the photographer's flash, his eyes glinting white and his mouth half-open. The Thais find no contradiction between the monk's photograph and the acres of naked flesh on the cinema poster behind it. Whether they are pimping, picking a pocket, or murdering a neighbour they all still wear Buddha images around their necks. "Jesus saves, Moses invests, but only Buddha pays dividends" – Buddhism is a part of daily life.

In the town's market, catfish drum and thrash around in old tin pails, their vendors – knotting their proceeds from the day's sales into a grubby square of cloth – quite unconcerned by their charges' show of life. Lok Tham, the Thai popular music, blares from every cassette stall, striking chords that at times sound Western, at times oriental.

Out beyond the noise of the tuk-tuks (taxis) that circle the town centre a soft drinks vendor sleeps on her bench, in the shade behind her stall, her block of ice dripping steadily into a well-placed bucket. A herd of buffalo splash through the padi beyond the town fringes, their hides matted with mud to protect them from the heat of the middle of the day. By the roadsides, entrepreneurs set up their own filling stations for the scores of small motor-cycles that buzz around the island. A drum of petrol, a shelter, a pump, a length of tubing and a calibrated glass jar are all that is necessary. Next door, bananas are battered and deep-fried; two baht will buy four slices, in a paper bag made from pages torn from school exercise books. I always found myself wondering, when I bought something from a food-stall, whether the children themselves sold their old exercise books to the stall-keepers, and whether they were at all embarrassed at the thought of their essays and sums being scrutinised by fried-banana eaters.

When the bus finally bumped the last bump into the bus-station, the island was rapidly getting dark, and it was far too late to start looking for Alison. I checked into the cheapest hotel I could find, consoling myself with the thought that the coming nights of togetherness would be all the better for having been delayed. The

Chinaman in the alleyway that constituted the hotel foyer didn't attempt to understand my Thai. He chalked up three prices on a board and indicated that I should choose one. When I chose the cheapest he grunted as if that was what he had expected, and thrust a flimsy key in my direction. Rats scuttled away down the dark corridor in front of me as I looked for a flimsy padlock that matched the key.

I found Alison's message waiting for me at the Poste Restante the following morning, as we arranged. She was staying in a bungalow on Karon beach, she wrote, and I noted with relief that her message was only two days old. I also caught up with a backlog of letters, redirected from Bangkok. Amongst them was one from my girlfriend at home in England. She wrote that she didn't want to continue receiving letters that were travelogues; she wanted to receive letters that were by me and about me for her – not for some onward audience. I noted the contents and stuffed the envelope into my bag, irritated. I had written her some of my best descriptions of Bangkok, I thought.

At Karon it was not difficult to locate Alison. Ominously enough, everyone seemed to know her and where she was staying. The door of her bamboo bungalow was half open and she was spreadeagled on the bed, half-conscious; the floor was littered with roaches from joints. Our reunion could not have been more unromantic.

"Hi, it's me."

"Uh . . ."

"How are you?"

"Ill, I've got the shits, so leave me alone."

"Oh."

Pause, and try again. "Nice hut you've got."

"Wanna sleep."

"Looks like a nice place."

"Bloody hot."

Pause. Then one last remark, to which I got a complete and cogent sentence in reply. "Coming out for a swim and a look around?"

"I told you, I got the shits, so go away and leave me alone," she groaned from the bed. I went, but I left my bag in her bungalow.

Back on the sand I gauged the extent of my dismay. Perhaps I had been expecting too much, I told myself, but was there really that little between us? I got little further than the first row of taliput palms at the top of the shelving beach. The sand was too hot for bare feet, so I slumped down in the shade. I found my English girlfriend's letter in my hand, and scanned it several times, not reading the words but feeling the strength of emotion behind them. Above my head the sluggish wind stirred the brittle taliput leaves enough to make a sound, the sound of the dead clapping. In the grass behind me a mynah bird belied its scraggy appearance by soliloquising and improvising endlessly in song.

The day dragged slowly into the afternoon, and I still hadn't moved from my shade – I didn't see any point in doing so. A group of fishermen gathered in the shade of a clump of taliputs and started playing cards. At first I presumed that they must have finished work for the day, but I was wrong: they were just starting.

At about three o'clock the surface of the sea boiled gently. I was not sure whether I had seen something stirring or just a wave breaking. A few moments later there was another movement, a little further along. The glint of thousands of tiny fish jumping desperately in unison as they tried to escape the jaws of hunting tuna and garfish. From beneath the taliput trees the cry went up, the fishermen dropped their cards and sprinted down the squeaky white sand to where their boat rested just above the water-line. Once afloat they paddled furiously, chanting all the while, and paying out a long net behind the boat. The net was anchored onshore by a gathering group of helpers, alerted by the shouts.

The beach was transformed, as if a charge of electricity had surged along it and brought everything that was alive into action, but on this first run the furious optimism went unrewarded. The cry went up, the sand squeaked, the paddles bit into the water and the net began to splash overboard, but then the fish stopped moving and the surface of the water stared back unruffled at the searching eyes of the fishermen. It was as if nothing had happened. The cries faltered, the paddles dipped half-heartedly, and then slowly the net-man hauled back on the line that he had just paid out, and dragged the boat back to the anchoring crowd onshore.

The second time the story was different. The fish continued to break the surface, and the fishermen paddled swiftly around the patch of twisting and turning sprats, jettisoning the net as they went. By the time that the boat had turned round the far side of the shoal and was returning to the beach fewer people were paddling: the younger ones had jumped overboard at intervals along the net, where they splashed and shouted to discourage the trapped fish from trying to escape the mesh. When the boat touched shore again the net was fully extended round the back of the shoal in an elongated U, and the onshore team set about dragging the U towards them. As the water grew shallower below the fish they began to panic: the more the dwindling pool thrashed, the more the swimmers on the net splashed and yelled, until, with a crescendo of shouting from all sides, the writhing and gleaming net was pulled on to the beach.

It was laden with tuna and garfish. The fishermen and their families got the pick of the tuna; anyone could help themselves to the ugly garfish, which were not such good eating. Other more prickly or indigestible species were carefully returned to the water. A stone fish blew itself up until its spikes stood out like a porcupine's quills, and was patted down the beach with a paddle to float off into the sea, where it was less likely to be vindictive. The net was coiled back on to the stern of the boat and the fishermen returned to their cards beneath the trees. The children disappeared into the trees in the direction of their family houses, long thin garfish hanging like silver threads from their hands. Peace returned to the bay for a while, and then the whole cycle repeated itself again.

It was exhilarating to be on the fringes of such a harvest. It seemed that the bay, which had all the picture-postcard appearance of a paradise, was also a paradise in its generosity. Whether they were young or old the fishermen all seemed carved from equally polished mahogany, their smiles gleaming white with success. I had found my noble savages without even trying. I returned to Alison in an altogether different mood to the one in which I had left her, but the new mood did not last long. Alison did not want to talk: she was hot, she was ill, she had been squatting all day, she did not want me to stay with her, and no, she certainly did not want to go out for something to eat.

On my way back from my solitary meal I returned in the darkness to the scene of the afternoon's excitement. The beach was littered with surplus garfish, and in the moonlight the landcrabs looked like pale, luminous ghosts of their brothers in the water as they sprinted silent-toed across the sands to disappear into their burrows with bits of scavenged fish. Beneath my feet little phosphorescent animals gleamed in the sand with each step, and seemed so bright that I quite expected to feel their heat through the soles of my feet. But there was no scorching – not even a tingle of a moving animal – and the sand remained cool and quiet. Where the garfish had been left untouched by fishermen or crabs they had died slowly, digging their noses into the sand, their long, thin bodies arching into question marks that shone silver in the moonlight.

On the beach the next day there were no repeat performances. The fair breeze, the surf, the song of the mynah – which had symbolised fecundity before – now seemed the trappings of sterility. In the evening the fishermen trooped home quietly to the slow hand-clap of the taliput palms, having spent most of the day in their shade.

Alison was a little better, and for the first time since I had arrived she even seemed quite pleased to see me. She thought that she could manage a bowl of soup, so we went to the nearby tourist restaurant.

I had gathered from what little she had said that she had got to know several other travellers over the days prior to my arrival. They had steered clear of her bungalow during her illness – and possibly because of my presence – but in the restaurant they welcomed her with open arms, making room for her at the crowded table. I tagged along, quiet, jealous and unhappy, and found myself a seat at the end.

My neighbour turned out be an American who had been on Phuket for over a year. He started talking to me straightaway, but this was not conversation, this was monologue. He described his daily life on the beach – I don't think I was expected to say anything. "Most days I git up early enough to be able to have mysell a good breakfast and go up to town with old I Ching Chinaman here, in his bemo." He took a slow look around the room to see if he could spot the restaurateur, and only resumed his slow narrative once he had. "I then spend around twelve minutes having my body refreshed by a Thai gurl, and when I say gurl I mean gurl. Anything that's over the age of twelve or thirteen is getting a bit loose, dontcha find?" He wound on. "Then I git mysell over to the market and have a good talk with some of those bast-head gooks over there about the prices of that rip-off fruit they sell." After an hour in the market selecting his lunch, he then returned with the restaurant owner, who had the task of preparing the meal. "And gawd help the bast-head if he gits it wrong. If he fucks up he has to git his ass back to town, I'm telling you!" The American found this idea very funny, and his laugh was as slow as the rest of his speech. The rest of the monologue was a kind of slow eulogy on the merits of pubescent girls, comparing them to those in their later teens, and on citrus fruit, which he preferred to the other sorts. Both girls and fruit were seen as fuel to his body. In the afternoons, after his nap, he oiled his skin with coconut oil and went jogging along the sand once the sun had dropped reasonably low in the sky. "My life produces one hotshit body. Just feel this here arm . . . and this . . . look here . . ." He went all over his body, cataloguing the evidence of perfection, and urging me to feel it to believe it. "And I'm telling you I don't drop nothing either – no junk, no shit, no acid, no way. I'm looking after my body."

After three months on the road I had met my ration of freaks, but this American was a new departure. His body may have been perfection itself – and was evidently the object of much admiration on the beach, where such things counted – but his mind had rotted in the tropics as quickly as the fruit which he so much admired. How he managed to continue renewing his visa, and where he found the endless source of money to support his life, I could not guess. I did not dare ask but I suppose that he must have come out of Vietnam. Rotting away in that tropical paradise, the American preached his sermon of citrus fruit and thirteen-year-old girls, on into the night.

The conversation rolled on and on and around me in that restaurant and I took no part in it, but I was still sitting there as the blinds were finally pulled down and the restaurateur started whisking the spilled rice from around our ankles on the earth floor. In a way I was grateful for the American, as I had not been called upon to say anything. I knew that if I had opened my mouth whatever I had said would have been a disaster, and I also knew that even though Alison had never turned to me and seemed engrossed in conversation she had been acutely aware of – and embarrassed and irritated by – my poor performance. We walked back in silence to our hut under the canopy of what should have been a beautiful night. Once inside the tiny room I said that I was going to leave the following morning: she agreed that that was a good idea. There was no need for further words – I was young, naïve, and I had seen romance where there was only companionship in travel. We then made love as if to set the seal on disillusion, wordlessly and emotionlessly. Images of twelve-year-olds, the market, and my girlfriend in England circled in my head as I lay awake afterwards.

I retreated to lick my wounds to a beach further south. There I set my mind to learning Thai with the help of an effete Thai boy who hung gratifyingly on my every word. I was never sure whether Noi ('small' in Thai) was gay, but on one occasion when the huts were all full we shared the same bed, and Noi's hands crept in my direction regularly through the night. I may have misjudged him: the line between normal friendship and homosexuality is not drawn as distinctly in the East as it is in the West, and I later was to walk hand-in-hand and share beds with other men on several occasions.

Prachuap, the local shell-fisher, took me out on his boat. Underwater he swam like a dog but he was far more effective than I, and by the time that I had pansied about equalising the pressure in my ears on my way to the sea-bed he would have already dislodged two or three giant clams with his crowbar, the brittle blows of metal against rock scattering clouds of electric blue fish, and his simple red, black and white-checked sarong swirling uselessly in the water. It was Prachuap who suggested that I go to Phi Phi, a fishing island some forty kilometres to the south of Phuket. He suggested the trip over a meal of clams cooked by his wife with coriander and chillies. The chillies were strong enough to power a rocket, and completely overwhelmed all taste of the shellfish. I desperately tried to conceal a severe attack of hiccups. Prachuap brought out the lao khao (rice whisky), muddied with a powder which he said would help me stay underwater for longer, but which cured my hiccups and brought with it such a deterioration in all our inhibitions that just practising the pronunciation of my name and those of his family was enough to keep us entertained for hours. At the end of the evening he suggested Phi Phi; he would take me there in his boat, he said.

The following day I questioned him further about his offer, but it transpired that the fee he wanted was far beyond my reach.

Nevertheless, the seed of the idea was sown. I had failed in the society of travellers so exile to an island seemed fitting.

The literary, romantic side of me had taken over, to give life a purpose again after my failure with Alison. I compared myself to Axel Heyst, the hero of Joseph Conrad's *Victory*. Heyst had retreated to the isolation of the island of Samburan after failure in the outside world, and I would do the same. Conrad had been the subject of my thesis in my last year at university, and he featured heavily in my diary, if not so heavily in my thoughts. I was fascinated by his recurring theme of crossing a shadow-line between youth and maturity or between sanity and insanity. I was also interested in subjecting myself to 'the power of the wilderness', as he rather mysteriously described it in some of his books.

After a couple of days of hanging around in harbours on the south of the island I attached myself to a party of travellers who had chartered a boat to take them out to Phi Phi for the day. I told them that I was in Asia because I was following in the footsteps of Conrad, and in the one-upmanship between travellers this earned me a point: I had a purpose, whereas they were just going to Phi Phi for fun.

Nevertheless my dominant emotion, as I watched their boat back out of the bay that evening, was anxiety – though I would never have admitted it. I was stranded on the shores of Phi Phi, and I told myself that I completely understood Axel Heyst at that moment.

In fact our situations were considerably different. Heyst's fictional island is located somewhere off the coast of Java, not so far down the Malacca straits from Phi Phi; but whilst Samburan was a single, lonely island, Phi Phi consists of two islands carrying the same name, and both are very much alive. One is inhabited by birds, and the other by people. The inhabited island is basically two giant rocks linked by a bridge of sand, and it is on this sand-bar that the main village has been built and most of the islanders live. They are small fishermen, but in addition they provide the base and accompanying services for the larger trawlers that come from the mainland. The bay at Phi Phi is well-protected and quiet, the jetty good, and the island situated in the middle of the prime fishing grounds. Here the trawlers tie up during the day, and the crew bask in the sun to sleep off their night's work once the on-board chores are completed. If the weather is not suited to fishing they find drink and entertainment in the open houses on shore.

Very little grows on Phi Phi. The sand-bar is covered in a carpet of flowers shaded by palms, but the rest of the island is either poor scrub or sheer rock. Besides the coconuts, the small fishing, a little charcoal burning and rumoured marijuana-growing the islanders also make a living in a more daring way. Bird's nest soup is a rare delicacy in much of Asia, especially amongst the Chinese (the Chinese will eat anything with wings except planes, and anything with legs except tables, so it is said), and in Hong Kong small boxes of unbroken nests sell for £60. Sea-birds nest in large numbers in the sheer and seemingly unclimbable faces of the second Phi Phi island, but there are caverns and crevices within the rock face that enable the more nimble of the islanders to get within reach of these little pockets of gold.

Accommodation did not prove difficult to find. One of the crew of the boat that I had travelled out with introduced me to a householder who agreed to give me food and lodging for a price, but to introduce me to one proved to be an introduction to the whole island population, and I spent much of the rest of the day trying to explain just how many brothers and sisters I had – invariably the questions were the same. Age? Nationality? What was my job, they asked. And why was I not married? And, more awkwardly, why was I alone, where was my 'puhlern', my friend? To have attempted my Conrad explanation would have been futile. So for the last question I had worked out a formula – '*con deo dee-mark*' – 'it's very good to be alone' – which I thought was quite satisfactory but which they obviously and probably rightly thought was not a complete answer. Solitude – lack of family and friends – is regarded as a terrible fate throughout Asia.

Chai, the local teacher, took me under his wing and gave me a guided tour of the village, all twenty-five houses of it. He had decided that I was a writer, as he had seen me poring over my journal. I didn't try to disillusion him. It all fitted with the Conrad-chasing idea. I watched Chai play Thai football with his friends, and then when it got dark we sat on the end of the pier and watched the trawlers slip their moorings one by one and chug out of the bay. Chai explained the routine of the fishermen, and though he admitted that they were rough and tough people they never made trouble for the islanders, he said. The whisky they drank and the marijuana they smoked was a way to quick relaxation he said, and it helped them to sleep in the few hours that were available.

Chai had arranged a passage for me next day on one of the local fishing boats, so I went in search of my bed early. At the end of the pier the planks jumped beneath my feet and ghost-like land-crabs zoomed off into the darkness. There was no light in the hut, but I knew my way well enough to reach the sleeping area without knocking anything over – besides, there was no furniture to knock. The rattan mat on the floor beneath my shoulders felt cool, and I pulled a sarong out of my bag to use as covering; nights by water are not as hot as they are inland.

In the half-light of dawn I found Nam and Tan waiting for me on the beach, as Chai had said they would be. No one in Thailand ever seems to be called by their proper names (except apparently by angry mothers) and these two were no exception. Thai names are anyway tongue-defying, and in a register of one class I later taught in Singapore the most accessible was Chungsumnoonmanbont; the rest, although shorter, were more unpronounceable.

Nam was scurrying around the boat making preparations for sailing and smiling all the while. He was obviously the crew, whilst Tan was the captain. The latter watched for a while in a rather indifferent, sleepy way, fiddled with a rope or two, checked that the fishing lines were on board, and then disappeared into his house for a while for no evident purpose. Nam grinned at me, but said nothing and seemed in no hurry to go and tell Tan that all was ready.

It was early morning before Tan at last re-emerged, looking as if he had just been getting a little more sleep. As we chugged away into the bay, Tan standing on the stern steering lazily with one foot on the tiller, the daylight was framing the great barren knuckles of rock of the two Phi Phi islands against the skyline. Both Nam and Tan were men of very few words at that time in the morning, though I got the impression that Nam would have liked to attempt a conversation but was under instructions not to. I decided that I would keep out of their way as best I could, and made myself comfortable just behind the bows.

The largest limestone knuckle of them all, the people-less Phi Phi, was our first stop, and for my benefit Tan steered into the lagoon inside the heart of the island. The boat leaned dangerously as we all peered over the one side at the colours of the coral below. Then they showed me the ropes hanging down inside the caverns above the waterline – ropes used by the villagers to reach the nests. Then, tour over, business began.

For the first couple of hours they fished with simple white feathers, hauling small fish aboard in twos and threes. These small fish were to be bait, and when the pile of the catch was judged large enough – by Tan, of course – Nam jumped down into the engine well, turned the engine over until it grunted into life, and emerged to wipe his oil-stained hands on the gunwales of the boat. We stopped again on the other side of the island and repeatedly dropped the anchor close to the cliff-face until it gripped and held. Judging by the colours, shapes and sizes of the fish that Nam and Tan then caught we were sitting on top of another coral reef. The fish that were worth keeping they called lai-oh, and the others they carefully threw back. Even many of the lai-oh (a term that covered many different species) had evil spines on their backs and required cautious handling. Nam was the better fisherman, concentrating eagerly on his line and shouting whenever he hooked or missed a fish. Tan sat on the roof and watched the waves wash in and out of the caverns, sucking and booming as they moved; his line trailed loosely into the sea.

Once the sun was directly overhead Nam set aside his line and started a fire to cook the rice for lunch. He made the fire in what is loosely translated as a fire-box, but which was more like a fire-bucket made out of brick and filled with charcoal. When the rice was done he returned to his fishing, but this time every fish he caught went straight into the fire, the largest amongst them flapping out several times on to the deck before it allowed itself to be cooked. Then we had lunch.

After lunch Nam stirred the motor into life again and we returned to the bait-fishing ground of the morning. Nam removed the stoppers in the hull between two of the major bulkheads, and the makeshift hold soon filled with water. Into this storage tank went all the fish then caught. It was some while before Tan was satisfied that the catch was sufficient, partly because the catching rate was considerably lower than it had been in the morning, and partly because we were competing with another similar boat doing the same, and Tan did not like to be beaten. So the two of them fished on, with Nam casting increasingly anxious glances at the sun, the number of fish swimming in the hold, and Tan, in strict rotation.

I understood his anxiety when we finally set off for the afternoon's fishing grounds; we must have motored for at least an hour and a half out into the open sea before Tan called a halt. How they knew where to fish I could not tell; apart from the island in our wake and the dim shape of the mainland far to the east, I could see no landmarks. But Tan was certain, and the engine coughed, spluttered and died.

I made a bad mistake on the long haul out to sea that afternoon – a mistake which I think the others thought would cost them the afternoon's fishing. Tied around the neck of the bows were a couple of coloured cloths, and whilst changing my position on the forward deck my feet had come to rest on part of one of the cloths. The first I knew of my indiscretion was a hiss from Nam, who glared at my feet. I swiftly removed them, but the damage was done and Tan had noticed. As far as he was concerned this confirmed his belief that my whole presence on the boat was a mistake, and thereafter he refused to even look at me. The morning's fishing had not been bad at all, and gradually Tan had started to smile a little in my direction, even directing a couple of remarks at me. He had smiled once when I congratulated him on a fine fish, and nodded in agreement when I remarked that it was hot, but my standing on the spirit-flags had undone all that in one easy move; it was no use my protesting that I didn't know what they were. So the atmosphere on board as the two fishermen baited up their wire traces in the hope of catching blah yai – big fish – was tight-lipped and pessimistic.

Fortunately for me that pessimism was uncalled-for. Within minutes Nam had landed a barracuda and then Tan did the same. The omens had been proved wrong, and Tan looked less thunderous. Nam looked mightily relieved. The barracudas were fearsome-looking things, and they fought violently in the water. Once on board they stopped struggling, and the only sign that they were still alive was the heaving of their gills as they fought to live. Nam hooked and lost an immense tuna, but laughed about it. The loss rate was high, and although losses were obviously a source of commiseration as they also meant lost income, Nam and Tan seemed to be enjoying the sport – something which I had not expected.

At the end of two hours' fishing came the sunset, which brought with it a string of trawlers. They came steaming out in lines from the islands and the mainland, and they obviously viewed us as an irritating sprat trespassing on their fishing territory. At first Nam and Tan affected not to notice them as they bore down on us, horns blaring. But in the end the wash and the near misses wore down their resistance, and Tan muttered to Nam, who disappeared down into the engine well to grind the engine into life; our bows sprang to point again at the broken knuckle of Phi Phi island.

It was a beautiful ride back. The evening air was renewed and fresh after the heat of the afternoon, and no land mass concealed the full strength of the sunset. Above Phi Phi large seabirds hung high in the sky against a vermilion backdrop. By the time that we reached the bay darkness had closed over, and the boat slipped gently in through the mooring posts that loomed up quickly out of the shadows. The jetty was silent; all the trawlers from the previous evening had put back out to sea. A handful of villagers gathered together to haul the boat up out of the reach of the tide and seemed impressed with the size of the catch, which some of them seemed to attribute directly to my presence on board. My sacrilege with the spirit-flags was forgotten. Just to make sure that Nam and Tan harboured no hard feelings I presented them with a large bottle of whisky before we parted awkwardly on the beach.

I was rescued from Phi Phi a day later by a couple of fat Germans on a chartered gin-palace. On the boat with them – besides the two crew – were a couple of Thai prostitutes. The journey was quite a contrast to my day out with Nam and Tan, and a never-ending stream of cans of lager, cold chicken and German sausage flowed from the icebox. I felt rather distanced from my two very generous hosts – just as Conrad's Heyst did when he ventured back into civilisation – and so did one of the girls, for she would not let her man come near her. The other girl kept taking her into a corner and speaking sternly to her, but it made little difference. The girl spent most of the return journey sitting cross-legged on the stern staring at the wake. The Germans resolved to ask for half their money back.

Phuket seemed a different place to the resort that I had left a few days earlier. In fact it was not Phuket, but my mood that had changed. I had succeeded on my own for the first time: I had stuck out my neck and been rewarded by an 'experience'. The thrill was considerable.

But there was no one to share that thrill with. Only a day later my mood of positivism had ebbed away. No one was interested in my exile on the island – not even the Thais on the beach who had seemed so keen for me to go to Phi Phi. After a day amongst travellers again I began to feel as if a cold shadow had re-attached itself to me and was following me around as my only companion. To make matters worse I found mail waiting for me at the Poste Restante. My girlfriend in England had sent me a carefully recorded selection of some of my favourite Schubert and Chopin piano works. The music replaced the chatter of geckos and the soliloquies of the mynah birds with an old order, with the feel of rich dark wood, of warm and cosy nights with rain on the window, with candlelight and carpets, and spring Sunday mornings. The tape served to make me acutely lonely for her, and it unearthed that question that all travellers try to keep buried: why am I here? What am I going to do with my life after travel? In my case I did what most travellers will do: I packed up and left. I headed south for Malaysia, and the onward rush of new places and faces banished for a time the inclination to harbour morose thoughts.

The daytime bus journeys were a great deal easier than the long haul down from Bangkok had been. The hills were supposedly full of communists, but the army at the roadside checkposts were flat out in the shade, taking it in turns to twitch the string that released the barrier and let traffic through. A young songbird in a covered cage by my feet repeated a single insistent note from beneath its cover, pausing only when the conducter lifted the cloth and poked a rice-daubed stick through the bars. Two turbaned Sikhs – a rare sight in Thailand – boarded at one stop with large bundles of textiles that they were touting from village to village. They entertained the whole bus by singing a medley of national anthems from all the South-East Asian countries they did business in.

I stopped for a night in the town of Krabi to have a look at the harbour. It was from here that some of the trawlers at Phi Phi had come. On the mudbank on the opposite side of the river estuary a large sailing vessel rested on its side next to the mangroves. At first I assumed that it was the relic of some bygone trading era, but this was in fact my first sighting of one of the Indonesian Bugis prahus, later to become a familiar sight. But my initial assumption seemed to be confirmed when the figures squelching around the hull of the old ship piled brushwood against it and set it alight, although this did seem a surprising act of vandalism. However, the fires flared only briefly, and then were extinguished before being rebuilt further along the hull. A man on the quay explained to me that the hull was being re-sealed with tar before the tide rose again, and that the boat was still very much in use. There was good trade to be done on the coast, he said, if you could avoid the customs: salt down to Malaysia, and charcoal and textiles back north. It was a traditional family business that must at one time have been in competition with the kind of tramp-steamer that Joseph Conrad once skippered.

I found myself a room in the only building in Krabi that owned up to being a hotel. It seemed deserted when I first arrived, but when I ventured upstairs in search of someone I found a girl asleep on one of the beds. I retreated to the bottom of the stairs and shouted 'hello' several times before she padded down towards me and sleepily showed me to a room. At the time I thought no more about it, but when I returned to the hotel that night I found a dozen men on the landing outside my room, waiting. As I sat on my own bed in my room the consciousness of that crowd, silently drawing on their cigarettes on the other side of my door, made me feel uncomfortable.

Hotel rooms in the traditional Thai hotels are divided by partitions that stop short of the ceiling to allow cool air to circulate. Unfortunately this also means that noise circulates with the air, and I lay on my back through the night trying to ignore the sounds coming over from next-door. At first I found this compulsory voyeurism an embarrassment, but as I waited for the next customer and for sleep, I began to see the lighter side of my situation. There I was, a decent, well brought-up kind of chap, separated from a grunting Thai fisherman and a giggling girl by a flimsy piece of board that was supposed to be a wall. What would my mother have thought? It may have been my naïvety that blinded me to the true nature of the hotel in the first place, but that naïvety did not extend to not being able to distinguish, in the dark safety of my room, what sounds meant what . . . A strange lullaby.

Farce continued into the daylight. When I rose reasonably early to cross the marshes and visit the village on the other side of the estuary I found that the iron hotel gates were padlocked, and there was no sign of the crowd of the previous night. I could well have been the only person in the hotel, but I wasn't going to go round knocking on all the doors until I found someone to open up for me. After retreating to my room and finishing the book that I was reading I decided that the best plan was to make as much noise as possible, so that if there was someone sleeping in the next room they would wake and remember that they had an innocent Englishman locked in their immoral premises.

So I slammed my door several times, thumped up and down the wooden stairs, dropped my bag on the floor and sang snatches of 'John Brown's Body', until finally a door creaked open and a bare-foot, heavy-lidded girl padded out across the landing with a key and gave me a sleepy smile.

So I continued south, crossing the border with Malaysia, not knowing really where I was going but following the urge of all travellers to keep moving. I didn't really like Malaysia – it was too civilised, not testing enough. With red pillar boxes, English clubs and notices, and Morris Minors on the streets, it was too much like home to be exotic.

I gravitated towards the edges, towards the islands and fishing communities, where life was more basic and more traditional. I travelled alone, with other travellers, on buses, on trains, and I hitched. One of my lifts was from a government minister in a chauffeur-driven Mercedes, the blast of the air-conditioning unit ruffling his otherwise immaculate hair. He was fat, wore a large ruby ring on one hand, and asked me why foreigners were so interested in drugs; himself, he blamed the fishermen. Fortunately he was sufficiently pompous not to want an explanation from me, but to air his views. It made a strange contrast to Thailand, where the white man in whatever shape or form invariably commands respect; here in Malaysia this educated, intelligent and prejudiced minister saw me exactly as I was: a young, dirty and rather confused traveller who was going to spend quite some time – and very little money – in the grubbier corners of his country, corners that would be most sensitive and susceptible to bad habits.

It took some while to find the best corners, but after two weeks' wandering through the country I arrived at the small fishing town of Mersing, at the southern end of the peninsula's east coast; I was to revisit Mersing several times over the next two years.

Fishing in Malaysia has become a minor industry in comparision with the fast growth areas of palm oil, rubber and tin, and the fishing communities are something of a backwater of traditional Malay society. Mersing has all the serenity of a backwater, but it is too close to Singapore for comfort. The town functions as a staging post for the offshore islands of Tioman and Rawa, favourite weekend resorts for the Singaporeans. When I first arrived in Mersing it was the monsoon season, however, and the town was quiet.

The river that bisects the town is a narrow creek that breaks the flow of a massive stretch of deserted and shallow-sloping beach. Lethal-looking king crabs, armour-plated and as large as dinner-dishes move slowly through the shallows: however dangerous they might look, they are completely harmless. At night-time on the beach the moonlight catches the rills of the sand so that even ranks of ripples seem to march down into the sea. A wrecked boat pokes its ribs up through the rills, while out on the water the red and white lights of a trawler glide into the river mouth. On the bar the quiet roar of surf makes a bass to the rhythm of the crickets behind the beach, and the thin whine of a small motor-bike adds the descant as it makes its way up the distant coast track.

In the town itself an old Chinese grandmother sleeps in the shadows of the edge of her grandson's coffee-shop. Portable food stalls accumulate in the darkness around the main roundabout, and a Chinese medicine-man lays out his cloth and candle on the pavement. One of the ladies behind the food stalls wears a T-shirt with the slogan: 'I like Champagne, Cadillacs, and Cash.' The shirt is stained with years of use. In the near-darkness on the fringes of the light cast by one stall young Malays watch sub-titled American 'B' movies on the stall's TV, glued to the technology both of the television and the world that they can glimpse through it. Many children in Asia will run crying from matsaleh (the original Malay word for white man) simply because the only vision they get of white society and behaviour is through the crime series they see on TV, where each starts with a murder and ends with a fight.

Mersing is a fairly typical small east coast fishing town. The

Chinese control everything that makes money: they own the taxis at the taxi-stand, the boats that line the creek, the Japanese cars that line the streets, the larger shops, the restaurants and the hotels, and all despite the fact that they are discriminated against in the nation's *bumiputera* laws, which are tailored to try to encourage more Malay involvement in the nation's economy. Next to the gold-engraved blocks in Chinese script above the doorways are neon signs in English. 'Golden City restoran', 'Happy Hotel' and 'Guinness is good for you'.

Close to the banks of the creek the air reeks of oil and drying fish, while up on the bridge at night schoolboys bait crab-traps and dangle them from the parapet into the water below. The bridge was built over the creek at Mersing for the benefit of the Mercedes and Bedford timber-lorries that snarl up the east coast road carrying loads of teak and chengal. The latter wood is so hard that it sinks in water. Before the timber exporting business made the route important the east coast was better travelled by sea than by land, and even now an old man still ferries passengers from one shore of the Mersing creek to the other, although the new bridge is only 100 yards away. His brain has been addled by years of sitting in the sun on the creek, and he does not acknowledge that the bridge destroyed his business years before. The fishermen keep him alive by sitting in his sampan when they have a few coins to spare.

The creek may be small, but it is well-placed for access to the fishing grounds and its banks are lined with boats well into the jungle beyond the perimeters of the town. The slow flow of the fresh water has worn a gap in the sand-bar over the years, but it is shallow and the larger boats have to wait for the appropriate tide before sliding through. Two marker poles, one stuck into the sand-bar on either side of the channel, tell the helmsmen when and where it is safe to move. The strength of the tide coming in through that narrow channel brings the boats back into the creek at a frightening pace, but I never saw a collision, and the old man in the sampan did not seem worried by the possibility of his boat being smashed to plywood under a stampede of trawlers.

The ferryman was gliding in and out of the quiet hulls on the first evening I spent in Mersing, and I paid him to take me across. I sat on a pier and watched the trawlers who had just sprinted in from the sea pack their catch in layers of crushed ice. In the darkness I could still see the white flecks of the monsoon waves breaking over the sand-bar, and the dark gap where I knew the deeper water lay.

Under the deck-light the crew shovelled fish from hold to packing case, jamming the case full with the ice that spewed out of the ice-factory chute. When they had finished sluicing the decks and cleaning and heaping the nets the light was extinguished, the generator silenced, and the factory gates shut. A fire-fly glow of cigarette-ends spread along the lines of the boat, and a sliver of moon slid about on the velvety-black water.

"Hey mister, you go to Tioman?" It was one of the crew.

"Perhaps." I hadn't thought of doing so.

"No good time for tourists," he said. "The sea is rough and it rains often."

He could hardly have been more provocative. I did not like to think of myself as a tourist, and I wasn't going to ignore the challenge of a rough ride, even though I had never really intended going to the island.

So at three in the morning I was sitting on the doorstep of my hotel, where Jay – the crew-member who had attracted my attention – said he would pick me up. He was late: I had been there an hour, during which time the village had been rustling with the sounds of sleepy fishermen dragging their steps down to their boats, when he finally turned up on his scooter. We joined the rest of the crew assembled on the beach, shivering a little in the cold morning. Phosphorescence streamed from the sides of the small dinghy that took us out to the trawler.

As soon as we slipped the mooring it began to rain, as if the monsoon was waking with the dawn. We idled in a bay, waiting for the squall to pass. The beam from a lighthouse some distance away stabbed into the darkness above our heads, lighting a searching ray of raindrops just before they hit the wheelhouse windows. Then it seemed to clear, and the Chinese helmsman agreed with the owner that it was safe to turn the boat into the open sea. In the cabin behind the wheel the dozen crew-members settled to complete their disturbed sleep on the four-hour journey out to the fishing grounds, but conditions were far from soporific. The bows bludgeoned into the surf, hammering sheets of water into the wheelhouse windows and reducing visibility to almost nothing. Then the dawn crept up over the skyline ahead, delineating the ugly scars of storm clouds.

Owner and helmsman held a whispered consultation, peering through the windows at the signs in the sky. Then the owner grunted something and the helmsman spun the wheel through ninety degrees. "No good fish today," he explained to me. "We wait on Tioman." The change in the boat's motion – smoother but more extravagant as it crossed the line of the waves – alerted the crew. "*Tak boleh – angin kuat,*" shouted the owner over his shoulder.

I could sense the disappointment behind; a day wasted on Tioman meant a day extra without family or salary. The crew received no wages, only a fixed percentage from the catch. Jay rolled an enormous joint. "*Kapan kerja tak ada, lebih baik tidur,*" he winked. "When there is no work it is better to sleep." I made myself a nest on the dry nets piled on the stern, but the boat's motion made sleep out of the question, and it was all I could do to keep myself from vomiting.

An hour later we banged alongside the jetty in the sheltered bay of Mukut, on the southern tip of Tioman. It had been light for an hour, but it still seemed dark. Night and day had compromised to produce a grey blanket. The cook had prepared the meal that the crew would normally eat as a prelude to the day's fishing, and we all squatted in the shelter of the cabin overhang on the stern and shovelled handfuls of fish and rice into our mouths. There was enough chilli and garlic in one plateful of that potent stuff to supply an English kitchen for a month. Then, after everyone had had a shit over the stern, they took me ashore, promising to find me a place to stay.

I knew it was the close season for tourists, but even so I was unprepared for the complete lack of tourist influence at Mukut. No restaurants advertised milk-shakes or pancakes, no badminton nets hung between palms, and not a single guest-house was advertised anywhere. There were no cars or motorbikes, and only the constant chugging of a generator hinted at the presence of technology. There most certainly are hotels and bars on Tioman, but they were on the other side of the island, and not even a path of the most precipitous nature could take me round. The villagers at Mukut went everywhere by boat.

I had visualised myself stepping off the trawler into the heart of an admiring beach community of travellers who would be impressed with my rugged method of arrival on the island, and who would remain impressed over the couple of days that I graciously agreed to stay with them. I had expected a community as at Phuket, but in the event my relief at having my feet on solid ground took the edge off my disappointment at not being able to show off my method of arrival.

I was given a deserted house not far from the surf. The house was next-door to the police station. My landlord, Mr Dom, was the policeman; he told me that the village of at most forty inhabitants only needed a policeman when a boatload of refugees landed, which was a regular occurrence. The police station was surrounded by a wired compound which formed the first sanctuary of many a Vietnamese family. To land in Malaysia is a better deal than Thailand: in the latter the fishermen often double-up as pirates, and will readily board a drifting refugee boat and search the terrified Vietnamese for any valuables they might be carrying. The Thais know full well that most of the people who can afford a boat will be reasonably well-off by Thai standards, and they won't have left their wealth behind them in Vietnam.

There were no golden beaches at Mukut, and the twin peaks of the mountain directly above the village were shrouded in low cloud. The shutters of the house I was in creaked in the monsoon wind, and a villager hurried past the balcony where I sat. "*Hujan datang*," he said. "The rain's coming." And come it did.

I saw little of Mukut, or even of Tioman, in the next thirty hours. The rain hammered the roof above my head and turned the mountainside into a thundering river. The weight of the water brought several coconuts crashing down through the palm fronds to strike the sodden ground with a sickening thud. A falling coconut can kill. I wondered what effect one would have on the roof above me. I sat and listened to the rain and the creak of my chair as I moved, my book damp and unopened on my knees.

The rain did not stop Jay and his boat setting out from the pier in the late afternoon. The crew were not prepared to waste more time without salary. Nor did it prevent the flying foxes from crashing about from tree-top to tree-top. Even above the hammering of the rain and chugging of the generator, the row in the tree-tops made my head almost shrink into my neck, and the more I thought about it the more I could visualise all the coconuts above me falling in unison on to the spot where I sat.

When the greyness of the day merged with the horizon and the rain blotted out all distinction between sea and sky only the black smudge of the trawlers between the curtains of rain showed me where the water was. Before the final word of darkness arrived all the boats marked out their fishing areas with floating wickerwork baskets. The baskets carried the hurricane lamps that would attract the fish, and as the boats sat in their semi-circles waiting for the night they looked like big spiders in the middle of their webs.

The rain stopped abruptly at midnight, and suddenly lights gleamed and sparkled on a smooth sea. The instant sudden silence made me realise that I had hardly moved from my seat for hours, although my book was no longer on my knee. The silence lengthened as the fishermen waited for enough fish to be attracted to the glare of their lights, and then one engine slipped into gear and then another, then another, and the air was growling with the concerted sound of trawlers hauling their nets through the water. So close did they sound across the still night that I could have been sitting in the middle of a field full of harvesting tractors.

As the night wore on the trawlers moved further out to sea, taking their lights up and putting them down again further away. The boats would then lurk as black shadows in the background before emerging into the light and growling up and down the pathway between the floating lamps. By the early hours of the morning all of the lights were just over the horizon, and the little haloes that showed up in the sky above the horizon looked like eyebrows without eyes.

I did try to do my bit as a tourist on the island, walking first one way and then the other on the short stretch of track. I even went for a swim in the rain-riddled sea and gazed down at a coral graveyard that drifted past below me. The dead coral was colourless and it was peopled with fiendish black spiky things with eyes, and large black-and-grey striped sea-slugs. The latter are thought by the Chinese to be good eating, but they are far from attractive to look at. What with that collction, and the razor-sharp coral itself, I made very sure that my feet never touched the bottom, and I didn't feel very encouraged to stay in the water.

There is something lonely about the monsoon season, and even though I was glad to be rinsed by the rain as I returned to my deserted house that day, the clinging dampness of the air inside the building seemed to work its way into my bones. The only sounds that penetrated the blanket of rain were the very close and isolated, and I walked around in a cocoon of my own making. The rain made curtains that sealed me off from the world outside, drumming on the roof so that I could hear nothing but the creaking of the floor stirring beneath my weight. The shutters banged and swayed dejectedly in an indecisive wind, whilst out of the sea-view window the downpour dissolved all detail, and a boat tied up at the jetty was no more than a dark lump in the greyness.

In the village, children sat cross-legged just within the shelter of the overhang of their doorways, staring at the sky over the top of the palms and arguing with their brothers and sisters. The monsoon brings out the worst in anyone. Life in monsoon countries is an outdoor life, and there is nothing to do and no money to earn from waiting inside for the sky to clear.

It was the time of year for murders, I reflected as I sat in my house, alone. The screams of a dying man would be suffocated by the driving rain, just as every other noise was, and his swollen body would deteriorate fast in the heat and the damp. If I had been a Conradian character, gradually rotting in an outpost of progress with no future, but only a constant continuation of the present, I'm sure my mind, too, would have rotted. The isolation of the rains would spur me to dig out the only photograph I had of myself as a young man – a cherished photograph because of the era of optimism that it reflected – dust it off, look at it once, and then smash it and hurl it as far as I could out into the rains. Then I'd let my hands tie a knot in a rope, stand on the only chair so that my head was up by the beams of the roof, and then watch my feet swaying against the lines of the planking in the dusty floor. Only the pressure of the noose around my neck would produce any semblance of expression on my face.

When Jay's boat returned to take me back to Mersing, he and the crew were also fed up. The monsoon had ruined their fishing, they said, because the stirred water diffused the light from the floating lamps and only a few fish had been attracted to their deaths, I tried to cheer them up pointing out that the monsoon was nearly over and that the dose that we had just experienced was probably just a parting shot. The day seemed to bear out my words, and by the time that we were an hour away from Mersing the sun had broken through the cloud.

On board, we had squid and chilli for breakfast, the squid taken directly from the nets, cleaned of their ink, and thrown into the frying pan. The sea was moving in our direction, and the waves frequently took the steering out of the helmsman's hands as the speed of the surfing boat overtook the power of the propeller. At the end of each ninety-degree swing the hull would wallow for a moment until the propeller caught up with the water rushing past and put control back into the helmsman's hands again.

Mersing was calm and quiet. Only the rustle of the palms high up above the atap houses in the mainland kampongs where the young fishermen lived indicated that there was any wind. Teenage wives of my teenage crew members (most were very young) sat on the wooden steps that led up into the family houses and compared children; by the time they reached twenty these mothers would be getting stout quickly, their faces lined by too much work, as the babies kept on coming. An overweight Magnolia ice-cream salesman weaved between the houses on his motor-bike, cursing the chickens. The colours in the pictures of his ice-creams that covered the large thermos box balancing on his back wheel had faded in the sunlight.

Then I decided. I shrugged off the listlessness of the monsoon and headed down to Singapore. It was time to look for work.

4 *Singapore and Security*

At five in the morning an old muezzin climbs into the dawn on the winding stair inside the minaret of the Telok Blangah mosque, switches on the PA system, taps the microphone twice and clears his throat. "Allah Akbar", rolls the chant from one side of the city to the other, with minaret echoing minaret as the shutters go up on the coffee-shops and Chinese dim-sum stall-holders stack their baskets high. In the river basin a jumble of tongkams knock together on the morning tide. Against the landscape of skyscrapers the Chinese lighter-owners scramble ashore for a thick, black and sweet cup of coffee before starting on their first trip out to unload the boats swinging at anchor to the south of the island. The early-morning hosing-down shift disperses at the entrance to the Alexandra Road bus terminal, whilst the buses' gears crash into life behind them. In the narrow passageway behind Komala Vilas on Serangoon Road, the heart of 'little India', not-very-little Indians tuck their dhotis up between their legs like sumo wrestlers before squatting down and plunging their arms elbow-deep into the dough for the day's breads.

'Instant Asia' the Singapore tourist promotion board calls it, and certainly there are threads from many cultures, both Eastern and Western, woven into the Singapore fabric. Choose the time and the place and you can watch the Japanese playing golf, the Americans playing baseball, the English playing cricket, and the Chinese moving jerkily through their morning's Tai Chi somewhere on this tiny island republic that became my home.

I hated Singapore when I first arrived. It was huge, modern and sterile, and not at all what I had come to Asia to see. It seemed to have lost its core. Chinese culture was imported from Taiwan and Hong Kong, Western culture from the US and the UK. The way in which the old shop houses were razed to the ground to make way for further shopping centres seemed to me a wanton destruction of basic Singaporean culture. When the oldest mosque in the city was demolished there was hardly a murmur of disapproval in the press. Three years later even the river-basin, just about the only venue in Singapore that inspired local artists to paint, was cleared of the tongkams. The houses are all old and dirty, says the government, and we need new ones.

Never mind about the old mosque, they say, the Malays will build a new one with the compensation that they have received from the construction company, and the new one will be much bigger and better than the old. They were quite right; property rose so enormously in value that some of the old embassies on Orchard Road were able to sell the land they were built on, rebuild in much grander style in some leafy suburb away from the shopping centres, and still keep an extraordinary sum of money in someone's pocket. Only the Thai embassy squats on, occupying a prime few acres between the super-stores and hotels, its presence a torment to every developer.

But even though the government placed no barriers in front of the developers and took little notice of the preservation of culture and traditions that the old buildings imply, it did take note of the effect that the changing face of the city had on tourism, Singapore's largest single revenue earner. Tourism in the late seventies grew fast, and by 1980 the number of annual visitors to the city-state exceeded the number of Singaporeans. Three years later the figure had dwindled substantially. The new strength of the Singapore dollar meant that shopping on the island was no cheaper than anywhere else, and anywhere else probably had more to see. Some of the best hotels turned their attention to local people, and offered discounted rates for Singaporeans to fill their empty rooms, even though their own homes can never be more than about twenty kilometres away.

The only remaining trishaws in the city were for the benefit of visitors, but however toothless the drivers may have seemed when they smiled, they were nevertheless sharks. One visiting academic who failed to establish the price of his tour before he started, ended up paying the driver the equivalent cost of his plane-trip to Kuala Lumpur the following day. The government took a dim view of most of this, and constantly cajoled shopkeepers, bus-conductors and taxi-drivers not to be unscrupulous and rude towards visitors.

Singaporeans were bombarded with slogans to improve them wherever they went. Besides trying to create a new national spirit to weld together the different races, the government was attempting to change the behaviour of the Singaporean by running a never-ending series of campaigns, and every month the banners changed their tune. The most common and necessary was the courtesy campaign, with banners like 'It's so nice to be friendly' outside the shopping centres. I well remember a very surly bank-clerk who I used to see every week actually smiling during one of those weeks, though when I returned later that month the banner above her head had gone and so had any trace of a smile from her face.

It was the forced disciplining that I found the most disturbing. Nobody would cross the street except at a Green Man crossing; the street could be deserted for miles up and down, but still they would wait religiously for the correct signal before setting foot on the tarmac. The streets themselves were fabulously clean, but the litter-fine signs that spelled out their message in four scripts (Indian, Chinese, Malay and English) were no mere threat, and people lived in fear of police spies and informers who they believed to be in the crowds around them. The press, in a well-meaning attempt to warn the population of the dangers of litter, developed the concept of 'killer litter' – heavy items disposed of by dropping from the upper floors of high-rise blocks. Unfortunately 'killer littering' caught on!

My first home in this ordered city was above one of the travellers' dormitories in the Bencoolen area. There were on average seven of us in two tiny and stiflingly hot rooms. The only furniture we had was a couple of chairs, a table and a couple of metal bedsteads. Eventually we got rid of the bedsteads. They took too much space and ants lived in their metal frames. Ants were a problem on the table too, where we kept our crusts of bread for breakfast. We put the legs of the table in pans of water, we sprayed the legs with acrid-smelling anti-ant spray, but sooner or later the top of the table would be swarming again.

It was a sordid place, to say the least. There was a French heroin addict who used to lie on her bed most of the day glistening with sweat, waiting for the cool of the evening and her night-time fix. We had to be careful when we barged into the bathroom at night lest we should jog the needle as it went into her arm. She ended up working as a call-girl for an Arab in the city. There were three Australian roughnecks (a technical term for a chunk of beef on an oil-rig who was supposed to do anything), a lunatic Frenchman who lived in fear of the French police tracking him down, a Belgian girl who slept with every man in the place except me, and all on the first night she arrived, and a Swedish girl who was hopelessly in love with the Frenchman but hated the kind of life that her love had dragged her into.

Singapore is not the place to be if you have no job and no money, and I had spent days sitting glumly beneath the frangipani trees on Fort Canning Hill. After some difficulty and a lot of depression I found myself a job as an English teacher. Knowing that I would need to work, I had trained as an English as a Foreign Language (EFL) teacher before leaving the UK. I was suddenly glad to have a core to my day and glad to get out of the squat. I worked hard, teaching all the hours that were possible. My students, mainly Chinese Thais or Indonesians, got so fed up with seeing me in the same clothes, that they began to bring back 'presents' at the beginning of each new course. I left for work at seven, and often did not return before nine at night. In the squat the bong would be bubbling away, a single candle in the centre of the floor, and within minutes the words of the day would float away in a haze.

Singapore officially had a horror of drugs, and the penalty for dealing was death. In the early seventies there were estimated to be some 13,000 addicts on the island, but a decade later that number had been officially reduced to 3,500. Rumour had it that the problem in the army was a massive one, but there were always rumours in Singapore, largely because the press was muzzled. Undoubtedly a great deal of drug trading went on in the city, but mostly it was for consumption elsewhere.

At one point I became tangentially involved. Tony, one of the beefcakes in our squat, had bought a rare Triumph motor-cycle in Penang, and drove it down overnight to Singapore with the intention of shipping it to Australia, where it would sell for a considerable profit. The only light that functioned on the machine was a front indicator, which was little help in that moonless night on the Malaysian roads. Tony had to wait on the roadside for cars heading in a southerly direction to light the road ahead of him. But Malaysians are superstitious, and when they became aware of the flashing orange light sticking close to their tails in the dark, they accelerated to try to lose it. Tony had to go faster and faster until tiredness overcame him and a near-plunge into the forest brought him to his senses. He rested at the roadside and waited for the next vehicle, and the whole process repeated itself.

By the time that he reached the causeway border with Singapore in the morning he was in a state of exhaustion, which combined with his everyday appearance (shaven head and earring) was enough to alert the customs. In the bottom of his bag they found a few marijuana seeds. His claim that he had only recently bought the bag from another traveller did not convince them, and the evidence that he had once been carrying drugs seemed to be enough to charge him. Between us, the squatters raised the money for Tony's bail. As I couldn't find any Singaporean willing to stand bail for him (perhaps it was rather unfair to ask them) I was elected – as the most 'respectable' member of the squat – to do the court work. Faced with the bald fact that no Singaporean would stand bail, but that I was there with the money in my hand, the clerk succumbed, accepted my signature, and Tony was released. Ultimately the police thought better of their severity and all charges were dropped, but it had been a narrow escape for Tony: during his two nights in the cells he had had a packet of opium in his boot.

Although the men in the flat found work, the women searched hard and long, before eventually joining a hostess agency. Officially agency girls just had to dress up well to be hired for the evening as company for visiting businessmen and sometimes this was how it was. But often they were pressed to do "extras", though this was something they rarely discussed. The money was good, and many European girls were tempted into something that they wouldn't have dreamed of doing at home. After all, who was going to find out? Very few ever admitted to extras, but the agency knew which were which, and farmed them out accordingly.

Sometimes the girls would find themselves hired for the night to local Chinese. On one such occasion a French-Canadian girl who was living temporarily on our floor was taken by an off-duty taxi-driver to his local coffee-shop, sat at a table and given a Coke. There she was told to stay whilst her hirer played Mah-jong with his friends at the next table. To every new arrival he pointed her out, boasting that he was now rich enough to hire a white woman. He didn't want the 'extras' – only the kudos.

As time went on and I got to know the city and people better I began to understand what it was that worried me about it. The state had moved too fast, and could not allow itself to slow down. The thin veneer of Western civilisation (for a while the government promoted the Japanese example, but that did not last) only covered the areas around the international hotels, offices and department stores. Beneath that veneer lay the not-so-dormant customs and traditions of three different ethnic groups (Chinese seventy-six per cent, Malay fifteen per cent, and Indian seven per cent) that made up the island's population. There is enough colour in the fabric of Singapore to prevent temporary visitors from looking too closely at the web of society beneath it.

Some of my students represented the new breed of Singaporean that this society was busily and rapidly creating. There can't be many countries where the school children wear T-shirts covered with slogans such as 'Knowledge through understanding, progress through knowledge.' British students wouldn't be seen dead wearing anything like that, and nor would they utter sentences like "We are a small island with no natural resources, yet our harbour is the second busiest in the world, our streets are the cleanest, our technology the most advanced in South-East Asia." It was amazing how often these sentences were slipped into essays done for homework, whatever the essay topic. Perhaps their state teachers gave them extra marks for it, but I found their constant reappearance irritating.

Sometimes I found the children quite frightening. Unlike the adults, they had no experience of another society with which to compare Singapore. They rarely travelled, and they had no counter-argument to the messages put across to them in their repressed society – nor even an appreciation of the need for debate. In a letter to the *Straits Times*, the main English-language newspaper, one child even went so far as to condemn the behaviour of parents – his own included – during the morning ceremonies at school. "Many adults continue chatting and laughing," he wrote, "while others sit in their cars listening to loud music, smoking or reading the papers. As Singaporeans we should stand to attention when our national anthem is played." The letter was signed, 'A proud Singaporean student' and was printed at the top of the page under a bold headline. I found it disturbing to speculate on how such people would develop as they got older.

Breed the right people and the business breeds itself – part of the philosophy on which Singapore is run. Premier Lee Kuan Yew repeated this idea in almost every speech, and his phrase, "Our strength lies in our human resources," was perpetually on every tour guide's lips. But Lee grew impatient, and he was not content to let the right people breed themselves, especially as the evidence showed that they were doing nothing of the kind. In 1984 eighty per cent of graduate women were remaining unmarried, reputedly because Chinese menfolk were not keen to marry women more intelligent than themselves (probably a true enough statement for any society); to keep up the momentum of Singapore's rapid development Mr Lee introduced a programme of genetic engineering.

Originally the message that all buses carried emblazoned on their sides was 'one is enough'. When the wrong people took note of it the message was quickly dropped: statistics showed that whilst graduates stuck closely to the instructions with an average of 1.7 children per couple, uneducated women had children at a rate of 3.5 each. The next step the government took was to try to redress the balance by financial incentives and the bait of better housing, whilst those who exceeded the limits were effectively fined by having to pay school fees, etc for the children over their allowance. The response to these moves was indignant, especially amongst those likely to be more vocal. "I feel deeply insulted by the suggestion that some miserable financial incentives will make me jump into bed with the first attractive man I meet to produce a highly talented child for the sake of Singapore's future," wrote one irate graduate, in the *Straits Times*.

The failure of that move did not deter the government. It then activated the Social Development Unit within government organisations. The SDU is basically a government dating agency. All unmarried civil servants and teachers have to attend the sessions at least once, whether they already have boy- or girlfriends or not. Sex education popped out of the woodwork and on to the curriculum of schools and polytechnics. But the crowning move came in June 1984, when the government started on the other tack and offered payments for uneducated women not to have children.

'Sterility cash' became the subject of everyone's conversation. The qualifications were simple, in both senses of the word. A couple had to have a combined family income of lower than $1,500 per month, no 'O' level passes, and no more than one or two children. Feelings were mixed about this new offer. Many thousands poured into the government offices to enquire about the payments, whilst others were scandalised by the government's crude approach. A rare piece of graffiti appeared on the hoardings around one construction site. "Help save Singapore," it read, "sleep with a college graduate." But the people who made the most noise were those who had already been sterilised on their own patriotic initiative, and had thus missed out on the reward of $10,000.

I soon began to appreciate that those existing human resources which were supposedly Singapore's strength and which were threatened by the imbalance of the birth-rate were in fact heavily subsidised by other nations. A large proportion of cheap industrial labour was imported from Indonesia, Malaysia and Thailand. Factory workers crossed the causeway from Malaysia every day – they were not allowed to become resident in Singapore. Every three weeks Thai workers returned in busloads to Thailand to renew their visas. Many of the higher management positions were filled by Europeans and the expatriate population of Japanese was second only in number to that of Los Angeles. Construction workers were imported from Korea, but by agreement with the government they were not allowed on to the streets. Buses took them from their work-sites to 'rest and recreation' in the seedier parts of the city. Every now and then a rash of deaths from falling off high buildings prompted the construction companies to relax their round-the-clock working schedules and postpone the opening date a day or two. Nevertheless most still made a point of completing their projects well before schedule.

No one can deny that Singapore's track record is impressive. When it became a nation in its own right only twenty-five years ago it was little more than a football off the toe of Peninsular Malaysia, fifty per cent mangrove swamp and jungle. By the time I reached the island it was criss-crossed with expressways, pile-drivers set the rhythm of the day as they sank the foundations of yet more skyscrapers, and politicians and populace alike were disappointed if the state's economic growth-rate dipped below ten per cent.

A topic of conversation was the ruling party's attitude towards its opposition, which it accepted as a political necessity, but obviously considered a permanent insult. Mr Jeyaratnam, for a long time the only opposition MP, had to fight case after case in the courts for 'defaming the name' of Mr Lee. When the opposition then won a couple more seats Lee's People Action Party cut some of the services in the offending constituencies.

The country's attitude to sex was equally confused. Paul Theroux's book *Saint Jack* was one of many banned from the national bookshelves. The 'sin' that Theroux described in the book was also suppressed in Singapore, but sin is a marketable commodity and business is business – one just had to look a little harder to find it. The transvestites who used to haunt Bugis Street were relocated, and tourists who went looking for the theatrical billy-boys found only photographs and expensive food-stalls where there had used to be flesh. Few of them realised that the billies had been moved just three blocks away, into back alleys which were blocked off from the public eye by new fences. In the Offshore Land Club and the Tropicana the prostitutes often outnumbered the offshore workers, but if you didn't know where to go Singapore was clean.

Racism was another issue on which the government was particularly sensitive. The official line was that there was no racism in Singapore, and in practice the state has had far fewer disturbances than in the Malay-favouring system in neighbouring Malaysia. The Malays, Chinese and Indians may not have mingled readily, but they did live together in relative harmony. It was the government's policy to distribute the different ethnic groups evenly around the housing estates: no ghettos were allowed. Moreover, the Singaporean identity of the nation's citizens was constantly impressed upon them through the media. For a while the Broadcasting Corporation screened national dances which had been especially devised to include elements from all cultures, but which unfortunately largely failed to impress any.

It was hard to gauge the success of these policies. Expatriate society nodded its head wisely and murmured that whilst harmony prevailed now, it was due to prosperity, not policy. Wait till the economy begins to crumble, the old hand added, and then judge the success of the new national feeling. My students were all adamant that they were first and foremost Singaporeans, with ethnic considerations coming second. They were good students, but they did what their teachers told them. The older part of the dominant Chinese community were less conformist. My only opportunity to understand them was via the cab-drivers, who were very forthcoming by Singaporean standards. One told me the story of how white came to be white, and black, black.

In the beginning all men were created black, he said. Then a lake was discovered, with water that had the power to turn the skin of those who bathed in it white. Because the lake was in Europe the Europeans had first go at it. The Chinese were quick to hear of the white magic but they had a long way to travel, and by the time they arrived the water was no longer pure and fast disappearing thanks to too much use. Thus Chinese skin did not entirely lose its colour. But the Indians were so lazy – and anyway they did not like washing – that they dawdled all the way to the lake, and by the time they reached its shores all that remained of the water was a muddy patch, just enough to wet the palms of their hands and the soles of their feet. This is why Indians have pale palms to their hands and soles to their feet.

This was hardly non-racist talk.

The older and more traditional society that the cabbies came from was altogether more inaccessible for a foreigner, and a talkative driver was a gold-mine. Their generation still held strong views, and they were prepared to express those views to visitors – to locals would have been dangerous. They were also prepared to make jokes about Harry, as they had nicknamed Lee Kuan Yew – jokes which were invariably extremely unfunny but which were then repeated endlessly from expatriate to expatriate. The state was well aware of the danger to its public image that 'irresponsible' cabbies posed, and gave them lessons in manners and in what to say to tourists. The Transport Ministry supplied them with plastic bags as spittoons, in an effort to curb the unwestern habit.

It was a cabby who told me that children's heads had been cemented into the bridge-pillars on the nation's most ambitious and newest motorway flyover, the Benjamin Sheares bridge. "Bridge stay good. No head – fall down, maybe five year. Have head, stay good many year," he said. I remembered reading several newspaper reports of children disappearing about the time that those pillars were completed, and I was inclined to believe him. Cabbies also provided an insight into the world of secret societies, which they always claimed – contrary to the government line – were widespread; no businessman could succeed in Singapore without the favour of the societies, they said. The cabby version of the more recent downward decline in the state's fortunes is less believable.

In the course of 1985 much of the work on Singapore's metro system was completed. This involved digging deep into the ground, and the digging coincided with the first economic slump in Singapore in the state's recent history. The older members of the Chinese community believe that Singapore is built on the tail of a dragon (the dragon's body is mainland China and the head Hong Kong) and that by digging downwards the workers disturbed the dragon and destroyed the nation's jobs. Thus the economic decline.

The cabbies gave me some insight into the older Chinese society; my students did the same for the younger end of the population. But I never really met the section in the middle – the intelligent, enlightened, professionals. The cabbies criticised this new breed for thronging the shopping centres and spending money on leisure, for wanting picnics and holidays, for belonging to squash clubs, and for having girlfriends and parking their cars late at night along Marine Parade . . .

After three months' work I moved away from the traveller's end of Singapore and into expatriate society. As my salary slowly rescued me from the breadline (I had little money left by the time I started work) so my life-style changed. I landed a good job teaching in the British Council; I moved from the Bencoolen Street squat to an altogether more salubrious spot amongst the island's rich in Binjai Park. This was Singapore's Hampstead, and here were extensive, security-patrolled residences hidden amongst the trees, set back from the lanes. Yet even here I saw little of the richer Singaporeans: often the only signs of life were the Malay gardeners raking leaves on the immaculate lawns, or the electronically operated gates swinging open to let the Mercedes purr through. The more exclusive and private of these houses even had mosquito exterminators on their perimeter fences; a steady light attracted the insects, and a high voltage spark got rid of them.

The flat, which I shared with three Frenchmen, was on the first floor above a tailor's shop. My flatmates had spent their national service in Singapore teaching French, which is accepted as a substitute for time in the army. They enjoyed it so much that they stayed on. They introduced me to the French subculture of motorbikes, girls, parties and good food. Sylvain worked part time in an art shop which specialised in Asian antiques. The shop was regularly restocked by an ex-CIA man who made sure his plane was well-filled with Buddha's heads every time he flew via Burma. Jules was a pâtissier who had moved from France at Sylvain's instigation: he was to have been the boss of a French fast-food bar which had never got off the round, but he stayed because he was in love with a Singaporean. Every morning he would get up, pull on his trousers and go out to the local shop. After two cigarettes and a bar of chocolate he would be ready to utter his first words of the day, and not before.

Jean-Claude, the third and most characterful of my flatmates, was an equally slow starter. He was multi-lingual, speaking Mandarin and Indonesian, as well as English, and he wrote on Chinese art for local publications. But his intelligence was largely wasted on his teaching work and he was bored through most of the day. Being tall, dark and very good-looking he spent most of the time picking up girls, with enormous success. One afternoon, after mooning around the flat for a couple of hours and muttering about how bored he was, he took his motor-bike up to the local supermarket. He returned half-an-hour later with one of the check-out girls riding pillion still in her uniform. She was the sixth that week.

I led a rather clean life, by comparison. I started rowing for the local yacht club, and then went with the crew to represent Singapore in the Regatta of East Asia in Japan, where we managed to come last in both finals. At work I was surrounded by English people of my own sort, who gave me reassurance; at home my flatmates and Asian girlfriends provided the entertainment. Only two things disturbed what could have settled into a secure home for years to come, and both were in my mind.

The first was that arbitrary two-year limit that I had set myself, and the feeling that I hadn't yet seen nearly enough. The second was a desire to become a journalist, a desire that was coming to fruition.

The press in Singapore was effectively under government control. As a European I always felt I could afford to laugh at the efforts of the state to bring itself into line with the leading developed nations (even as I scoffed, the standard of living in Singapore overtook that in the UK). As a white man I could wander in and out of the magnificent hotels in my shorts and sandals; I used the swimming-pool on the top of the Mandarin Hotel unchallenged; I crossed the roads wherever and whenever I wished (the policemen may have turned a blind eye but the good old cabbies always hooted, however far away they were), and above all I spoke my mind without restraint on the streets and in the restaurants. But once I started going into print, with a series of short articles on odd subjects in the *Straits Times* features pages, I found myself having to be careful. Even what I considered to be flippant remarks were carefully cut.

At the beginning of 1983 Patrick Smith, the bureau chief of the *Far Eastern Economic Review*, was effectively expelled from the republic. No explanation was given for the non-renewal of Mr Smith's visa, but he had written extensively on such potentially sensitive topics as the defence policy and the release of political detainees. I wrote only bland feature material that was unlikely to attract anyone's attention, and yet my work was censored. In public I said it was a scandal – the topic made a good focus for anti-Singapore discussion – but privately I was pleased: censorship made me feel like a real journalist. I had a business card printed.

I told myself I was not made for journalism in Singapore, I would become a freelance travelling journalist. I gave up my job and my place in the flat (even though I frequently returned to stay on later occasions) and I wrote a long, ideological letter dismissing Singapore to my English girlfriend, who had persisted with my memory all this time. "What worries me about the place," I wrote, "is the total lack of freedom for individual characters to develop in their own way at their own pace. What is worse is that most Singaporeans seem to have no desire to change the status quo. People here have a lot of security, and that security is more important to them than their freedom. For us in the West this is too high a price to pay for security." She probably thought I was a pompous ass.

In truth I envied the Singaporeans for their green and clean city, their bus-services and their police efficiency. I envied them their food, their hotels, the then strength of their economy and the cheapness of their telephone bills. I envied them their new airport and the way the post office handled their mail, and I admired my students for the diligent way in which they noted down carefully whatever I said or wrote in class. But I never talked of my admiration. It was just not fashionable to talk about Singapore in favourable terms, and in sticking to the fashionable expatriate ways I ensured that much of the place remained a closed book to me; I remained a foreigner.

5 *Seven Islands*

I left Singapore from Finger Pier. When I had arrived in the city-state, nine months previously, I had crossed over the causeway from Malaysia to the north, so it seemed only logical to leave by the sea for Indonesia in the south. That was progress – I was travelling again.

There were other reasons for the choice of route. For nine months I had worked as a teacher in the British Council's Rubber House on Collyer Quay, and every day on the quay I passed dozens of Indonesian seamen, drawing on their familiar kretek clove-scented cigarettes to give them confidence as they gazed at the skyscrapers and banks and the Western faces and fashions that whirled past them at a very un-Indonesian pace.

These seamen were the descendants of the Bugis sailors, Indonesia's sea gypsies. The Bugis come from the south-western arm of Sulawesi, but they are found in pockets throughout the whole archipelago. They are shipbuilders, sailors, merchants and modern-day pirates. For them today's seagoing vessels are even easier prey than they were 500 years ago, when the Bugis terrorised much of the peaceful shipping in their corner of the world. They are a rough people, especially towards white men – as any westerner who has wandered through the dockland area of the Javanese port of Surabaya will testify. The Bugis were the scourge of the various colonising powers who tried to control the whole Indonesian archipelago, and when some of their own men were killed the Dutch rounded up 30,000 Bugis and Makassans and shot the lot. The Westerling Massacre is still a relatively fresh memory – early 1900s – so it is hardly surprising that the Bugis still feel some antagonism towards white men.

For many of them, however, their sailing lives have changed. Indonesians, like Filipinos, make up many of the crews of flag-of-convenience vessels, and it was these men who crowded the Singapore quays. Instead of risking life and limb to move a few coconuts between uncertain markets they lived a life of oiling moving parts and watching videos.

Nevertheless the traditional Bugis have not gone, not even from Singapore. Not so far from the kretek-smokers on Collyer Quay is a Bugis camp. A piece of the bank of the Sungai Pandan river is fenced off and designated as Indonesian soil in order to receive the passportless Bugis and their boats. They come from the rough timber yards on the islands of the Riau archipelago, no more than a dozen miles to the south of Singapore, and their boats scud between the hulls of massive container vessels that are just pausing for a few hours on their monthly trips around the world.

The Bugis on the Sungai Pandan – whose boats are little bigger than a single container – are not interested in long trips any more. The mangrove-pole business between the Sungai Pandan and the eastern coast of Sumatra is a good one, and the journeys are sparrow's hops for the Bugis compared with the treks that they used to do.

Mangrove poles have played a surprising part in the literal growth of modern Singapore. The strength, length and lightness of the poles means that they are ideal for scaffolding, but change is on its way. The Singapore government does not particularly like the sight of the rattan-lashed mangroves leaning against the walls of some of the most modern architecture in the world, and has ruled that the mangroves be phased out in favour of metal, on safety grounds. When the poles go so will the Bugis, but where they will go is anyone's guess. The luckier amongst them might follow their brothers and make the giant leap up on to the decks of the massive vessels anchored in the roads that sheltered them on occasions from the area's angry squalls. Until then they watched from the sterns of their boats the tugs buzzing up and down the river and the oil platforms growing taller day by day in the shipyards of Jurong near-by, and from the fenced off compound this is all they were allowed to see of Singapore. They also used to watch me in the company of other white men as we rowed up and down the Pandan, training hard for our regatta in Japan. They must have thought us mad, paddling for sport in their toilet. For us, looking up at the sterns of the boats as we sweated past, the panorama of the Bugis shitting was an enervating sight.

I had told myself as I prepared to leave that I was merely picking up the old Conrad trail again: I was following the prahus to see what lay through the narrow passages in between the Riau islands. I told myself also, as I packed up my teaching notes and bought myself a typewriter, that I was now a journalist, and my first job would be to get into the refugee camp on Pulau Galang, to get some stories. In this I was encouraged by a sympathetic section editor on the *Straits Times*.

So when I arrived at Finger Pier I was bristling with optimism. The pier – which featured often in accounts of Singapore in colonial days – has long been swamped by the growth of the harbour around it, but it has resisted the impact of modernisation and sophistication which has invaded the commercial sections of the port. In the middle of the pier building a couple of school desks stood on a floor that was unaccountably covered with puddles. Signs on each desk informed me that there were two options for going to Tanjung Pinang, my chosen destination. I could go with the desk on the left – faster but dearer – or the one on the right – slower but cheaper. As if to symbolise the kind of service his company was offering, the man behind the desk on the right had his feet up and was reading a Chinese newspaper. I chose the slow and cheap way, in order to celebrate the end of employment and the beginning of travel once again.

When the time came the few other passengers (most of them turned out to be crew, or friends of the crew) and I boarded a big old motorboat, clambering over sleeker and faster boats en route. The boat was Indonesian made, and owned and run by the Chinese living in the trading centre of Tanjung Pinang, the pivot point of all travel and most trade in the Riau archipelago. Just how pivotal it was it did not take me long to discover; I passed through Tanjung Pinang twice more in the following nine months – both times against my better inclinations.

At the time, however, it felt good to be going to Tanjung Pinang. I watched the boat-owner's father – a sour, foul-mouthed Chinese gentleman – scatter paper money to the wind to earn us a safe journey. The squares of paper fluttered down into the wake of the boat, whilst the skyscraper skyline of Singapore melted slowly into the haze beyond.

Smuggling is an everyday and piracy an every-week occurrence in the narrow gap between the first Riau islands and Singapore. Scores of small sailing vessels skidded between the giant hulls swinging on their anchors on the tide, ladders left hanging by crews who had gone in search of the delights of Bugis Street. I had witnessed the speed-boat smuggling across the northern Johore Straits, and if smuggling was worthwhile between Singapore and Malaysia, where the two standards of living are similar, then it was even more so between Singapore and Indonesia. My boat was certainly not making money from the dozen or so fare-paying passengers it was carrying.

Even so, I was unprepared for the rigorous checks that we were subjected to on that five-hour trip. Midway between the last of the anchorages and the first of the islands an armed patrol vessel slowed alongside, and we rocked together in water that was churned by the meeting of currents.

Nor did the maze of islands that we meandered through thereafter hide us from watchful customs, and we were checked twice more, the crew now plainly exasperated by the delays. The patrols seemed highly efficient, and yet only the boat's papers were checked in the wheelhouse, behind a firmly closed door. No search was made of the boat, despite the evidence of more cargo than passengers, and I wondered if the closed door signified that money was changing hands. All I could be sure of was that none of the cargo disembarked through the customs shed on Tanjung Pinang, as we did.

That shed was the most distinct feature of the town. When the bows of the boat finally pointed to a thin line of corrugated roofs sheltering in the corner of a long and low bay it deflated the last balloon of optimism that had buoyed my spirits at Finger Pier. It was the rainy season, and it had begun to drizzle on the journey; the grey sky made a poor backdrop to an already unprepossessing shoreline of straggling shacks.

When we finally bumped up against the jetty teeming with people, the few passengers on board were shooed off the boat into a wire cage in the customs shed, where we clucked and scratched about like a load of chickens, wondering what was to happen to us next. Our passports were taken by men in uniform and removed to a back room, then a man with a loudhailer called out names individually and the lucky ones were let out of the cage, stamped passports in hand.

As I stepped out into Indonesia I was immediately picked up by a young man who called himself Paul who suggested that I stay with him in his uncle's house. I hesitated, but then the heavens opened and the drizzle was drowned by a monsoon downpour that thundered on the corrugated roofs and stuck my shirt to my back with the first half-dozen drops. This was evidently a sign for me to let events take their course; Paul's presence was obviously pre-ordained, and I was not intended to do anything but follow him. Being a great believer in the guiding force of circumstances I nodded my agreement, and together we sprinted down the pier to solid ground. At Paul's suggestion we hired two ojeks (motorbikes and drivers who act as taxis in the poorer Asian towns) and whined up the hill to his uncle's house. By the time that we reached the back room where he slept with his brother we were both drenched.

The room was dark, and the damp air laden with mosquitos. The only decoration was a cracked mirror mounted in the middle of a plastic ship's wheel. I was moderately dismayed, and I must have shown it, as Paul mumbled something about it being small, whilst he quickly busied himself in replacing the light bulb in the corridor outside. But I was following events, I told myself, and I had to accept where they took me.

For a couple of days Paul showed me around Tanjung Pinang, as he had obviously done for many a traveller before me. He had a much-thumbed book of names and addresses of those who had shared that little room with him over the years. At night he read them to me slowly and deliberately.

"You know Andy from Sydney?" I shook my head.

"Pete from Miami?"

"Never heard of him, but I do know a Rupert from Southend." We added my name to the list.

Picking up tourists was the only way Paul could earn money. Tanjung Pinang has an enormously high unemployment rate, as many young Indonesians fleeing from Java – the densest agricultural population in the world with over 1,500 people per square kilometre – came to rest on the jetties of the town either because they were sure work must be available in such a busy crossroads or because they had simply run out of money to take them any further. Scores of young men drummed their heels above the water every day, waiting for boats to come and boats to go, in the hope that someone might grab them and ask them to do something, or offer them a working passage to somewhere new. Ultimately they all aspired to go to Singapore – and the arrival of the Singapore boats was the main landmark of the day. In Singapore there was work and money, but to get there one had first to buy a passport from the highly corrupt Tanjung Pinang passport office.

Around the corner from the customs shed and the boat-spectators was another jetty with more people in it, though here there was more activity, and work to be done. It was here that the goods that had come on my boat from Singapore had been landed, out of the line of sight of the customs shed, for form's sake. But the officers in the shed knew full well where the goods landed, and they were not slow to exact unofficial duty for it when their day's work in the shed had finished.

The water next to this alternative jetty was too shallow for larger boats to approach, and everything was ferried by sampan and transferred into trishaws on land. Every boat or trishaw owner wanted a share in the load, for only by doing so could he earn any money. The more runs made then the more money earned, so the pace of life on the end of that jetty was frantic. Paul and his unemployed friends envied the workers on the jetty. Although there were far too many of them and stiff competition meant very small earnings, at least they were doing something for some return.

Paul's uncle was one of the favoured few. He was a customs officer in the shed on the jetty, and a customs officer at such a crossroads could earn a fortune however small his salary. On my third day in the house I was called in by the uncle – with all the dignity that he had earned with his money – and requested to construct an electric organ he had just bought from Singapore. I wondered, as I read the instructions and laid out the labelled parts, which jetty it had landed at. That evening there was a little party in the house, and all the neighbours came to admire the new organ. From the back room, Paul and I listened to the rude sounds it made as the visitors tentatively placed their fingers on the keys.

Paul's dream was to become a customs officer like his uncle, but he didn't have the money. To buy one's way into the favoured shed on the jetty required family connections (which he had) and 100,000 rupiah (which he didn't). Although at the time he despaired of ever getting hold of the money, he eventually succeeded in getting the treasured post, as I discovered on my third and final visit to the island. But he needed two years' salary to pay off the price of buying it.

His new position didn't even require him to work. On my later visit he was doing exactly what he had been doing when I first met him – waiting on the jetty and showing travellers around the town – but he wore a cap on his head and one of his uncle's cast-off jackets around his shoulders.

On that first visit we both soon ran out of enthusiasm and ideas. There wasn't much to see or do on the island. Paul took me to a palace on an island out in the bay which he said was made of egg. It transpired that the mortar had been fortified with egg-white, and there was nothing unusual in the palace's appearance at all. We went to visit the Chinese marsh-temple, hidden amongst the mangroves to the east of the town. The place was deserted apart from the old Chinese caretaker who kept the incense burning and filled the lamps with oil. Grass grew through the cracks in the concrete floor.

Then there was nothing more to do. I was a problem for Paul. His two days' worth of sights was usually enough for most travellers, who then moved swiftly on. But I had made no onward plans. I had tried to pursue the idea of the visit to the refugee camp, but the office of the United Nations High Commissioner for Refugees (UNHCR) was unhelpful. I would have to go to Jakarta to get permission to visit the camp, they said, and even then it was unlikely, because an American television crew had recently made a programme about conditions in the camp which the authorities had not liked at all. The next boat to Jakarta was scheduled for five days' time, but in the monsoon season anything could happen, they said. If I had had a plan B, I would there and then have dumped plan A, but I hadn't, so I hung on for that theoretical boat. Besides the option of returning to Singapore it seemed the nearest prospect of leaving Tanjung Pinang.

Over the next couple of days the sense of helplessness and hopelessness that obviously dominated the young unemployed on the island infected me. The thoughts of the monsoon on Tioman all came crowding back. Paul gave up the pretence of showing me around and reverted to his usual daily routine, but with me as an addition to it. I became quite a familiar face on the jetty. Whenever Paul and I sat down for something to drink or eat – which was often, for not even the jetty could entertain us constantly – three or four of his 'friends' would inevitably drift in off the street and sit down too, and I would end up paying for everyone. I suspect that he did not know half of them any more than I did, but a foreigner with a full wallet was a prize that had to be shared.

On one of those afternoons on the jetty there was a new arrival swinging at anchor in the bay. Paul told me the *Barlian* was a tramp steamer on what was locally known as the Seven Islands route. She provided the only regular source of supplies and communication between a semi-circle of islands in the South China Sea, pausing for a few days on the west coast of Borneo before making the return run. And could I go on the boat? "Is no good, no good. Very long journey and very big wave. Better to go to Jakarta when boat come. Wait more three days." Although I thought him to be right – after all, what would be the point of depositing myself in a place even more remote than Tanjung Pinang? – there was something that attracted me to that junk-heap in the bay, with its canvas awnings flapping and tearing in the wind.

In the end events again took a hand, and a simple but sordid encounter was enough to dislodge me.

It was the fourth morning, I think. Paul had expressed a wish to go to the jetty and see his friends, as he always did. I said that I would walk in the town, pretending that I had business to do. I had none, but the weight of having to make conversation was bearing down heavily on us. I found myself incapable, then and now, of progressing beyond a certain limit in friendship with someone of a different language and culture, and sharing that tiny room and our daily lives was putting much too much of a strain on our relationship. Despite the fact that I genuinely liked Paul, I began to feel irritated by certain of his mannerisms. He had a strange series of nervous twitches which he used to run through in a pattern. He would snap his jaw as if he was a dog trying to catch a fly, and then twist his head suddenly from side to side, cracking his neck joints, ending the process by cracking all his finger joints in succession. I didn't usually object to the cracking of joints – many Asians do it as a habit – but it was the inevitability of the sequence that got me down. The irritation grew so strong that I could hardly stop myself from grabbing him and shaking him whenever he started his shuddering and clicking programme. Half of me knew that I was over-reacting, and that same half was also secretly dismayed by my own lack of initiative and stagnation that allowed such irritations to become important.

So that day I wandered off by myself and felt pleased to be alone. I sat for a while on the end of the busy jetty and watched the sampans ferry load after load of prawn crackers from a small motor-vessel lying a little offshore. After a while I noticed a long, cool wooden corridor that led off the side of the walkway at the end of the jetty, out of the heat and the noise. At the end of the corridor an open door led into a small Chinese club. An old man in a string vest sat with one foot up on the bench opposite, watching a game of pool. Seeing me gazing in he beckoned, and made room for me on the bench.

My arrival brought little more than a glance from the men playing pool, and the gent who had beckoned me in didn't seem inclined to try a conversation. I was grateful to be accepted so readily, without being barraged by the usual questions. Only the soft click of the balls on the green baize broke the peace in that room, with the hustle of the town little more than a murmur in the background. The smoke from the old man's cigarette curled up into the silent sunlight that streamed in through the window behind my head, and I could see the reflection of the water outside in the glass of a picture hanging above the doorway on the opposite wall. The picture was of a mountain, painted in Chinese style, with Chinese characters below it presumably explaining what and where it was. On the frame someone had written 'Gunung Bintan' – Bintan mountain, the highest point on the island.

I think that I must have dozed in that place, for the next thing I knew was that the game had ended and the two players had gone, stirring the dust floating in the sunlight as they went. Without really knowing why, I felt a lot better for the loneliness and the quiet, but at the same moment I felt that I had been rather anti-social to Paul. I set off back to the house to wait for his return, intending to suggest a trip round the island – something that he had wanted us to do.

It was when I had got half-way up the hill that I first became aware of the shuffle of footsteps behind me. At first I ignored them, thinking that a child was playing the usual prank of following a white man and imitating his walk. But there was no giggling, and no audience to appreciate the daring, so I began to feel a little disconcerted. The footsteps were very close behind.

Anxious not to show my discomfort, but to test my follower, I slowed. The footsteps did the same. I turned slightly and affected to look across the road at the houses on the other side. Out of the corner of my eye I caught a glimpse of a blue shirt, a pair of off-white trousers, and a Chinese youth, considerably smaller than me. For a moment I ceased to feel threatened. I had size and strength on my side, and if necessary I had my knife in my bag.

So I continued to walk, quite pleased that events had begun to roll for me and that I was sufficiently in control of them. A few steps further on I became aware of a low hissing coming from behind me. I stopped suddenly, pretending to scratch at a mosquito bite on my foot, and Blue Shirt was so close that he almost collided with me. As he passed he placed a light hand on my buttocks and squeezed, whispering something that I didn't catch but fully understood. Any sensation of fear turned at that moment to anger and then disgust, but Blue Shirt had taken me by surprise and was well ahead.

Now that I had him permanently in sight, scuffing his sandals along the gravel and turning his scraggy neck from side to side to keep tabs on my movements, I felt powerful enough to squash him like a mosquito. The frustrations of the past few days came together to produce a strong abhorrence that translated into hatred. I walked faster and faster to try to tread on his heels and hurt him; after a moment he broke into a run and crossed to the other side of the street, out of reach.

For a moment I reviewed the situation coolly, and thought how ridiculous it would seem to an outsider, this little comedy. The last thing I wanted to do was to attract attention. There were people on the road in the distance, and others behind me, so to have assaulted a local in broad daylight would have caused an outcry. Nevertheless, I had plainly acknowledged his presence, and I could hardly ignore him now, even if I had wanted to. For his part, Blue Shirt seemed pleased with progress, and was now openly gesturing for me to follow him from the safety of the other side of the road, slinking his skinny hips and crooking a thin finger. He was grinning at my discomfort.

I faltered for a moment, uncertain of what to do. I did not want to turn and go back, because that would have been admitting defeat, but to have walked on would have been worse, now that he was sure of my full attention and getting bolder by the moment. So I just stopped where I was and waited for him to go away.

As soon as he saw that I had stopped then he stopped too, turning to face me. "Misterrr . . . misterrr . . ." he hissed. "Come here misterrr . . ." His meaning was plain. He wrinkled his nose like a dog sniffing a dog, nodded first at me and then his groin. "Yes misterrr . . . yes." Then he started rubbing himself.

The complicated frustration of the last few days, the disorientation, the boredom, the closeness of my relationship with Paul, all crystallised. Something inside me exploded, and I charged Blue Shirt over the sun-scorched gravel. I had no idea what I intended to do once I reached him, and it was probably just as well that I didn't. The surge of rage was clumsy and he must have seen the lunge coming from miles away. He sprinted away up the road before I had even left the shadows on my side.

I followed for a few paces, and then suddenly the rage melted as fast as it had come and I stood foolishly in the middle of the road. Blue Shirt reached the next junction before he stopped, realising that I was no longer following him. I could hear his voice, tainted with insinuation and evident enjoyment, repeating "Misterrr, come here misterrr, yes misterrr, yes." I didn't move from the middle of the road, not really aware of what I was doing. To my relief it seemed that no one had witnessed the little drama – or almost no one. As I collected my thoughts and struggled to pull the semblance of a reasonable expression over my face, I found myself looking directly into the eyes of two little girls, sitting on the steps of their house. They were staring at me, open-mouthed and petrified. Probably they were the only people in the street to have been aware of the whole episode. Quickly I tried to force my face into a smile, but the attempt must have gone disastrously wrong: with a small frightened sound both girls scrambled to their feet with one accord and disappeared into the house.

I could hear them wailing indoors, and I knew that sooner or later one or other of their parents would come to find the cause, so I had to move on. To my relief Blue Shirt had decided there was no more fun to be had from taunting me, and he had disappeared. I walked stiffly but slowly up to the junction and past: nobody followed, nobody shouted, and nobody jeered.

It had been a humiliating and disturbing experience. I kept my head low as I skirted the side of Paul's house, below window level. I didn't want to be seen by anyone, least of all Paul. To my relief the back room was silent and empty. It took only two minutes to pack what I needed. Seconds later I was back out in the street again, heading for the town. My head was empty, the strap of my bag nagged at my shoulder. Back on the table in the room that I had just left a banknote quivered a little as it unfolded like a flower to the sun. Beside the money I had left a note which read "Gone to Gunung Bintan. Back in a few days. Please look after my things for me. Thanks. Andrew." Above the stained table-top a few mosquitos hung dispiritedly in the quiet air.

A dozen old Hudsons stood mudguard to mudguard in the pitted and rutted car-park outside the town's lone cinema. These cars were the island's only transport, apart from the motor-cycles, and their drivers were inevitably Chinese. My request caused a certain amount of amusement. Sure, I wanted to go to the mountain, but where would I sleep? Where would I eat? There were no shops. And how would I find the way to the top? After a while they seemed to concede that I was serious. Squatting by the wheel of one of the cars the drivers discussed what was best to do with me, and then one stood up and motioned that I was to get into the car nearest the wall. Although he himself said nothing, it seemed that by general consensus he had been elected to take charge of me.

It was too hot to sit inside the taxi. In the monsoon spells of sunshine between the rains are often fiercer than in the dry season, and one could have fried the obligatory egg on the leather upholstery. I leaned against the bonnet and bought an ice-cream from a boy with a thermos tin mounted on the front of his trishaw. He watched me eat it with great concentration from beneath the shade of his umbrella. After two mouthfuls I dropped the bulk of the ice into a puddle and watched it dissolve: it was made of condensed milk flavoured with artificial coconut, and was so sweet that it made me feel unhealthy from the gums down. I grinned at the boy apologetically, but he didn't seem to have noticed the fate of his ice-cream; his concentration did not flicker from my face.

I thought that I was the only passenger for the taxi, but as soon as my appointed guardian climbed into the driver's seat the shadows emptied of people, and as we bumped along the stretch of tarmac that led through the outskirts of town I counted thirteen of us in that car. As a foreigner I was accorded a central place in the back seat, but other males hung half out of the side doors, and two sat out on the bonnet. The car seemed not to notice the load at all.

At the twelfth kilometre we stopped at the local brothel. Business was slack in the heat of the day, and the girls were sitting out on basketwork chairs, playing with their children. The two men who had been on the bonnet paid their fare and disappeared. Thereafter there were no more villages, and the road turned into a rich, ochre-coloured mud track. Gradually the crowd on the back seat thinned, disappearing out of the car down thin paths that threaded into the jungle. We picked up no one. At one point we rounded a corner to find a poorly dressed and austere man silhouetted motionless against the sky. We stopped. There was a short conversation at the roadside, and the man handed over a single banknote. Then we were off again.

I spent most of the journey with my face directed out of the window. I didn't want to talk to the other passengers because I knew that they would be curious as to where I was going, and I didn't want to admit that I had no idea. Fortunately my immediate neighbours seemed embarrassed at having to sit so close to a foreigner, and only stole glances at me when they thought I wasn't looking. After about ninety minutes' bumping, when the solitary tape in the cassette-player tied to the dashboard was coming round for the third or fourth time, the driver turned to me and pointed to two humps that rose above the forest. "*Gunung Bintan – bukit yang lebih besar*," he said. "Bintan mountain is the larger hill." Hill? Neither of them looked much higher than giant ant-heaps. I had come all that way just for that? I cursed the picture in the club for the artistic licence that had deceived me, but events were leading again, and it was only necessary to sit back and follow.

We finally bumped to a stop in the yard of a rambling group of buildings in the forest. The cassette-player died with the engine, and the driver signified that this was where we got off. He led me towards the house, explaining as he did so that this was his family's pineapple and rubber estate.

I was escorted through a wicket gate that swung lightly to behind me and found myself in a dark room. For a moment I could see nothing, but I could hear many things: the crying of a baby, the shouting of a child, something frying, old people talking, and the wheeze of an old man quite close to my ear. Slowly the dim brown light of the day coming through the bamboo walls showed me the furniture of a kind of scullery. Three old men were sitting on a bench. One of them coughed and shuffled his feet, and the others watched me steadily and silently. Behind a table a small Chinese grandmother stood chopping onions. She was dressed in the usual pyjama suit, but she seemed more alert than most Chinese grandmothers. As she smiled a welcome she seemed for a moment to be the Chinese equivalent of the American mid-Western farm-lady pictured in the happy autumn of her life, all kindness and good home cookin' . . . which was just what she was. She took immediate control of me, and led me through another wicket gate into a different room and indicated that I should sit down. I was grateful not to have to say anything in explanation of my presence, so I sat.

The new room was more of a living area. There was a roof, but on two sides it was open to the forest. On the dry and concrete-hard earth floor children and dogs were the origin of the crying and the shouting, which stopped when I arrived. The arrival of white features often silences children. In the middle of the room a bundle bounced and swung on the end of a long spring suspended from the ceiling. A young woman passed the bundle at regular intervals and gave it a tug to set it bouncing, and the baby inside slept peacefully on. There were three smells: the sweetish one was the cooking, the second was the earth floor, and the third was more pungent and acrid – fresh-tapped rubber that was drying out in the open, draped over a pole like white bath-mats.

Two young men came and tried to talk to me in scrambled English. Then the old lady came back with some boiled eggs and sweet bread wrapped in polythene. I wasn't hungry, but it seemed rude to refuse and she seemed pleased when I started to eat. As I ate an old Chinese gentleman came and sat beside me on the bench. He nodded a greeting, and when I had finished eating he indicated that, if I wanted to go up the mountain, then it was time to go, and that he himself would take me.

From the little conversation that we managed as we walked it became clear that this gentleman was the towkay, and the taxi-driver and the other young men were his sons. He was dressed in an old shirt and shorts, and he had a parang tucked into the waist of his trousers. Although he must have been in his sixties he was agile and tough, and quite unlike the Chinese that I had come across before in the towns. One of his sons set off with us, and his clothes were a marked contrast to those of his father: whilst the old man looked like the labourers that I had seen sitting on the bench in his kitchen waiting for their midday meal, the son looked like a well-to-do shopkeeper, and he found walking a bit of a struggle. The towkay showed me his fields of pineapple with some pride, explaining as he did so that he had once lived in the town of Tanjung Pinang and had kept a shop, but that Tanjung Pinang was full of bad people.

There were a few poor houses in amongst the trees and the towkay stopped in front of one and shouted a name. One of the Indonesians who had been sitting in the kitchen earlier came out to join us. By the time that we had passed the last of the houses three more men had dropped their tasks in order to join the expedition to the top of the mountain. We caught up with and overtook a group of children on their way home from school. They had removed their shoes – presumably their only pairs – and carried them carefully as they padded through the mud. Shoes were for wearing in town and in class, not for walking with in the forests: bare feet were good enough for that.

The towkay and the other – who seemed to be a kind of foreman – had gathered momentum, and I struggled along behind with the others to keep up. The men discussed the best route – whether to go straight up the hillside or to skirt it to find the remains of an old path. The old Indonesian settled for the latter, and the rest agreed. The towkay explained that no one from his estate had been to the top of the hill for a few years, but that although they were no longer sure of the best way the climb would not take us more than an hour. I was disappointed that it was to be no more – it seemed feeble to have such an escort for a simple walk up a simple hill – but surprisingly enough the men seemed to be enjoying it more than me, talking in low tones as they pushed through increasingly dense undergrowth. One of them cut me a stick to help keep my balance on the hillside; we were all behaving as if we were all out hunting tigers rather than going for a walk to the top of a hill. We found the path and lost it; the young man in the smart clothes decided that he had had enough and that he would wait for us to return.

Near the top where the slope grew gentler we came across an open suitcase in a clearing, with sodden clothes strewn around it. Neither the suitcase nor the clothes looked Indonesian. Near the case a small cheap cosmetic mirror reflected the greyness of the sky, a forlorn eye of light in the muddy centre of the clearing. It had a bright red plastic frame. My guides looked at the case and turned away with a single comment: "*orang gila*" – "mad man". I wondered if this meant they knew whose case it was, or whether it was just a common expression to use. They are easily superstitious, the Indonesians, and I feared that they would take the rather enigmatic and unsettling suitcase as an ill omen, but they seemed happy enough to go on.

At the top we found a small clearing and a trig point. Between them the saplings and the drizzle obscured any view that there might have been. My guides apologised for the fact that the trees had grown since they had all been up there last, but they pointed out the directions of the villages, and named the various rivers that surrounded the hill. They seemed disappointed that their island was not spread out below for me to see.

Now that they had got me to the top – something that I had obviously come a long way for – they expected me to do something or signify that something had been achieved. They had done their bit, and now it was my turn. So I climbed the trig point and took a couple of pictures into the mist, took out my compass and pointed it north, and generally looked around me as if I was just where I wanted to be, and a very valuable experience it was too. Someone discovered a leech on someone else's leg, but once that was removed with a cigarette butt there was not much more to do.

"*Pulang?*" queried the towkay, after I had completed my antics on the trig point. "Go home?" I nodded, feeling rather foolish.

We descended in silence. What little adventure there had been was over, and there were serious matters such as the afternoon's work that had been missed and the following day's meals to be considered. We all walked wrapped in our own thoughts, and the spell of unity which had been so strong on the way up was broken. At one point I tripped and fell and we all laughed, once it had been established that I was not hurt, and for a moment the unity returned. But once we reached the flat land again the men began to melt away. Finally there was only me and the towkay left, his son having also stopped off at one of the houses.

The old man set a good pace and said little. My shoes were covered in mud and completely sodden, so I slung them on either side of my stick and carried them as the children had done earlier that afternoon. The towkay – who had been barefoot throughout – grinned in appreciation as the mud squelched up between my toes.

Back at the pineapple farm we were welcomed as heroes. I was shown where to wash, and we all sat down to eat after dark. Then I withdrew a little from the circle of light on the grounds that I wanted to write my journal. But although I was too tired to write anything it dawned on me as I concentrated on the shapes of people moving around the light that even though the act of climbing the mountain had not been adventurous, nor a great achievement, it had still been a success. My tired brain threw up the idea that somehow or other the walk had been just as important for the towkay and his men as for me; I had been the catalyst for improved employer/employee relations. Then the light slipped away and I fell asleep on the bench.

The beam of the torch of the taxi-driving son woke me well before daylight. It was time to go, he whispered. With his torch he pointed out the pieces of bread that had been left for my breakfast, and with the torch he also showed me the bill that had been prepared for me. I paid for the services of every one of the men who had joined us on the trail, but for accommodation, food and the taxi-ride I paid nothing. The driver said that the towkay had seen to that.

At the time I did not try to analyse why I felt infinitely better as I returned to Tanjung Pinang than I had in leaving it. My encounter with Blue Shirt seemed long in the past. My confidence had been restored, and in the towkay I had met someone I had really liked in the most unlikely of situations, someone of wisdom. I think also that he had liked me. Paul was delighted to see me, and I was equally pleased to see him. In my new, positive mood things just fell into place. I decided to catch the boat that I had seen waiting in the bay, and do the trip of the Seven Islands. Gunung Bintan may have been a washout as far as expeditions go, but it represented a turning-point in my morale.

I had been warned that boats going places in Indonesia were hardly likely to leave on time, but even so I was unprepared for the unexplained twenty-six-hour wait on the bridge of the KM *Barlian*. A constant hammering came from somewhere within the bowels of the boat. We swung at the end of the anchor in the bay, whilst the monsoon brought a queue of heavy clouds down over the water. I found myself wondering how that one-ton lump of metal that was the anchor could possibly secure the 650-ton boat in the teeth of the wind, but secure it it did.

The *Barlian* was a Dutch-built cargo ship nearing thirty years of age – and the scrap-heap. She dated from the time when the Dutch – colonisers of the then Dutch East Indies – tried to curb the number of unregulated boats plying between the 992 inhabited islands in the Indonesian archipelago. Their attempt was doomed to failure, for with such a range of islands and weather conditions Indonesia is far better served by hundreds of thousands of small sailing-vessels than a few hundred motorised boats of varying sizes which would create infinitely fewer jobs. Nevertheless, they did build a large number of boats for the islands, and the *Barlian* was one that remained as part of the government-run Pelni and Perintis fleets.

Although she was primarily a cargo ship there were scores of passengers on board, huddled in nests of sacks and possessions. Passengers who were on their way to visit married sisters or brothers on the other islands, who were returning with full pockets from a period of work offshore, who had just been on a shopping-spree in Tanjung Pinang – and of course those hopefuls who were finally disillusioned with the chances of finding work in the harbour and who had decided to move on. But out of the whole lot I think that I must have been the only passenger who believed that the ship would leave on schedule. Throughout the day following my installation on the bridge both passengers and goods continued to arrive, even though by then we should have been well on our way.

Loading the ship was a lengthy process because everything had to be ferried by sampan, and the wind was such that it took a lot of time and muscle to reach the shelter of the ship's side. Nor did the problems cease there, for the sea tossed the boats like corks against the hull, and everything had to be passed by hand to the deck-rail above.

The largest items were sixty-kilo sacks of rice, and the rice-laden sampans rode so slow in the water that waves broke over their sides. Whilst the sampan-owner sculled steadily away his boy would scoop feverishly with a plastic bucket at the water washing around the sacks. With the ship's steps too crowded with passengers and small cargo, many of the sacks had to be hauled up over the rail by means of a rope and noose, but in the whole time that I was watching only one was lost – snatched away by a wave before it cleared water level. Other common cargoes included sweets, soap, batteries, bicycles, and even monkeys in boxes, ready-trained to climb the palms for coconuts. The monkeys' arms waved frantically through the gaps in their wooden boxes, desperately trying to grab something solid in their alarm at the rocking of their sampan.

The *Barlian* was far from being a beautiful ship. It was difficult to decide for what purpose she had been built. From a distance she looked cluttered, with a stack of cabins behind the bows and another on the stern, and tarpaulins stretched between to protect the passengers – or was it the rice? – from the driving rain. The crew too were a motley collection from all parts of Indonesia, ranging from the barrel-like negroid second engineer from Maluku who rolled his rrrs and roared with laughter every time he saw me, to the rather timid purser, a Sumatran Muslim who liked to mention Shakespeare every time we met, and who spent most of the trip praying to Allah and looking at a photograph of his wife and children. A supertanker these days may not need more than a dozen crew-members, but the *Barlian* needed every single one of her thirty-five crew to coax her along. The captain was having shore-leave, as he apparently did rather often. The acting captain was the first mate, and he looked more like a pirate than all of them, with a broad face and curled moustache, wide-brimmed hat set permanently at a jaunty angle. However alcoholic and interested in my photograph of my girlfriend he may have been in the bar, once on the bridge he became abrupt and commanding, striding from one side to the other and firing questions and orders out of the side of his mouth which didn't carry the cigarette. "How many?" he would ask the quartermaster, and the quartermaster would reply in ringing tones with the compass reading. The captain would then make an alteration to the course, shouting it even if the two of them were standing shoulder to shoulder peering at the wheelhouse compass together.

On the bridge the first few moments of departure were tense. I couldn't understand why until the captain pointed back at the wake, where widening patches of mud marked the passage of the ship over the blue-blackness of the sea. She must have been virtually scraping the bottom.

The ticket for the six-day journey 'deck-class' cost me 8,000 rupiah (£14), inclusive of food. If an Indonesian passenger had wanted a cabin then he or she could pay a member of the crew to relinquish his, but for me the privilege of being the only white man they had had on board for quite some time was to share the cabin – and the bed – of the radio officer. The tiny room was crammed with a mountain of antique radio equipment that hissed and gurgled like an ancient boiler as soon as it was switched on. The radio officer was called Siregar but, surprisingly, the rest of the crew called him 'Sparks', a nickname I had never come across outside of war-comics. While he waited for the valves to warm up he would smoke an endless chain of kretek cigarettes, and the crackling of the burning cloves blended with that of the radio waves. The Singapore weather forecast was in morse, but English morse, and it was strange to see English flowing fluently from Siregar's pen as he decoded it – English coming out of a chaos of noise via the pen of someone who could speak no more than a few broken phrases.

This forecast told us much the same as the last: "Serious monsoon disturbances ahead." It wasn't long before I found out what that meant.

The pitching and tossing began as soon as we were out of the lee of Bintan island, and for the remainder of the day, the night, and much of the following day we crashed from wave to wave, the boat quivering from stem to stern. The passengers were in hell, and even the crew became irritable and silent, looking up from their games of cards whenever a particularly large crash strained the bow-plates. I was grateful for Siregar's bed, where I crawled early on and curled up around my sickening stomach. The decks below were covered in vomit, and even the passengers' nests of rice sacks could not protect them from the spray. I slept fitfully, half aware of the voices on the bridge just outside the cabin door.

I was woken by the ringing of bells and voices from the bridge. Even lying in bed I could tell we were near land: I didn't feel ill and the boat was moving steadily. This was Tambelan, as I was told when I staggered groggily on to the bridge. By the time that we had docked at the jetty the ship's siren had already summoned a mass of people. The late afternoon sun was warm and the ground felt welcomingly solid beneath my feet. Boats appeared from distant corners of the bay and homed in to surround the *Barlian*'s hull like barnacles, and receive the cargo that was moving on to more inaccessible neighbouring islands. It was the mango season, and I felt secure enough on dry land to think of trying to eat. Turning back into the open sea again that evening I was confident enough in my stomach – even as the ship began to roll again – to accept the officers' invitation to join them in the mess for dinner.

It was a grand-sounding invitation from a scruffy bunch of people, but then as I soon discovered the mess itself was rather grand, and it cast a spell over the crew. The white linen, waiter service and polished panelled walls with their paintings of Dutch sailing ships all reeked of colonial days and of Conrad. But the food was not grand – it never varied from cold fish on rice with chillies – and the waiter was an engineer who couldn't get a job. The surroundings impressed the crew just as much as they did me, for once inside the mess they became uncharacteristically formal. They sat strictly according to rank, did not make the usual jokes, and indeed hardly spoke at all. The acting captain even took off his hat religiously as he sat down as if he were attending a funeral rather than a plate of rice and fish. When the meal was over they ceremoniously wiped their mouths on the starched white napkins kept permanently by the side of their places, waited politely for each other to step out into the corridor, and then hared off to the bar at the stern of the ship to drink and gamble into the night.

We arrived at the island of Midai on Christmas Day. The significance of the date only dawned on me as I came to write up my diary for the previous day, and it seemed completely incongruous in the circumstances. As far as I knew the crew were all Muslims and the festival would mean nothing to them, so I told myself to forget about Christmas for that year. But I was wrong; several of the crew were from Catholic islands which still followed the creed that their colonisers had left behind them: the second engineer announced to me solemnly that he had a tape of Christmas carols, and if I would like to join him and a few others in his cabin that evening I would be welcome. I said I would.

Midai was a depressing place. The *Barlian* anchored about a mile offshore, and a single motorised boat struggled bravely to and fro between the ship's steps and the debris of corrugated iron onshore that was the village. The boat's hull had once been painted blue, but a combination of continuous repatching and the strength of the sun had peeled off most of the colour, leaving the bare grain of the wood to face the sea. A few passengers disembarked, taking with them a few bags of rice; no sweets or bicycles were going to Midai. I had noticed one of the disembarking passengers before, largely because he had an expensive new cassette-player tucked under his arm, and wore a conspicuously new suit. Presumably he had been working either on an oil platform or in one of the Singapore factories, and here he was returning to his family with the spoils. The contrast between his clothes and the rags of the crew on the battered motorboat was dramatic. If they knew him they did not acknowledge it, and he took his place on the bows without a word, staring out to sea holding firmly on to his cassette-player. He didn't seem to be relishing his homecoming.

Most of the crew, whether Muslim or not, turned up for the party in the chief engineer's cabin. We sat in a circle on the floor eating biscuits, drinking beer, and listening to the engineer's tape of carols. After hearing it several times through the crew voted 'Hark the Herald Angels' the best, though recorded as it was in Indonesia it sounded very different to what must have been echoing around the roof of King's College Chapel that same day. No one stayed long; the Muslims were a bit embarrassed by attending an alien festival, and the Catholics were embarrassed to be drinking beer in front of the Muslims who were technically teetotal (plenty of them broke that ban in the *Barlian*'s bar). But despite its brevity and slight awkwardness, that Christmas party remains fixed in my mind as one of the best and most original that I have been to: biscuits and beer in the engineer's cabin could not have been more different to a lifetime of fully fledged family occasions.

At the island of Sendanau we arrived with the early-morning sun to find the usual crowd on the jetty. Sendanau, and the next day's island of Serasan, are rich in cloves, which are used to flavour the kretek cigarettes nearly every Indonesian smokes, and the people were obviously more prosperous than the islanders from Midai who had only copra and fishing to keep them alive.

As at every other port those on board were desperate to get off, and those on the jetty keen to come on board, and soon the crowd onshore and the crowd on deck had changed places. As the sun climbed the sky the jetty emptied slowly into the shadows of the town, and I went inland to look at the clove trees and the villages.

When I returned I found the crew playing billiards in a darkened room, cool and quiet in the heat of the afternoon. The cargo on the boat was left untouched until the evening, when the strength of the sun had diminished. Even then the only person to lift a finger was a crooked old man of enormous strength who raced up and down the plank between land and boat bent almost double beneath drums of oil.

The evening was well advanced before the old man had carried his last load. Our departure was framed by a blue seascape with a mist that took the edge off the mountainous islands marking our passage. At the entrance to the archipelago a small liner rested at an unusual angle. The ship was a skeleton – everything of value removed. Siregar explained that it had been doing the same run as the *Barlian* six months previously, when the captain had deviated by a fraction from the recommended course, ripping open his ship's hull on a reef.

Like Sendanau, Serasan was enjoying the peaceful period between clove crops, and the islanders sat talking on their verandahs, or walked arm in arm down the main village street. As if to emphasise the atmosphere of leisure there were billiard halls everywhere. Rows of young men slumped on benches in the darkened rooms snoring to the accompaniment of the clicking balls whilst they waited their turn on the table. Siregar assured me that the prettiest girls were to be found on Serasan.

But there was one discordant note to an otherwise harmonious island. Half-way down the disused jetty that led out from the main village street on to the mud flats were a couple of wooden shacks jammed full with Vietnamese refugees. I was quite unprepared for the reception I received. It seemed that the boat people thought that I had come to rescue them. As they surrounded me on the jetty, talking excitedly, I heard the word 'America' repeated several times, though I understood nothing else. They spoke no Indonesian and I knew no Vietnamese, so there was no way of telling them that I was a travelling white man who had strayed from the beaten track. I assumed their presence on the island was known to the authorities and that they would soon be 'processed', but those thoughts were useless without the words to express them. It was not a hostile meeting, but nor was it friendly. There were few smiles on the faces of those refugees, and understandably so. In the end all I could do was smile, and smile, and walk away. I felt the strength of their eyes on my back as I retreated into the village.

Back on the boat that evening things were reassuringly familiar. The navigator, who was a devout Muslim, disappeared up on to the roof of the bridge to get a few readings as we left. He kept a prayer mat up there, and I allowed myself the irreverent thought that presumably he had no problem in finding the true direction of Mecca, up there with his compasses and charts.

The night when it came was one of the darkest I have ever seen. Overhead a patch of clear sky sparkled with stars, but where the sky met the sea dense cloud made the join indistinguishable. Not far from the centre of the deepest blackness was a lighthouse that should have functioned as a reference point, but the depth of blackness around it after each flash gave no clue as to where it would show itself again. On the bridge the quartermaster pulled at his cigarette, and the glow of the compass below him silhouetted his face against the darkness. Siregar had been in the bar most of that day, and I woke in the night to find his arm over me and his heavily laden breath in my face. It had grown to be a common situation which I no longer minded. At least it indicated that I was accepted.

In the morning mist we chugged steadily up a broad river into the flatness of western Kalimantan, the Indonesian part of Borneo. It was fitting to arrive in such a way, as much of the island's inland transport is still by boat. Fishermen were anchored against the breadth of the river, which slid in a single sheet towards the sea, but there was no other sign of life or habitation. The port of Sintete, when we rounded the last bend and it swung into view, proved to be no more than a railway-station platform in the middle of the jungle with a compound and a couple of Nissen huts. Tied to the jetty was a small tanker, and the *Barlian* docked gently alongside her. Looking at the featureless mangrove banks and the tiny, dwarfed compound, I felt that I could easily have written pages of Conradian description.

I shook the hands of all the crew with great solemnity, and shepherded them for a group photograph. It looked like a school photograph as I composed it, and it occurred to me that they had been my fellow-students, my caretakers and my teachers, all at the same time. Then I dropped my baggage down on to the deck of the tanker, nodded to its captain who was trailing a fishing-line over the stern, and stepped off the other side on to the dry land of Borneo. At that point my priorities were simple: I had a craving for hot food that was not fish; a cake or two, and a bed I did not have to share. Little did I know that only a month later I was to make a much longer, much more primitive sea-voyage, one which I would be lucky to survive.

I lost three of the films that I took on the *Barlian*, thanks to the Indonesian postal system. But I can still remember that final group photo of the crew as I composed it through the lens, and the single image outweighs pages and pages of Conrad.

6 *The* Chun Bhatera

In my little tour of the Seven Islands on the KM *Barlian* I had barely scratched the surface of Indonesia. There are 6,067 named islands in the Indonesian archipelago, of which 992 are inhabited all the year round. Yet more are inhabited outside the monsoon period.

Modern Indonesia was only created thirty-odd years ago, and the spirit of national identity has taken a long time to spread down through areas where there are no newspapers and few radios. Older people on many of the islands often don't speak Bahasa Indonesia, the new national language, and many of them speak Dutch as fluently as they do their own dialect, indicating the last of the outside influences that had a real impact on their communities. The *Barlian* would be luxury travel for many of these islanders, but only twenty of the nation's recognised ports are capable of handling vessels of more than 500 tons, so most of the inter-island communication is provided by many thousands of prahu layar, sailing boats. Before long I too was aboard a prahu layar and looking back to my time on the *Barlian* with envy.

Between the better known islands of Bali and Irian Jaya (Indonesian New Guinea) stretches the Nusa Tenggara archipelago, a chain of islands as different from each other in as many ways as it is possible to be. The inhabitants live quite distinct lives, speaking quite different dialects from their neighbours, visible across the water. Indeed, on the island of Alor alone there are reputedly seventy different dialects. Moving from Hindu to Muslim to Roman Catholic, from names like Made on Bali to Paulus Diaz on Flores, from fair skin on Java to negroid features on Tanimbar, from lush tropical paradises to volcanic wastelands, it is hard to believe that this is all one nation.

Foreigners have been trading with these islands for centuries and have ruled many of them. Inevitably some traces of their cultures have been left behind, and the new culture has yet to wipe them out. In many cases the outside influences have been assimilated into local traditions over the years, and are now regarded as part of the islanders' own heritage. Thus on Flores hawkers still sell ivory that traders brought with them from India centuries ago (there are no elephants on Flores); on Solor the villagers hand down cobwebby lace-work from the Middle East, yellowed and mildewed with age, from generation to generation; on Sumba one of the designs on the local kain, the hand-woven cloth, is taken from the lion's head motif that appeared on a Dutch coin. The very isolation of these islands means that any new influences will take a long time to leap from island to island down the chain, and their idiosyncrasies look set to remain largely unmolested for many years.

This was the chain that I was to sail down, in the company of seven other Europeans, on a prahu built many years before in Malaysia. The plan was to follow the chain as far as Timor, and then to turn southwards and cross the 300-mile stretch of open sea to Darwin, in Australia's Northern Territory. We estimated that the journey would take us about six weeks to complete if everything went according to plan. Of course, not everything did.

The name of our boat, the *Chun Bhatera*, is Sanskrit for The Ark. We were ourselves following the ark tradition in some senses, and on board we had two Australians, two Americans, two Italians, one New Zealander and myself, all but one headed for the promised land of Australia.

I had first heard of the existence of the *Chun Bhatera* many months before. One of the beefcake Australians sleeping on the floor in those stiflingly hot rooms of my first squalid home in Singapore had worked for some time alongside the boat's skipper in preparing her for the sea, and he used to talk of the *Chun Bhatera* in glowing terms. He was far less enthusiastic about the skipper, an Australian called Jamie, and had come to Singapore after a series of disagreements with him. With the Australian I had sailed on the *Chun Bhatera*'s sister ship, the *Anak Duyong*, in Singapore harbour, and loved it. Both boats had been built in the same yard in the estuary town of Kuala Trengganau, on the east coast of Peninsular Malaysia.

The design of the boats has an interesting origin, which makes them unique. Story has it that in the late 1880s a French frigate sank in high seas off the coast, and one of the very few survivors came ashore at Trengganau. Eventually he married and settled down to live in the town, and to make his living he turned his hand to boat-building in the only style he knew – French. For the rigging he followed the example of the Chinese tongkams that were then plying up and down that coastline. Thus was born a strange hybrid boat, Chinese above the gunwales and French below, that was peculiar only to Trengganau. For a while these Pinas/Bedor boats (as they came to be known) were very popular, and they dominated much of the salt and charcoal trade along the east coasts of what were then called Malaya and Siam.

Some decades later the new Malaysian government started to subsidise coastal dwellers to enable them to motorise their boats; the craftsmen who produced the Pinas/Bedor began to die of old age, and with them went their skills. In 1982 there were just two or three original boats still in genuine use for the traditional trades, but interest amongst foreigners in the style of the Pinas had injected new life into the boatyards at Trangganau, and the old-timers reached back into their memories for the details of the style their fathers used to make. Over the space of five years some eight new boats had been built for foreigners, and several more hulls have been dug out of the sands of the estuary and refitted.

The *Chun Bhatera* was one of the latter. Some ten years before we sailed on her she was spotted as an unfinished hull lying on the shores of Pulau Duyung, and bought by a French woman married to a Malay islander. She then went to Australia and left both her boat and her children on Pulau Duyung. The children were still there when I revisited Duyung in 1984 and they had become more like Malays than French, shyly watching the half-crazy foreigners who slept rough amongst the palms alongside their developing hulls.

Jamie had fallen in love with the boat as soon as he saw it. After a certain amount of negotiation by letter the French woman allowed him to hire it for a minimal fee (which I don't believe was ever paid) if he would work on it to make it sea-worthy. Together with various helpers who passed through Trengganau on their hike round South-East Asia he worked hard, and the boat was ready within a matter of months. There then followed a period of local sailing to test the rigging and the handling, after which he decided that the boat was sound enough to take him down to Australia and his home town of Darwin. This is where the rest of us came in.

I spotted the *Chun Bhatera* for the first time in Bali's Benoa harbour. I was looking for a boat that would take me down the Nusa

Tenggara chain, and I recognised her instantly from photographs that I had seen in Singapore. Even so she was considerably bigger than I had thought. Her 56-foot length was exaggerated by a 12-foot bowsprit which reached out like a thrown punch over the sea. She would require several crew-members for a long journey, I thought to myself. After watching the boat for some while I concluded that there was no one on board, so I approached the ibu (literally 'mother', but a name for any woman in authority) who ran the coffee-shop on the harbour side.

The ibu was enormously fat and earthy, but her coffee was excellent and she knew every boat in the harbour – where it was going, what it was carrying, who was on board. She also ran the lives of the girls who lived in cubicles next to her shop, where they serviced most of the crew-members of the ships in port. Benoa was not a large harbour, and apart from the Indonesian coasters themselves, most of the vessels that called there were oil-tankers from Korea. The Koreans would make a beeline for ibu's shop, and she would make sure they were entertained for the time they spent ashore.

I was all politeness. "*Selamat sore, ibu. Nak minum kopi susu.*" I sat down on the bench outside the shop. When the coffee was placed in front of me ibu returned to combing the hair of a young girl in the shade of a nearby tree. She was obviously in no hurry to make conversation. I plucked up courage. "*Ola, ibu, ada se-orang Australia bersama dengan prahu layar putih itu?*" I asked. "Was there an Australian on that white boat?"

"Yuh," she said, without looking at me. "Dat fuckin boat got one fuckin Australian and girl. Jamie."

Her command of English was brutal but effective, and I gave up my pretence at speaking Indonesian. "Are they going anywhere?"

"Yuh. 'Stralia."

"Have they got enough people?"

At this she looked at me as if she did not think that I could possibly be a suitable candidate to make such a journey, but she didn't put her thoughts into words. "*Bagaimana saya tahu?* How I know this questions? You mesti ask this questions Jamie," she shouted.

"Is he there?"

"*Tak ada.*" She shook her head.

"*Kapan sampai?*" – "When will he arrive?"

She shrugged her shoulders. I took this to mean that there would be no further conversation between us, so I got up and paid her for the coffee. As I turned away to leave she called out: "Jamie come *di-sini* the evening," she said. "Always come my shop evening-time."

She continued to comb the girl's hair, and didn't look up as I thanked her.

"I need at least six crew members," said Jamie that evening. Ibu was quite right; he, his girlfriend Lorraine, their two-month-old baby and their only other crew-member Alex were already in the coffee-shop when I arrived. Jamie was wearing a sarong, and his shoulders and arms dominated the table. He spoke with an over-deliberate charm that suggested something dangerous, and a heavy beard served to accentuate the power of his hard blue eyes.

"The topan and the agung are both laced with bamboo batons. They're pretty heavy, and it takes the three of us to raise the agung." He was interrupted by Lorraine, who explained to me with a smile that the topan was the foresail and the agung the mainsail. She was breast-feeding the baby. Jamie continued, this time speaking as if I were a greenhorn. "To tack - y'know what tack is, I suppose? – good. To tack she needs someone on the tiller, someone on the agung sheet ropes – that's the ropes that control the angle of the agung from the poop deck on the stern – someone on the topan sheet ropes and a further couple of guys for the stays port and starboard of the main-mast. Y'know what stays are?" He looked at me suspiciously, and I nodded. Until that moment I had always thought of myself as quite a knowledgeable and experienced sailor, but dinghies only had one mast.

"Right," but Jamie did not sound convinced. "We got down here from Singapore with just the three of us, but it was too much like hard work, especially with the kid. Three more should be enough."

"Heaps," Alex grinned in agreement as he bit into his chilli sandwich. He too had a beard, though his was straggled. He looked far more piratical than Jamie, and when he smiled he showed several gaps in his teeth which he had won in bar-room fights in his home-town, Sydney. He had a massive bandage around one foot – "stuck my stupid foot into a propeller, dint I" – seemed overweight but was massively strong, and when he grinned it split his face from side to side. Ibu passed him a joint she had been rolling and he belched appreciation.

Jamie was looking at my shoulders, arms and legs. "You look strong," he admitted, "but can you sail?" I told him of my wind-surfing experience, of dinghy sailing in Scotland, and of my trips on the *Anak Duyong* in Singapore. When I had finished he just nodded and said, "Sure thing. You want to come, you can come. We leave in two weeks." As I left the coffee-shop my vision blurred with the excitement of the forthcoming voyage. Jamie shouted an afterthought. "You do realise that this could be dangerous, don't you?" I shouted arrogantly back that I didn't think the danger would be a problem as far as I was concerned. On the contrary, I told myself as I walked away, it was what I wanted. In my pursuit of Conrad, this journey would give me the chance to cross that shadow-line of his, that invisible line between youth and maturity or sanity and insanity that his characters crossed in the most dramatic moments of his books.

I went on board a couple of days later.

Four more crew joined the boat in the course of the next two weeks. Like me, they had drifted down to the harbour looking for a passage. Americans Frank and Alma and Italians Riccardo and Largo did not strike me as natural choices, but I told myself to reserve judgement until we were afloat. There was plenty to do on board during the preparation period. We built a bamboo shelter over the rear cabin, we sewed patches on the agung and measured up new material for a replacement topan, we re-beaded much of the deck planking and re-spliced many of the stays. For a week the boat was on the beach whilst we scraped and painted the hull with anti-fouling, sleeping at nights at an angle of 30 degrees inside the beached boat, too stoned and tired for the angle to prevent sleep.

Every night we joined ibu on the harbour side. Once I had become one of the crew she accepted me, although Lorraine, Jamie and Alex were always the most welcomed. Her laugh was as enormous as she was, and whenever we scrambled ashore she would boom with laughter as she set about preparing eight platefuls of food. She kept an excellent stock of the local arak and supplied most of the harbour with marijuana.

She liked the foreigners, and even though she had never set foot outside Bali she knew all the ports and islands between Benoa and Australia. The white boat-people who stopped in Bali on the long haul from South-East Asia down to Australia all knew ibu, and many of them stopped off just to see her. There was an element of hardness in them that matched the toughness in her, and she argued constantly with all of them – breaking off in the middle of a rough and crude tirade to cackle with laughter. But above all she loved children; she had never had any herself. She called Lorraine's baby Anak (Indonesian for child) because she could not pronounce the real name. Anak stuck, and even though I spent two of the first four months of that child's life living cheek by jowl with him, watching him develop from a wriggly white thing into something approaching a human being, I never learned his real name. 'Anak' was enough. Ibu used to look after him for hours; his blond hair and grey eyes fascinated and delighted her just as they were to fascinate and delight many other Indonesian mothers on our journey.

In the end – or at the beginning – we had to leave Bali before we were ready. It did not worry us crew-members, but it did worry Jamie, who knew what still remained to be done. We were all dying to get to sea, but he was worried that he had not had time to re-step the bowsprit to make it stronger and higher. Events in the end proved his worry well-founded – but we had to go.

Our early departure was prompted by visa problems. Indonesia only gives one-month visas to foreigners, and we had already extended ours beyond that limit. The harbour-master at Benoa had watched us making the boat ready, and eventually he decided that he could not allow us to stay in his harbour any longer. We were ready enough, he told Jamie, and we were to leave the following morning. He gave us sailing-papers that allowed us to stay within Indonesian waters on our route, but officially we checked out of the country at Bali, even though we were to be in Indonesia for at least another month. Bali was the last immigration office on our route.

And so we worked late into the night loading the boat with ballast, stacking wet bags of sand deep into the bilges and covering the cabin planking with coconut logs that Jamie hoped to sell in Australia. On the deck we lashed down a Balinese Jukung (a traditional out-rigger sailing boat) which was also destined for sale on arrival, and our own dinghy. The dug-out canoe which we used for shore trips was to trail along behind, as there was little room left for it on deck. Then we went over to ibu's in the darkness and drank until we could hardly stay awake. She wouldn't say goodbye to any of us except the baby.

The anchor came up with the dawn, and we swung away from our mooring out into the channel that led to the sea. The wind was slight, but the *Chun Bhatera* had an old motor that was sufficient to move us at a couple of knots in dead calm conditions, so we chugged happily down the channel, hauling up sails and tightening stays whenever the wind blew the cotton-shreds on the rigging enough to give us a hint of its direction. Then, just as we were beginning to relish the opening-up of the shore-line and watch the receding shapes of the other boats with a mixture of disdain and hidden anxiety, the boat lurched. I recorded that first disaster in my diary:

> There was no noise, but an invisible fist gently but firmly stopped us dead, lifting the bows unnaturally high in the process. At first no one knew what had happened; the sea was calm and there was no sign of any hazard. We looked to be in the middle of the channel. We could not have been more than a kilometre away from our mooring, and yet already we had gone aground! Ignominious – in full view of all the other boats. Tankers can come and go into the harbour, but we could not. Not a good omen.
>
> After a moment of dismay we all realised that we were not going to sink, and there was a frenzy of activity as we all went over-board to push. The keel was wedged in a coral graveyard; we shoved and swore and splashed in four feet of water and succeeded in riding her a little higher, carving our feet up on the razor-sharp coral. The sails flapped idly like elephants' ears, as if our efforts were just an irritation.
>
> Jamie unloaded a torrent of abuse at the harbour-master's henchman, who came out in a launch to watch the fun. Then we had a coffee, a cigarette, and watched the sun climb the sky, waiting for the tide to carry us off. Eventually it did.

Once outside the harbour mouth we were greeted by a short, sharp squall that got us truly under way. The day settled, and soon we were rolling on the long swell coming up the Lombok strait, watching the elegant Sanur Hotel on the distant shoreline come and go as we tacked into the current.

Currents that rip between the islands are a hazard of Indonesian waters, and it is often their existence that isolates one island from another, although the two might seem only a stone's throw apart. The current that flowed through the Lombok strait effectively divided tropical Asia from Australia; on the south-east side of what is termed the Wallace Line after the scientist who discovered it, the islands have much the same flora and fauna as the Australian continent, whilst to the north-west tigers stalk through forests, mynah birds sing on street-stall tables and buffalo lather their hides with mud to keep cool in the tropical sun. But to us in the straits and on that crucial line both shores looked much the same.

There couldn't have been eight better friends in the world on that day. Jamie, rugged, tough and experienced, had just the right edge of temper that a captain should, I thought. Lorraine was equally tough in her own way, but at the same time calm and reliable. She discreetly acted as an interpreter for Jamie when he was too technical for us newcomers, giving his authority an edge of kindness. If she was nervous about the first experience of life that her child was undergoing she didn't show it; she breast-fed Anak throughout the voyage, even when she herself was exhausted or sick. I never saw any baby-food on board. Alex hobbled around the deck, grinning and checking our work. He was shitting blood from his chilli sandwiches, as he told us with some glee as we gathered round to help change the bandages on his gored foot. Riccardo, the fatter of the two Italians, was foolish, soft and likeable, and he rapidly became the crew buffoon. Largo, his skinny friend, was less approachable, slow-moving and abstracted, although he earned our admiration by playing his guitar on deck in the evenings. Alma, the American girl, was lightweight and easy to get along with, although she used to complain that we never treated her seriously. Frank, the other American, was . . . well, ordinary. There was a mean streak in him which I never defined but that I didn't like and he was openly hostile to the Italians at times. But Frank didn't exist as far as our sailing papers were concerned. He intended to come with us as far as Flores, and then turn back. Therefore his character mattered little, I told myself.

In those early days the weather was very kind and it gave us the time to learn the feel of the boat and how to master the rigging. It gave us the time, but it didn't force us to learn enough. Life was too idyllic for learning.

> My night watch has lead into the dawn. As the light hardens Largo pokes his head up through the forward hatch and grins wolfishly. I know what he means. The northern end of Bali rears blue-green above a quiet sea, a sea flecked with brightly coloured sails that catch the morning sun. Fishermen in jukungs are returning home to houses that seem to perch on the hillsides, the morning breeze rippling their latteen sails. Snatches of song reach us across the water as the fishermen begin to enjoy the warmth of the sun after a cold night riding the swell. We waylay one of these returning boats with cries of "*ada ikan? ada ikan?*" – have you got any fish? He is so stunned by the sight of so many foreigners on board such a boat at such a time and in such a place that he forgets to ask a high price for his fish. So we have fresh tuna for breakfast.

Cooking was done on a rota basis. We were all to share the tasks equally (some shared the tasks more equally than others), and there were many tasks to do. Everything down below, from the bottles of cooking-oil to the plastic dustbins full of rice, had to be tied down so that nothing broke in rough seas. The bunks had to be built from bamboo and then hung from the deck-beams. The hull had to be cleaned on the inside, the bilges pumped and the drum of engine-fuel secured. Up on deck the new roof on the cabin needed varnishing, and the even newer one of the captain's cabin on the stern needed finishing. Many of the stays needed re-splicing again, the dinghy leaked like a sieve and needed repatching, and a spider's web of ropes needed to be strung up the sails. Every hour or so the deck needed washing down with water to prevent it from cracking under the assault of the sun, and this treatment demonstrated that yet more beading between the deck-planks needed renewing where the water leaked through on to our few possessions, hanging in nets from the deck-beams below. We had plenty to do.

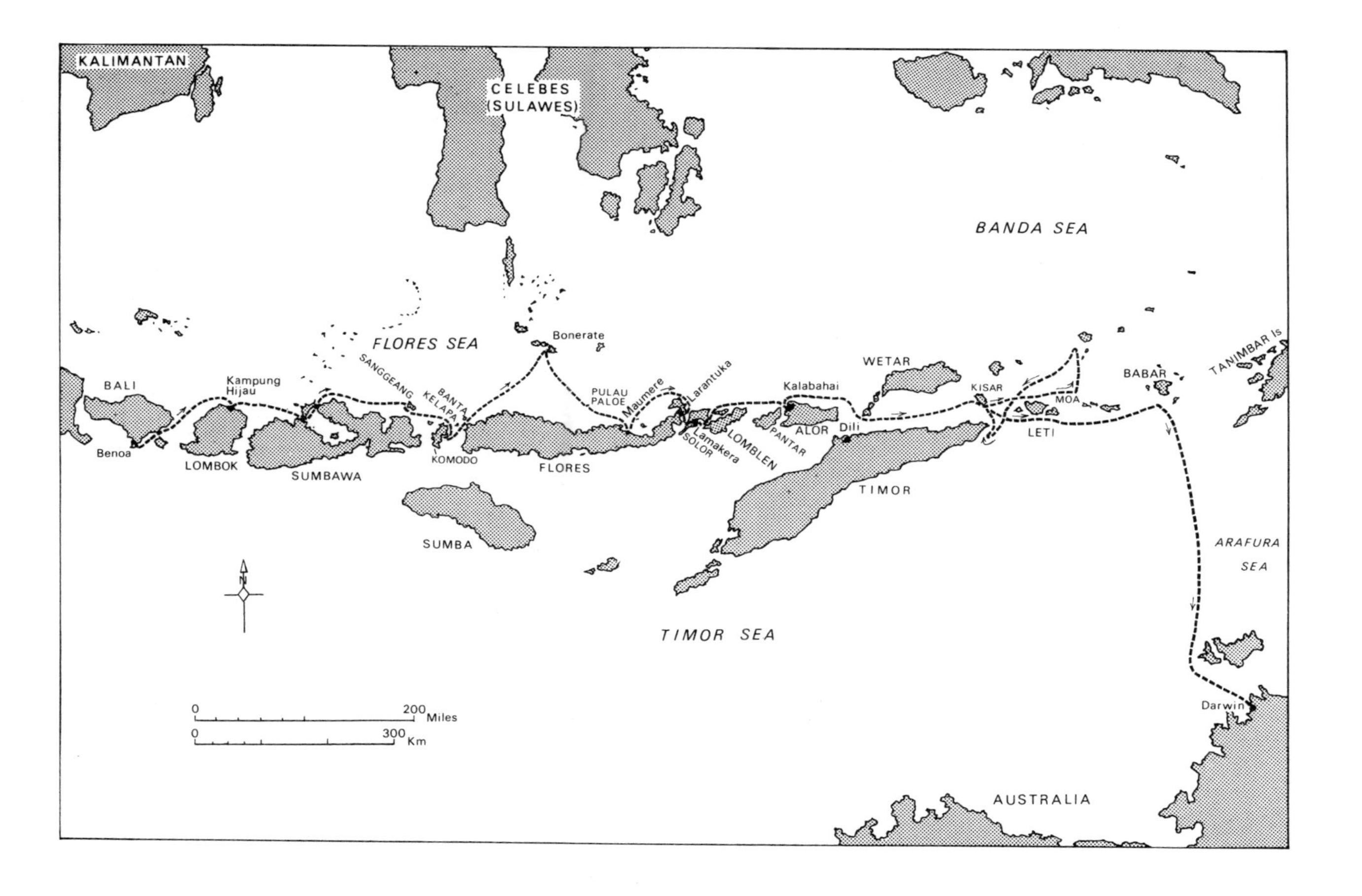
KALIMANTAN
CELEBES
(SULAWES)
BANDA SEA
FLORES SEA
Bonerate
SANGGEANG
BANTA
KELAPA
PULAU
PALOE
Maumere
Larantuka
Kampung
Hijau
BALI
Benoa
LOMBOK
SUMBAWA
KOMODO
FLORES
SOLOR
Lamakera
LOMBLEN
PANTAR
ALOR
Kalabahai
Dili
WETAR
KISAR
MOA
LETI
BABAR
TANIMBAR Is
TIMOR
SUMBA
TIMOR SEA
ARAFURA
SEA
Darwin
AUSTRALIA
N
0
200
Miles
0
300
Km

Our first stop was on the northern tip of Lombok, the neighbouring island to Bali. We re-stocked on fresh water and investigated a leak in the hull that had kept us busily pumping the bilges at frequent intervals. The water was coming in round a piece of the keel that had been badly renewed in Benoa. We arrived late in the evening and rode at anchor some distance offshore of a village that our charts told us was called Kampung Hijau – green village. The two Italians played their guitars and we learned the words of a couple of their songs, cool at last in the offshore night breeze that was to carry us on our way for several weeks to come.

In the morning the boat was swamped by curious villagers who had come to look at the foreigners and their strange boat. The odd outline of our rigging against the night-sky and the foreign music that they heard the previous night had made them rather frightened, they said; all Indonesians are very superstitious. They asked many questions, and couldn't understand why we didn't have a motor-boat, or tinned food, or television, or why we did not eat bread instead of rice. Many had their faces powdered white, like ghosts, to protect them against the sun.

They told us that the policeman from the neighbouring kampong had been informed of our presence and was on his way. When he arrived he came aboard and checked our papers, reading every word on every page as if he was looking for a misprint or even a missing word. He cannot have read them too intelligently – our papers were for seven adults and a baby, yet there were eight of us. There was no objection to us going ashore, he said eventually, as long as we did not stay too long. He just wanted to be sure that we were not intending to settle on his island and thus get him into trouble, and once he was sure that we had every intention of leaving his patch quickly he was all smiles. He was particularly impressed by Jamie's muscular forearms and by the women. He sat for a long time on the cabin roof watching us closely from behind his sunglasses, and we were relieved when eventually he said he was 'pusing-pusing' – a little seasick – and returned to dry land.

Kampung Hijau was a Muslim village, and made quite a contrast to the Hindu villages on Bali. The sand was dirty, the houses poor, the people much less free and open. For us as foreigners the pockets of Catholicism on the islands gave us much the best reception. By the end of our journey we had all developed a slight antipathy to

Muslim strongholds, which generally were a good deal less friendly. On one of the later Muslim islands (the further from central Indonesia and the more remote the people, the more fanatical the isolated religions seemed to get) a couple of boys threw stones at me whilst their parents looked on indulgently.

Fortunately at Kampung Hijau they were friendly enough. A lady sitting in the midst of a litter of bits of decaying fish called us over as we landed. Did we want to buy one of her delicious dried fish? she asked. The flies buzzed frenziedly around the fish as they baked in the sun on sticks stuck into the sand. The sand itself was heaving with insect life. In unison we declined her offer.

The fresh-water well was next to the mosque. We waited with our jerry-cans whilst the men of the village washed quickly before entering the building for midday prayers. One or two of them decided to forego their prayers in order to watch the antics of the foreigners, and they were rewarded with the sight of us struggling to fill an obstinate well-bucket. The bucket was made from the lower half of a plastic container, and it insisted on floating. One of the older spectators eventually stepped forward and gently took the rope from my hands as I jigged at the bucket and swore. With a few expert flicks of his wrist he filled the rest of our containers for us, and then watched us struggle back to the boat without a word. I found the episode a little depressing: what could they have thought of us? I had gone ashore with the swagger of a tough, experienced seaman, but I had not even been able to use a well-bucket effectively.

The repairs to the keel went on all day, and we took it in turns to go down to scrub the barnacles off the hull; they would reduce our sailing-speed considerably if they had been left to grow. In the evening we again went ashore, this time at the request of the headman, who had heard the guitars the previous night and wanted us to play to his villagers. The occasion was a great success, as I recorded in my diary.

> Riccardo and Largo played Italian love-songs. The headman is very impressed with our orchestra, as he calls it, and has given us heaps of bananas. We now have great stalks of them hanging from the beams below decks. We had a large audience last night, with rings of people sitting on the sand way out beyond the circle of fire-light. We've got all sorts of percussion instruments on

> board: a Jew's harp, a small drum, sticks, tambourines and a bamboo tube with a soft hammer that makes an excellent hollow note, and these instruments were passed around the crowd. Many joined in for the choruses. Some of the percussionists had no idea of rhythm, and some were naturals. I wonder whether the kind of Latin beat to Italian music is strange to them? One of the teenagers could never get the chorus of 'Juantaramera' in the right place, and made the rest of them roar with laughter. One of the old men was hot stuff with the bamboo.

When the keel was declared finished Alex and I took the dug-out canoe out fishing. We lost the line on the bottom on the first cast, and then had to spend hours struggling back in the darkness against a current that roared around the end of the island. The following morning we were off again, and this time we spent a longer period at sea.

> It is surprising how we've all adopted roles that we determinedly act out. Jamie of course the boss, and he complains about everything. Alma maternal, smoothing our hair down as she talks to us. Riccardo is deliberately slow-witted, but funny, Largo deliberately bolshie. Had an episode this morning with him. He was late for his watch, half asleep when he dragged himself up on to the deck from the forward hatch. Jamie jumped on him. He was to do this, and that, and the other, and quickly. Largo just ignored the torrent of commands. "Today is not a good day," he said, "today my biorhythms are low. I cannot work hard. It is dangerous for me to work with bad biorhythms." Of course we all exploded at the idea. What if we all had low biorhythms? What if there was a storm, and we had to rely on each other? Lorraine stepped in and cooled tempers as she always does, but we won't forget that row for a while. The day has been clouded by the morning's burst.

The close conditions of life on board and our isolation began to work on us.

> It's funny how we all react to being on board. If someone sets a mood in the morning with a sharp word – or even with a happy

Above: Outside commuting hours the main users of Bangkok's Chao Phya Express river taxi were Buddhist novices, fruit and vegetable vendors heading for the floating markets, and me.

Below: Malaysia's fishing communities are by far the most colourful corners of the country. Here one of the night trawlers anchored in the creek at Mersing waits for high tide before crossing the sandbar.

Spirit flags hang above the chief's hut in a Yellow Lahu village. My party stayed in the guest hut opposite. Seven hill-tribes live in the rain forests of Northern Thailand, spread across the borders of three countries – Burma, Thailand and Laos – but citizens of none.

The *Chun Bhatera*, photographed from the back of Pastor Romano's motorcycle as we bumped along Solor's coastal path. The bowsprit was later torn out of its foundations by the storm. Outrigger canoes are very common in these fishing communities.

Above: The only catamarans in Indonesia, off Komodo island. They are hopelessly unmanoeuvrable, and the village headman regularly had to rescue the fleet as it was swept out to sea on an outgoing tide. He owned the only boat with an outboard motor.

Left: There was plenty of rigging to master – and plenty to trip up over – on board the *Chun Bhatera*.

Below: The *Chun Bhatera* glimpsed from Solor's coast track. The islanders could never understand why we didn't have a large motor boat, and why we didn't eat bread.

Above: Riding the surf at Puri. The hardwood boats were virtually unmoveable, and their crews were swept overboard like skittles by the heavy surf.

Below left: My saviour on the Thorong La melts snow for tea.

Below right: The Puri boats could only be moved once they had been unlashed, and had fallen into three or four pieces.

The edge of nowhere: the friendly-sounding village of Sam, in Rajasthan's Thar desert, is no more than a teashop sheltering behind a cactus. Nevertheless, Sam was a good place for buying camels.

Faces of Asia: a Lisu boy (*above left*) presents the innocent side of the hill-tribes whilst a 'sky pilot' Lahu prepares a bowl of opium (*above right*). The crew of the trawler out of Mersing shared their breakfast with me (*below left*), but the Paharia in the foothills of the Himalayas were very wary of the foreigner with the camera (*below right*).

word, though that is less likely – then that mood is picked up and carried by the others. We watch each other shitting over the sides, we can see every inch of each others' bodies, so there is no chance of hiding moods on a boat this size. There are times when you know instinctively that it is important to say nothing at all, for if you do you know that it will inevitably attract a bitter response from somewhere. Then there are other times when there's a kind of mutual egging-on in happiness, but it's fragile, and I am always so conscious that the surging wave could break and fall, and bitter words fly again. We have no privacy here, and no freedom. Our lives are tied to each other and we all fight to keep independent. We are hanging on to the tail of the wind, and if it chooses to lash out then we must jump to attention. So far it hasn't. Only Anak seems unworried by everything. We lavish attention on him because he can't answer back. Mind you, he does pee on everyone to make up for it.

Sunrises came and sunsets went, each magnificent, but we became blasé about their beauty. The sun was always impossibly hot, and there was little wind to do more than keep the sails pressed flat. Only at night, when the wind veered to come at us from the land, did we make good progress. By day we erected a sheet above the deck by the tiller to protect us from the sun, stretching it from the boom-rest to the back-stays of the agung. The breeze was so predictable that the boom stayed out and the shade could stay up for hours at a stretch. The cool that it provided saved both the soles of our feet and the edges of our tempers.

I started to smoke for the first time in my life. I started because the only legitimate excuse that Jamie recognised for taking a break from work was to stop for a roll-up. At the beginning we had had some dope to put us at ease and give us the space that we didn't actually physically have. Then the dope ran out and tempers grew correspondingly thinner. But even this had its positive side, for the lethargy of dope-smoking would not have helped us in the foul weather that we were to meet, and even though the way in which we bitched at each other was unpleasant at the time, it was probably necessary to goad us all into fighting for survival. Anyway, to go and roll a cigarette and smoke it was to have a moment of quiet away from everyone else. The local tobacco was strong and sweet, and it went straight to my head. I usually dropped the bulk of my mis-shapen roll-ups into the sea, after only a few drags.

Apart from smoking the other pleasure was the bowsprit. Like the poop deck above the stern and behind the aft cabin, the bowsprit was away from the centre of activities. From the poop deck we fished constantly, but the speed of the boat was insufficient to attract any tuna to the lure. Each time we went about (which was not often those early days) the line would get wrapped around the rudder, and if we were not careful we would lose it. Both bowsprit and poop deck exaggerated the motion of the boat, the finger of the 'sprit describing a gentle arc against the sky ahead. To reach the platform at the point meant scrambling out along the whiskers that stretched out from the bulwarks and converged on the platform. The jib flew from the end of the 'sprit, and to raise or lower it involved going out on to the platform to guide it and furl it. In calm weather this was a reasonably easy feat to achieve, but when it was rough the bowsprit's gentle arc changed into a wild dipping and rearing, and anyone struggling to control the live jib as it cracked in the wind would have most of his work cut out in just staying on. At its most violent the 'sprit would bury itself into the waves as the boat plunged and rolled, and the salt-water would threaten to tear the body on the platform off into the sea. Then the 'sprit would free itself with an agonised judder that ran the length of the boat, and the struggling figure on its end would be tossed into the air like a speared fish, dripping and gasping and wriggling to keep his balance.

But during those first weeks the weather was calm, and the ride on the platform was gentle and smooth. In shallow waters it was the lookout's position, and I spent many hours staring down into the translucent water idly watching transparently long and thin garfish as they loitered in the water and sucked at anything that looked edible on the surface above them. Through the inland sea on the corner of the island of Sumbawa the ride on the bowsprit was excellent. The water was calm, the wind fresh, and the bow-wave curled and gurgled below. It was a Rolls-Royce of a ride, and the sea was always deep enough to be safe. At one stage in the afternoon a school of dolphins torpedoed the boat in pairs. I spent several hours on the bowsprit that day, lying back against the jib-stay as it sang gently with the strain of the pulling jib. When evening came and we were almost out into the heavier seas again I returned to the safety of the deck, staggering with sunstroke, my skin tight with the sun and the salt. I had never been so brown and probably never will be again. Our diet of rice, fish, fruit and vegetables kept us well. All the men had piratical beards.

Sumbawa is a large, barren-looking island. One major road links the towns, but in the wet season all of the bridges collapse with regularity. Jamie had once been ashore there, and he didn't recommend it. The people are fiercely Muslim, and white Catholic missionaries (of whom there are several in the islands) no longer dare set foot on Sumbawa since one was stoned some years ago. In the island's capital, Bima, a pig was placed by person or persons unknown in the mosque and there were riots in the town. Several of the Catholic minority were hurt, even though they denied having anything to do with the sacrilege.

So in the end we thought it better not to land on Sumbawa, but anchored just off the western tip for a pause in our journey. The sea was running high, but there was no wind. The boat crashed and banged on the swell through a sleepless night. On deck I felt companionship with a local fisherman on his tiny boat some 150 yards away from us. Every now and then snatches of song would carry over the chop as he tried to keep himself warm. The light on his boat winked at me between waves.

A fair wind took us straight past the Bima inlet the following day; we could see the sails of vessels heading into the port, which acted as a trading centre for many islands around. In the evening we stopped at Pulau Sanggeang.

Sanggeang is a volcano of an island which rises sharply out of an otherwise empty sea, just off the eastern tip of Sumbawa. Its sides are so sheer that there was hardly a purchase for our anchor on the bed of coral before it shelved off into the darkness of very deep water. We dived again and again from the boat into the colours of the corals. The water was so clear that the reef looked only inches from the surface. Swimming above the rocks was warm and reassuring, and shoals of brilliantly blue fish would change direction simultaneously to let the swimmer through. But if you strayed out over the deep water there were no fish, and you felt an instant physical and psychological chill. Down below could be a beady eye watching you struggle clumsily through the water, silhouetted against the sky above, and it could be picking you out as an easy target.

On shore the sand was so hot that it was more comfortable to walk amongst the brittle grasses, even though the latter lacerated my feet. With a parang I collected some firewood. I saw no wildlife except one bird that darted out from a sand burrow beneath my feet. The sparse mountain-side was a little forbidding. Someone caught a shimmering blue fish before we left, the first fish of our trip caught by our own hands, and we celebrated by cooking it on a wood-fire in the firebox on deck. The swim at Sanggeang had boosted our morale, as reflected in my diary entry.

> Tonight is a magic night. A land breeze picked us up just after the beginning of my watch. I padded round the deck as quietly as I could, adjusting the sails for the best speed, and have been rewarded with the creaking of ropes as they take the full power of the wind. We have passed between the volcano and the mainland already, and must be doing a good five knots. To the south I can see the lighthouse on Pulau Kelapa. There is no moon, but I have never seen the canopy of stars so bright, nor the darkness between them so intense. On deck the wood fire is still glowing, fanned by the breeze, and the scent of burning embers mixes well with the salt of the sea.
>
> She feels so sensitive at this speed, a bird, I feel so powerful with the tiller resting lightly in my fingers. Our course seems OK, but there must be huge currents squeezing up between these islands. At one time we seemed quite far from Pulau Banta, but now it looms frighteningly close. I cannot trust my eyes to judge distances, and the harder I stare at that low-lying piece of darkness the less I can tell how far away or how close at hand it is. Pray God the currents don't decide to squash us irresistibly against the steep side of the island, like a fly on a window-pane. On nights like these I can just feel the suppressed power of the elements, which only just tolerate our presence on the sea.

We had compass and charts, and a pilot book that told us the speeds and times of local currents together with the safest anchorages. We had all learned relatively quickly to calculate our position with reasonable accuracy. Later I recorded: "I've checked the chart, bearings and speed. No danger."

The morning light showed us the bare northern shoulders of our next destination, Komodo island. Tall lontar palms were silhouetted like lollipops on the horizon, but they were practically the only growing things on these northern slopes. The currents were strong, said our pilot book, and so we followed a prahu along the coast, trusting his local knowledge. At one point the sail seemed to disappear into the hillside, but when we reached the spot we saw that there was a narrow channel through to the main strait, with a tidal current ripping through the middle. At times motionless against the current we skirted the edge in the wake of the other boat, praying for the wind to keep its strength. Eventually we emerged into the main strait. Here the current was with us, and we were swept southwards like a matchstick on a storm-drain. Fortunately it looked as if the tide would push us where we wanted to go, but it was an unnerving experience.

> We are taking turns at being lookout on the bowsprit – not that we would be able to do anything about a collision course. At times the current eddies and twirls us around in idle circles. The tiller has no grip at all. It feels like a ghost ship, with no wind in the sails but nevertheless a steady, silent progress, taking us somewhere quite deliberately, as if in a bad dream.
>
> The sheer power of this current is humping water up on the shoulders of the rocks that break up the channel, and the air near those rocks is full of the heavy roar of a torrent. If we were to get between one of those rocks and the current we would be smashed to fragments. Just now it was my turn on the bowsprit; out of the darkness below me the sea-bed rose with frightening speed and I shouted a warning to the rest. But the bottom disappeared just as fast as it had appeared, leaving me with a glimpse of a large pilot-fish hanging over a patch of sand.
>
> Around us huge turtles lie sunning themselves on the water's surface, making heavy splashes as they dive when we get too close. On the sandbanks to our left fishermen pole themselves through the shallows in a line. Their presence is reassuring, but they are not in the grip of the current as we are. We've all just eaten about ten bananas each.

Then suddenly we were opposite Komodo bay, and the current released its hold, gently pushing us into the quieter waters. It was a charmed arrival in a charmed place, with tuna leaping all round us in the joy of the evening and the fleet of catamaran fish-traps anchored in readiness for the night. We had come to the island of the Dragon.

Komodo was first inhabited in 1900 by criminals exiled by the Sultan of neighbouring Sumbawa. It was such an inhospitable place that no one had attempted to live there permanently before; just to survive was thought to be sufficient punishment for the criminals. Then the exiles began to send back terrified reports of the existence of a huge *buaya darat* (land crocodile) on the island, which they said was preying on the village. At first the reports were ignored because they came from convicts, but later they were supported by a similar story from visiting pearl-divers. Finally in 1912 rumour was so persistent that the Dutch authorities sent someone to investigate, and the Komodo Dragon was officially discovered.

The dragon is in fact a monitor lizard, the largest and fiercest of its kind, which was thought to have been extinct long ago. It lives only on three islands in the world – Rintja, part of Flores, and Komodo. There are rumoured to be 2,000 of them in the acacia parkland of Komodo, and they outnumber the residents of the island several times over. Every now and then the beasts show their power by eating a local or a visitor. Komodo is now well-known and has been declared a sanctuary by the Indonesian government. The sanctuary officials take the line that the dragons are not basically aggressive, but there are several recent case-histories of unfortunate victims. The last was supposedly a young French tourist who fell asleep beneath a tree; only his shoes were found. But the most famous episode was the disappearance of the nature-lover and huntsman Baron von Reding, who strayed from the path taken by the rest of his party in 1974. The only trace found of him was his camera, its strap broken. On the savannah above the valley where the dragons lurk is a cross in his memory.

In the only village on the island, built on stilts half into the sea (so wary are the villagers of their co-resident nightmares) we found the hut of the dragons' keepers. We bought a goat in the village, hired a guide who would take us to the *ora*, as they called the dragons, and set off inland.

We crept up a jungle path through a valley buzzing with wildlife. Occasionally the raucous cry of a cockatoo would make us stop in our tracks, but as the walk went on we became more flippant, shushing one another and giggling. In a dried-up stream-bed, the same spot that David Attenborough's expedition visited in 1956, the guide tied the goat carcass to a root; we were glad to be rid of it, as even on the walk up the valley it had seemed to begin to smell through the sack as it rested in turn on each of our shoulders. The stream-bed was a perfect arena, and we watched and waited on a high bank some ten feet above.

At first the jungle fell disappointingly quiet, a quiet only broken by the occasional shriek of a jungle-fowl. We began to worry that our goat had not been smelly enough to attract any attention, but before long the first Komodo appeared on the edge of the bowl of sand, blinking in the sunlight. It was small, no more than three feet long, and it showed no real interest in the carcass. It wavered on the edge of the light, then turned and lumbered back into the darkness. Stagefright, someone whispered.

But it wasn't long before a real monster arrived to please the crowds. It must have been all of ten feet in length (Komodo grow up to about twelve feet and can weigh 300 pounds), and as it waddled into the centre of the arena it looked like a log on legs. It stopped and surveyed the spectators above, its flat head high and motionless, scarred skin hanging in folds around its muscular neck. Its forked tongue flickered rapidly in and out of a cavernous mouth. Then it scented the putrefying goat and made a beeline for the carcass on the stake. Komodos can articulate their jaws as snakes do, and once our beast had torn the carcass away from its stake with one sharp movement, it broke it into three pieces and set about swallowing them whole. By this time a couple of smaller and more timid beasts had swayed into the clearing and were watching with evident disappointment as their more fortunate relative polished off the snack.

But they were not to be disappointed for long. When we set off to retrace our steps down the path to our boat, satisfied with what we had seen, we met the advance party from a large liner that had just entered the bay. The *World Discoverer* apparently called at Komodo once every three months with a crowd of all nationalities who were touring the wonders of the wilds almost in their armchairs, by virtue of spending a lot of dollars. The advance party had walkie-talkies and goats, both live and dead. Behind them came the passengers, and we watched them with almost the same fascination as we had the Dragons. We hadn't seen any other white people for weeks, and to meet a group of pensioners in those surroundings was almost surreal. Few of the visitors were under sixty, and some of them would have made decidedly tough eating for the Komodos. One gent had a mosquito net covering his whole head, and he looked very hot beneath it. He was wearing a tie. An old lady came up the valley path supported between two bronzed locals, looking as if she was enjoying every moment of that contact. Another held a battery-operated fan under her chin as she walked, complaining bitterly about the heat. A fat German with a walkie-talkie ran around them all making sure that they did not lag behind and that they had what they wanted. He also made sure that we did not get our thieving hands on any of their supplies. We watched incredulously as they consumed apples and fizzy drinks. But if they looked out of place to us, they seemed to think that we belonged. "Do you live here?" asked one lady who was obviously determined to make conversation despite her apprehension at our appearance. I wondered whether she meant the jungle or the village. We looked wild enough to have been in the jungle for months.

We spent a couple more days in the bay at Komodo, watching the fleet of catamarans coming and going with the tide, crows circling above them waiting for their chance to pick the drying squid off their decks. We left when the tide was going in our direction. Someone had pulled the plug out of the northern end of the Komodo strait and we took our position on the swiftly flowing current. It was like catching a train.

We followed the coast of Flores for a day with a good wind beside us, then headed north into the open sea for the island of Bone Rate.

> We have our own pet turtle on board now. We were taken by surprise this morning when Jamie leapt overboard with a cry. I thought something awful had happened and was mighty relieved when he surfaced clutching the tiny but perfect animal. We have named him Max, and he now lives in a bucket on deck, which he shares with a limpet. Alex feeds him flies and talks to him in the same tones that he uses for Anak.
>
> Tonight during my watch I heard my first whales. At first I had no idea what the heavy snorting sounds near the boat were.

In the darkness they could have been anything. Some of them sounded so close that I could hear the jets of water spraying back into the sea. I felt small in a land of giants, and found myself praying that one of them would not take it into his head to try to surface beneath the boat. The loneliness of the darkness seems to exaggerate small emotions felt on deck, until everything becomes pregnant with unseen danger.

We saw the whales clearly in the daylight, long black shapes that shouldered gently above the water to snort and spurt. Dim, rippling smaller shadows alongside some of the mammals marked where the young calves swam by their mothers' sides.

Then the wind dropped but the swell increased. The ship banged and crashed more than it had done ever before, the sails rattling against their masts, dangerously heavy with no force to keep them steady. Everything below was shaken loose and had to be secured once again. I cooked an appalling meal (we had run out of fresh vegetables) that no one ate, though no one complained.

We are all depressed and silent. Not a word on deck as we wait for the wind. Even the whales have gone. A huge ray leapt in the distance, but only Alex and I saw it, and it didn't seem worth mentioning it to any of the others. The hugeness of everything seems to flatten us into nothing. With no land to look at, with no outside stimulus, only a wide, wide sea with us in the middle of it, going nowhere, we are nothing.

We know each other too well to find each other interesting, so we stare at nothing, read, and smoke more. The sea makes time seem listless and unchanging, and it is a real test of our characters. It shows us whether we are leaders or followers, whether we can or cannot hold ourselves together with no outside help. Here there is no one to say "hello, how are you – it's nice to see you." How are we standing up to this test? I suppose it's harder now because of the weather and the empty sea. This is the first time we have been out of sight of land.

The next day brought more whales and a little wind. By the evening we were in sight of the island, a low smudge on the horizon.

Bonerate is an unattractive, enigmatic island. It is a centre for boat-building in the middle of nowhere, and rows of half-finished hulls stand between the palm-trees on the shoreline. The wood comes by boat down from Sulawesi; the customers come up from Bima, where they find the prices too high. We were asked constantly as we walked whether we wanted to buy a boat. How much? *Limabelas juta* – fifteen million rupiah. Not cheap.

> The beach here is horribly filthy, but the kampung is neat and symmetrical. As we walked through it this morning we accumulated a trail of children who got more and more excited as we went. We had to split up to try to reduce the noise.
>
> We called on the various khaki-clad officials, sitting behind desks in dark huts that doubled as offices and schools. They wanted to see our papers, but really they were more interested in our women. Another Muslim village. Riccardo bought some black coral off a toothless lady who couldn't understand what he wanted it for. He intends to make bracelets out of it. Apparently the Indonesian sailors believe that black coral keeps them free of disease.

I made myself a bracelet out of Riccardo's coral, bending it above a candle flame and oiling it to prevent it from burning. Only when I finally returned to England did the bracelet suddenly break: I still have the pieces.

Jamie found an ancient cannon lying in the sands on the beach; it had been left behind by the Portuguese, and was 300 years old. He gave the village headman 7,000 rupiah for it on the excuse that he needed it for ballast – any other motive and the price would have been enormous. The villagers were all very amused as we floated it off the beach in our dinghy, which almost submerged under the weight. We used the masts as cranes to lift the great lump of brass on board. It was worth it all, as the museum in Darwin bought the cannon for several thousand per cent more than Jamie had paid.

We visited Bapak Weka's family boat-building business which was building a boat for someone in Darwin. Bapak explained at length why the boat was behind schedule: no tools, no money, no wood, no labour . . . the list was endless, and hard to believe. Jamie gave the family a drill with a set of bits, but as most of the hulls that I could see on the shore were held together with wooden pegs there didn't seem much point in giving them even that. I was glad when we finally set sail from Bonerate: it was a depressing place.

My depression showed itself the next day, when Bonerate was still in sight in our wake. Its featureless shape did not seem to have moved all day, and it seemed determined to drag our morale down further even than when we had left its shores. Weather conditions had not changed much, and the swell made the boat roll heavily without the weight of a wind in the sails to hold us steady. We all went about our tasks listlessly. I picked an argument with Jamie, who was trying to steady the tiller against the hammering of the swell.

"I think that you did the wrong thing giving that drill to Bapak Weka. What if we need it?"

"It's nothing to do with you. They need it more than we do. We can always get another."

"But that's not the point," I said, getting angry. "The point is that once you give them something – "

"I know what you're going to say. 'Once you give them something they'll expect something from every visitor.' I've heard that trotted out so often that it makes me sick. You've been listening to too much tourist talk."

"But you'll make them think that you're incredibly rich."

"And so I bloody am, compared to them." Jamie got very angry. "We are all bloody rich compared to them. We're just playing at doing things their way on this fucking boat. They have to live like this all the time."

I tried to control my voice. "But don't you think that you're spoiling it for – "

"I'm not spoiling anything for anyone. I'm doing a bit to help people, which is more than you're bloody doing. Anyway, who are you to criticise me. I have done this fucking trip three times, which is three times more than any of you. In future I'd be grateful if you kept your high and mighty opinions to yourself. Why don't you just piss off and leave me to steer this boat."

I went. My head was flooded with argument, but at the same time I knew there was no point in arguing: in the normal run of things no harsh words would have passed between us. We were both wrong and both right. I escaped to the bowsprit, to get as far from the others as I could.

A couple of hours later I pulled myself back on deck just as the sun was setting. All traces of anger had gone, and I felt regret at having started the row. Jamie was still on the tiller, studying the hard patches of skin on his hands where working the ropes had worn them.

"That," I said, studiously avoiding his eyes and looking out to sea, "is what they would call a glorious sunset."

"Glorious sunset number twenty-six," he said, without looking up. "I think I got bored with them after the first half-dozen."

We both watched as the sun dipped lower and lower. It swelled like a bloodshot eye as it descended, glaring across the uneven sea at the insolent boat. Then the horizon pulled the lid over it swiftly and cleanly.

I apologised to Jamie for starting the argument. He apologised for continuing it. We both laughed. The darkness had released the grip of the spell of Bonerate. I went below to fetch the hurricane lamps up on deck to give the glasses their daily clean before lighting them.

The rest of the trip down to Maumere, the port in Flores where we intended to spend a week, was uneventful except for the seascape that greeted us on the last morning before landfall.

> We were going to visit Pulau Paloe to see the pearl-fishers and the boats, which Jamie says are unlike any others, but there is no chance of that now. It looks as if the island, which is basically just a volcano as Sanggeang was, is in the process of erupting. A great pall of smoke is hanging over the place, hiding the top of the peak. What must be a lava flow is scarring the near slope, oozing smoke as it crawls down to the sea.

At Maumere we were told that the island had started erupting five days before. All of the islanders had been evacuated, and no one injured. They were quite accustomed to the quirks of the island on which they had built and re-built their villages.

We stayed in Maumere for a week. It was the time of the national elections, and the advance party ashore came back with excited reports of streets full of crowds and lorry-loads of islanders coming in from the hills around. Even from the boat we could hear the drums and cymbals of processions moving around the streets of the small town. Very soon the local police arrived on board. They asked for our papers and surveyed them in critical silence, stern-faced. They all had guns, and we began to wonder what it was that we had done that merited such heavy treatment. The captain relaxed a little after he had established that we were who we said we were, and he told us that President Suharto was in town canvassing. Apparently there had been fifty deaths in Jakarta that week in pre-election demonstrations, and they were taking no chances on the same thing happening on Flores. Security was tight, he said, and to prove his point he indicated a tank landing-craft and a naval destroyer hovering out to sea on the edge of horizon. We could be infiltrators, he said, political extremists come to upset the elections and maybe even assassinate the president. He admitted that he didn't think it likely, but nevertheless confined us to the boat until the president had gone the following morning, just to make sure. They had counted us up and found seven, as the paperwork stated. Frank hid below.

When we finally did touch land, after having kept our promise to stay aboard, the town was quiet. Solid ground felt strange after a rolling deck and we moved inland cautiously, as if just learning to walk. Many of the young people were wearing Golkar caps (Golkar was the ruling party), but there were few other signs of the presidential visit. Trampled streamers blew sadly along the gutters. One local said that the president had not moved from the government offices the whole time he was in Maumere, others claimed that he had led the procession. No one seemed to have actually seen him.

During the week that we stayed in Flores we went our separate ways, thankful for the chance of a little freedom to reassert our individuality. By night most of us reassembled to sleep on deck – when the boat was stationary the heat below was intense. We lay on the deck-planking and stared up at the ceiling of the world; the point of the mainmast circled slowly amongst the stars, like an unsteady finger trying to point out the galaxies. Not for the first time I intensely regretted not knowing the first thing about the night sky.

Someone had to guard the boat so we took it in turns to stay on board by day. The locals were inquisitive, and soon we had to make a rule that no one, barring specific friends and officials, was to be allowed on board. But even this did not ensure privacy, as fishing boats rode at anchor within metres, and there were always eyes trained on our decks. At times we would wake to find a group of new arrivals in the harbour clambering slowly around the boat staring at the winches, the masts, the anchors – anything that was in the least foreign. And of course us. The women grew tired of trying to be discreet, and deliberately started using the more visible side of the boat for their more private personal needs. This tactic seemed most effective and as the week grew older we were left more and more to our own devices.

Most days Alex would paddle across to the motorised fishing boats when they came in in the mornings. He bargained hard for the fresh tuna that they brought, often getting a cheaper price than the locals. He relished the daily haggling, and the fishermen were amused by his daily visits. Fishing went on even round our boat, with shoals of tiny sprats leaping and pattering back into the water like showers of silver rain. We had more luck with our own attempts, and supplemented our diet of tuna with deep-fried sprats almost every day.

Jamie had friends on land, and one of them, Paulus, took us to his family's house on our first night. We had our first fresh-water wash for six weeks from the well in the middle of the family courtyard, and sat down to dinner at the family table. Mr Diaz was a reasonably well-to-do Chinese from Kupang on Timor, and he and his family were strict Catholics. He was a clock-maker and electrical repairer, and his shop was littered with broken machinery and old wiring. He gave us a lecture on sin over dessert, quite unintimidated by the presence of so many white people around his table. The incongruity was that whilst the rest of the family were Chinese, Paulus had dark skin and Portuguese/Melanesian features. Somewhere surely, Mr Diaz must have committed an indiscretion that belied his commentary on sin – or perhaps Paulus was the work of some nefarious brother? Riccardo and Largo produced their guitars by popular request and played until late. Many people crowded in off the streets to listen, and one of the sons made them repeat most of the songs again so that he could record them.

I spent a couple of days in the hills looking for Catholic missions and hand-woven and tie-dyed materials. I found both. Every village had its large church, and every household seemed to have its own hand-loom, where the wife made her pocket-money. On the beaches dyed strips of cotton dried in the sun, ribbed with streaks of white where they had been tied with palm strips to protect the material from the dye. There were some fabulous cloths and rich colours; very few chemical colours broke the natural hues that the women wore. They knew what I was after in those villages, the women, and I was assaulted from either side by cries demanding that I step in and look at their ikat and decide upon a price. I bought two on each visit.

Most of us also went on a gruelling trip to Mount Keli Mutu, in the centre of the island. Flores is built like a squeeze-box, all ridges and valleys as if some giant had bunched it up to show his strength, and consequently all roads are tortuous and broken by landslides and fallen trees. To make our journey worse, the driver of the van we had hired had been up all night drinking with the two Italians. We nearly went over a cliff on the way back, but after the rest of us threatened to get out and walk, he seemed to wake up. It took us about five hours to cover the eighty kilometres.

Keli Mutu's claim to fame is the view from the mountain tops and the colours of the crater-lakes. From the peak we could see from one end of the island to the other, and down below us, to the north, the island of Paloe was still billowing smoke into the heavy air. Each of the three lakes on the top of Keli Mutu were supposed to be different colours, one red, one white and one blue. But both the red and the white were near enough to a burgundy hue, thanks to a change in their mineral composition. However, the blue remained a true blue, and it seemed as if the sky was staring through a hole in the mountain-top. They say that the souls of sinners live in the darkest lake, the souls of the elderly in the less dark, and those of virgins and the pure in heart in the sky-blue water.

On the night of Good Friday we went in search of more bamboos to replace some of the battens in the sails. As we bounced up through the Catholic villages in the darkness the gardens and forests seemed full of flickering lights. The villagers had lit candles on the graves of their relatives and were sitting, talking quietly in the candlelight. The flickering lights in the trees gave the evening a kind of biblical peace.

Today we are making ready to leave Flores. Alex and I went to the market for the last time, he to do his haggling and I to do the carrying. I am amazed how the locals take to him. He rolls his eyes and speaks appalling Indonesian – he just tuts and repeats '*mahal, mahal*' – expensive, expensive – all the time, but they find him funny and usually take a bit off the price. They all call us Belanda, which technically means Dutch, but is now a term used for any foreigner with a white skin. On board we are well-stocked again, with coconuts rolling around the cabin-floor and green papaya hidden in the darkness to stop it ripening too quickly. The plastic bin for the rice is full to the brim, and bananas are hanging from the beams behind the engine. We have had to lay a lot of them out to dry on deck to make storage easier and longer.

Ignatius and the rest of the family from Magapanda came aboard for lunch. The old mother was quite terrified at first, afraid that we would sink there and then on the end of the anchor-rope. It was ages before she would say anything. I think that it was the first time the women had been aboard a ship. The family are poor hill-farmers, and their corn-crop failed badly this year, so we fed them until they could take no more, and made them carry the remainder away with them wrapped in leaves. The old lady warmed up so much that she sang us a selection of songs that she had learned at school under the Dutch. One was about a plane-crash in which two young Australians were killed, and she was so involved in it that she was in tears by the end. The tears doubled when I played back the recording that I had made of her voice. We offered her some arak to make her feel better, and she made the sign of the cross before sipping some 'for medicine'. Fortunately the anak was there and in the end the attractions of a fair-skinned and well-behaved baby conquered all sad memories. One of the daughters was incredibly beautiful, and we were all hypnotised by her grace. When they came to leave there were more tears.

Then the anchor came up covered in slime. Alex blew on the conch, and we turned out to sea with the echo of the sound ringing around the bay behind us, the shore lined with waving children.

We had had a couple of personnel changes. Frank, the American, had left us on the first day of our arrival in Flores, to try to make his way back up to Bali by land and plane. I was not sorry to see him go, and I don't think anyone else was either. He had not been much of a contributor to crew morale. We had a new crew-member in the form of Pas, one of Ignatius's sons, who we were taking around to the other side of the island to visit his relatives. The trip round to Larantuka was relatively peaceful, but Pas didn't seem to think so. He curled up at the foot of the mainmast below decks and didn't move for twenty-four hours, and when he finally emerged he was horror-struck to see that we didn't wear any clothes on board.

Opposite Larantuka we dropped anchor in the lee of the neighbouring island, Solor, and there we were welcomed by an Italian missionary who had been on the island for eight years.

Romano Gentili was an unconventional picture of a pastor. In his mid thirties and over 6 feet 2 inches tall, he rode the only motorcycle on the island, wore jeans, open-necked shirt and a peaked cap, and the islanders loved him. His outpost of progress comprised a mission school, a hospital and four churches, two of which he had built himself. He was not averse to a quiet drink, and had a monopoly on the sale of the local drink called Sopi, produced on his part of the island. Sopi and Tuak (fermented juice from the lontar palm) are both vital to the social life and the economy of the community, and the latter is especially important because in the higher parts of the island it can be hard to find water. So, whilst the villagers are up in the hills working on their gardens they rely on the lontar palm for their drinking supply. Even the children sometimes come down to the mission school still tipsy from their breakfast.

Romano's shed was stacked with bottles of Sopi, and as he ran his eye over them he admitted to being reminded of the wine-cellars of his native Italy. But these bottles hardly had the time to collect dust, for this was Solor's bottle-shop, and Romano by no means tried to suppress sales. The Padre had entered into the business side of his community with a flourish. He was the largest single employer in the area, with twenty-seven employees, and he paid out 400,000 rupiah a month in salaries. Apart from the staff of the hospital and school, most of these people were employed in the construction of housing for the parishioners, and the standard of houses in the village reflected Romano's priorities. Besides this he was a supplier of materials and expertise to other businesses, he was supervising the building of a boat, and also beginning to get involved in agricultural projects.

He hadn't learned these skills in his native Italy, nor were they taught at the seminary in Ohio, where he was ordained. He had learned what he could from reading and observing, and from the early mistakes that he made. The village had progressed in leaps and bounds after the day that the young Romano landed on the jetty of his first parish ever. He was six months late through illness and problems of communication, and his superior had tired of waiting and gone on well-earned leave. Standing on the jetty with his luggage, surrounded by fascinated villagers who thought that his beard and stature made him look like Jesus, with practically no knowledge of the language and no one to interpret, Romano admitted that he had aged several years in those first few days.

The Indonesian government is tolerant of all religions but doesn't give anything in the way of financial aid to church-backed projects. An organisation called the Divine Word Missionaries, based in Germany, provided Romano's keep. His family and village in northern Italy were proud of their son and sent what they could. For special projects such as the building of new churches he wrote an assessment of his needs and sent copies of that assessment to fund-raising organisations in Europe. He had always got what he required. Once a month he had his only contact with the other pastors in his diocese. They played cards, drank beer and prayed together. This was the only check kept on him to make sure that he hadn't turned heathen or died.

Romano said that his parishioners were meticulous about their worship. Every meeting of the village elders had to be started with prayer, and in church the trappings of the faith (vestments, altar-pieces, etc), were vitally important. His parishioners were increasing the strength of their faith, he claimed, though at the same time there were definite traces of animism ingrained in their everyday lives. Many still went to the local bomoh, or witch-doctor, before attending the mission hospital, despite the fact that the former was the more expensive.

Romano was modest about his own achievements. The government had, he said, vastly improved health on the islands over the years, though the principal problems of eye and skin infections lingered on. On the shore one morning I met an underwater fisherman who had a large open ulcer on his leg, and I asked him how long he had had it. "Not long." How long was not long?

"About two months." He asked me if I had any medicine to give him, and when I suggested that he go to the mission he shrugged his shoulders and muttered something about the expense.

Romano's main ambition was to be able to hand over his parish to a suitably capable local man as soon as the moment was right. It was a measure of his own self-sacrifice that whilst he had applied for Indonesian citizenship to be closer to the people that he loved, he was simultaneously working towards a situation where there would no longer be a place for him in the parish. In the not-so-distant future he hoped that his parishioners would be strong enough in their faith to dispense with their Western figurehead.

He told us stories of his time on the island that would be enough to spice his sermons for the rest of his life, stories of the idiosyncrasies of his people, of the dangers that he faced (he had been stung by scorpions and had his feet chewed by rats) and of the hopeless misunderstandings of government administration as it tried to rule the islands from afar. And yet, despite the amusement and frustration that alternated through his life on the island, it was obvious that whether he was lecturing from the pulpit on the evils of polygamy (common on the island) or telling his foreman how many parts sand to mix with how many cement, his people loved and respected him, and he them.

Thanks to Pastor Romano those hours spent on Solor were enthralling, and we were sorry to leave the following day. He presented us with two flagons of sopi to remember him by. The Italians had been delighted to find someone else to share their language, and they were particularly sad to leave, but in the end we were all beginning secretly to long for the completion of the journey, and wanted to get on.

I wanted to take some pictures, so Romano took me up the coastline on the back of his motor-cycle whilst the *Chun Bhatera* sailed up the straits. Then the dug-out came ashore and I went back on board. As the pastor turned his bike and bumped away down the tree-lined avenue that the Portuguese had left behind them he made an incongruous but absolutely integral picture. With a string of beads around his neck and a black coral bracelet around his wrist he was an unconventional pastor in an unconventional situation, but he belonged. I had found a Kurtz but he wasn't Conrad's Kurtz.

That night we stopped at Lamakera, a whaling village on the

other end of Solor. The whaling season had not yet begun and the boats were under rush-matting shelters on the beach. The villagers had an unusually perilous way of hunting: the spear-thrower stood on the bows until the whale was close enough, then jumped on the animal's back before stabbing it with his spear. The boats were often dragged huge distances before the whales died – and sometimes the spear-throwers themselves died too.

The beach was littered with massive jawbones, but there was not a lot more to see at Lamakera. An old haji gave me some raw eggs to drink, someone else gave us some papaya, and we returned to the *Chun Bhatera*.

Over the weeks a rift had developed between the English- and Italian-speakers on the boat. It was unfortunate, and we tried to resist it, but everyone had to pull their weight on board, and not everyone did. Jamie had threatened to throw Largo off the boat in Maumere on the grounds that he did no work, but Lorraine had dissuaded him, supported by the rest of us. True, we all thought that Largo was lazy, but he was also a scapegoat for all of our frustrations and some of the criticism was undeserved. The heavy discussion that had followed Jamie's threat seemed to clear the air somewhat, and either we felt ashamed of our own meanness or Largo did in fact improve; certainly for a while there were fewer disputes. Morale was further improved when we left Maumere by a breeze that filled the sails by day and night, and the bow-line curled up from the ruffled seas as we moved swiftly past the smaller islands on our route. Padre Romano had also helped morale by focusing attention on things outside the domain of the boat and the sea. But the peace did not last.

The fresh winds that took us round Lomblen and the neighbouring island of Pantar were exhilarating but tiring, and when we finally dropped anchor in the straits of Alor that led up to the town of Kalabahi, we were all fairly low. Scenically it was a lovely anchorage, but the current swung us round the little bay at will. We had to reposition the dragging anchor constantly. In the mornings scores of sailing-sampans passed us, their masts little more than a pair of sticks with a patchwork of pieces of cloth stretched between them as a sail. The people landed in our bay, ascended to the hills to their gardens, and then returned again in the evenings to re-cross the strait to their houses.

Someone brought a huntsman on board. His skin was pock-marked, and hung loosely from the bones of his face. The home-made poisons that were instantly deadly to the animals his arrows pierced had affected his own skin. After a demonstration of his skill ashore, Alex and Jamie bought bows-and-arrows and spears, and the huntsman departed well pleased with his visit. There was something rather unsettling about that man with his repertoire of poisons and quivers of carefully crafted deadly arrows, and it was evident that the other islanders left him well alone. I was quite glad to see him go, as if the air had got cleaner suddenly – but evidently it hadn't: over the next day most of us were affected by tropical ulcers, and my left foot swelled up to an impossible size and made it very difficult to walk.

We've all come down with infections. I suppose it's obvious why. It's almost impossible to move around on deck without gathering a catalogue of small cuts and bruises. Rough pieces of wood, bamboo sharp enough to tear skin, metals and tools and cutting edges – they are all waiting for the movement of the boat to throw us on them. It doesn't seem to have mattered up till now, though Jamie did warn us to be careful of all cuts. There are flies here, and they must in part be responsible for carrying infection. Also the sea-water stops cuts from healing. We have run out of fresh vegetables and high protein foods, which can't help.

I'm boat-bound. Cannot get my foot wet. It's impossible to go ashore in the dug-out without getting wet to some extent. Other people are here too, but we are hardly talking. Every morning and every evening we gather around the medical kit and replace bandages and creams. The baby also seems unhappy, screaming a lot for no apparent reason. Lorraine says he won't drink, and I think she is a bit worried, though she gives little sign of it.

The Italians have got off lightly. I don't know why. They've spent most of the day onshore with Alex. His foot is still bandaged, but he said when he left this morning that he wasn't staying on board a moment longer.

There is some disagreement as to how often and how long we should stop from now on. Some of us want to stop often, some want to go straight as possible to Darwin.

In the end we agreed to go up to Kalabahi to buy more vegetables and re-stock on fresh water, but we also agreed that we would stop only once more, on the island of Kisar, before Australia.

The market at Kalabahi was poor, the hillsides around obviously producing little. Women squatted on their heels behind small piles of chillies and talked about the harvest. We made up the lack of green vegetables by buying a dug-out load of pumpkins. Pumpkin curry became our staple diet, and we got thoroughly sick of it.

Jamie bought a Moko drum in town. It was scratched, but nevertheless the price was high. The drums, which are Vietnamese in origin and date from the second-century Dong-Son era, are found in large numbers on Alor. Locals regularly find them buried in the ground, and they are handed down from generation to generation within the families as part of bridal dowries. We were taken to view the drum in a decaying rush-house next to the tide-line. The family selling it had had a bad harvest and needed the money badly, said a spokesman. They would have preferred more than the 55,000 rupiah that Jamie gave them, but they could not afford to wait for the arrival of another foreigner on the off-chance that he would be prepared to offer more; foreigners came only rarely to Alor.

When we left Kalabahi that night we glided out with the tide on the top of a mat of jellyfish, so thick that there hardly seemed room for the water they floated in. The moon was bright and the mat of jelly reflected its light, gleaming sickly-white. There was little wind to move us on the water, and it seemed as if the jelly itself was carrying us out to the open seas.

It was then that the difficulties with the weather began. Previously we had been blessed with steady winds on the beam or even aft, but after Kalabahi the wind veered round to take us on the bows with renewed strength. We had to tack into an increasing swell and a considerable current. We began to doubt the capabilities of the boat, as we never seemed to get closer than about 70 degrees to the wind. This put an added strain on the relationships between crew-members.

> I've been staring at the same bloody piece of Alor for two days now. We tack out away from it for a day, turn and come back, and there it bloody still is. Waited and waited for the land-breeze

tonight, but it didn't come. In the end the wind dropped and we just banged on the swell until the end of my watch. Doesn't sound as if things have changed much since then, either. Very glad that I did not have to share my watch with Largo tonight. He's getting really irritating – accuses me of not knowing what I am doing. Why don't we push the sails out wide and steer the course we want, he says, and he just will not believe me when I say that it is not possible. It got so bad that I had to ask Jamie to take him on his watch – he wouldn't take it from me that he was wrong. We almost came to blows on the deck last night. I know that I am stirring a potentially explosive situation making him watch with Jamie, but I can do nothing with him.

Also having a hard time staying awake for the whole four hours. It never used to be a problem. The night sky really gets me down, staring down at me. I don't know why it is called a canopy – no canopies have such depth and such indifference. Without the moon – it rises right at the end of my watch at the moment – the stars seem to bore into my head and yawn it open. They even gleam back at me from the moving water. There's no escaping them, they are malicious, they seem to concentrate evil energies on me as I hang on to the tiller. It is as if I shouldn't be there, they conspire with the sea and the dome of the sky to make me feel inadequate. The sails don't hide me from them – only the moon, when it comes, seems to banish some of them.

My foot is not better, despite the antibiotics.

There were times when the darkness was illuminated by flashes of lightning, a common feature of the night-sky over tropical seas. Sometimes the lightning seemed to show something lying on the water – was it a reef or a boat or a wave or what? I would stare, and stare, and stare until my eyes hurt; consult the pilot, the compass, the shape of the island on the horizon, the ship's log, and then another flash from the sky would show me that I had just been imagining again. Every three or four hours we would go about, which meant rousing everyone. Once awake it was hard to go back to sleep, and forms shrouded in blankets and wrapped in their own thoughts would sit on the lines of the boat, staring out unseeing across the black sea. At this time Jamie decided to use the motor to try to help the boat get closer to the wind; I hated it. The machine belched evil smoke into the cabin, and the smoke and the noise made it difficult to rest below decks. When we pumped the bilges the water, which previously had been quite clean, coated the deck with a film of rainbow slime. The boat juddered along, the noise of the motor scarring our nerves. Eventually we left Alor behind.

Then a dipstick reading into the drum revealed that we did not have much fuel left, and we decided to save the rest until we really needed it. The gas for the cooker had also run out, and we cooked twice a day in the fire-box on deck, using wood that we had gathered on Alor. Our diet was down to dried fish, rice, pumpkin and dried bananas; we had cream-crackers and raisins for lunch. The cooks had stopped trying to make anything taste interesting.

The baby kept on crying, the tiller banged from side to side in the swell and the sails hammered against the masts. We stared at the sea, the sky, the sails and the land, expecting something to change, but it didn't. There was nothing to do except keep on plugging away, the emptiness of the days leaving our minds wide open to the sway of our emotions. Out there in the middle of the wide ocean I found myself thinking of London's red buses, the face of an old friend, the garden at home – all part of another and unreal world that had absolutely no relation to the present. It was as if time before the voyage had not existed, and time after it would not exist. My life before the start of the journey had become infinitely remote, a fast-fading memory of light-hearted youth. I knew that I should have been relishing every moment of what was presumably to be one of the finest experiences of my life, but what was there to relish? One night I slept with Alma. Alex told me later that he had slept with her the following night. It meant nothing. Our characters were being stripped bare.

After days of labouring in heavy seas and constantly re-adjusting the sails in pursuit of a better grip on the wind, we managed to slip through the gap betwen Wetar and Alor, with the coast of Timor on the horizon ahead of us. With the shelter of islands on either side the swell was lessened, and we made better progress without the heavy waves to block every inch of forward progress. We even had a pleasant surprise.

> Rain at last! It was quite plain to see on the water, only about a mile from us; a little patch of rain. We headed for it, for where

> there is a rain-shower there is usually a good breeze, a breeze that might be more favourable than the prevailing wind. I think the rain came to meet us rather than us it: one moment it seemed to jump on us. You could hear the water trickling sternwards in the bilges as the sails caught hold of a better wind on the edge of the shower. At the same time the sea flattened, and we suddenly seemed to be flying along.
>
> The rain itself was delicious. For a moment we stood like statues in a park drinking it in. Then we all went mad, dancing around the deck crying 'soap', 'a wash', 'where's the shampoo?', 'it's raining, it's pouring, it's raining . . .'. The heavy sails stood out like concrete in the wind, pouring streams of fresh water down on to the deck. It actually hurt like hell after a while; perhaps it was the salt coming out of my hair into my eyes, but for a while half of me was laughing and the other half screaming.
>
> Although the rain has now stopped the wind has kept fresh. Looks as if we shall make a lot of way suddenly, and might even be in Kisar by tomorrow. Everyone the best of friends.

The guitars came out on deck that night, and we all sang for the first time in weeks. There were several compliments to the cook on a particularly ordinary meal, and we drank the last of Pastor Romano's sopi, remembering him as we did so.

The fair wind continued through the night, and dawn brought with it the shape of Kisar lying a few kilometres to the east, but conditions had changed. Instead of the typical unclouded day the sky was heavy and low, and the wind that had pushed us all night suddenly dropped and left us drifting with three or four kilometres still to cover. It had deposited us in the lion's den, for it was then that the squalls started.

It was a disturbing experience, watching small but violent squalls circling us like prizefighters sizing up their victims. We could see their progress by the steel shafts of rain and dark patches of water that marked their presence. These were what the Bugis sailors called 'sumatras', presumably because they are most common around the island of that name. Singly they are not too difficult to master, but our problem was that there seemed to be two or three moving around the same stretch of water. Our mistake (in fact it was Jamie's mistake, but the rest of us would have made a worse mess of it) was to have the sails close-hauled. The wind seemed at first to be about to come from the port side, and we raced to adjust the sails with that in mind, but then all trace of it died, and we waited with the mainsail amidships, standing by the stays and the sheet-ropes for the next alarm. The wind hit us from starboard, with none of the usual tell-tale racing scratchings on the water's surface to warn us of its approach. I really thought that the end had come as it hammered at 90 degrees into the sails and laid us almost flat. It was not so much a sudden blow as a steady one, confident in its power to scatter us into the sea, and with a sickening, inevitable movement the *Chun Bhatera* laid her cheek on the water. Nobody said anything – and nobody would have heard a word that was said. Possibly if we had not all been hanging on to the ropes and stays ready to alter them, some of us might have gone over. Everything loose on deck slid rapidly into the sea; fortunately that wasn't much. Down below the bottles and jars had been tied, but not tied to meet the possibility of a capsize. Lorraine screamed once – she was below nursing the baby – and her scream was followed by the sound of breaking glass. Water slid up the deck from the port side and started to pour down the hatchway into the cabin. I could feel the stay that I was hanging on to vibrating with the tension of holding the mast on to the boat. We watched what we believed was the disintegration of our lives around us, frozen into our places waiting for the next thing to happen, the next thing to break.

It seemed to last an age, that awful sickly lunge of the boat for the bottom of the sea. I visualised myself clinging to the upturned hull. But nothing more gave way, and – barely perceptibly – the boat straightened up a little as some of the power in her sails was channelled forwards and not sideways, and she gathered way. In the same moment Jamie came to life, yelled to someone to let the stern-sheets run free and himself dealt with the foresail sheets. The boat bobbed upright. Suddenly I was trembling, and beside me I heard Riccardo's teeth grind together. We all came back to life again, as if someone had clicked their fingers and un-frozen us. We tightened the agung stays and checked that none of the splicing had been torn apart, and then we evaluated the damage. There was little. The cabin floor was a mess of glass and coconut oil and rice, but that was easily cleared up. Lorraine had screamed because water had come through the side wall of the cabin where it protruded above deck-level; the torrent had given her a shock, that was all, and she was unharmed. As for the baby – he didn't even cry.

Our only casualty was Max the turtle. His green bucket had skidded across the deck and toppled him and his friend the limpet into the sea. We were sorry to lose them both, especially as Max had seemed to enjoy his diet of flies and had grown rapidly, but altogether they were the best casualties there could have been: there were no living things on board that boat more suited to being ditched into the sea than Max and friend.

A couple of hours later we tacked into the bay at Kisar, and dropped anchor with a collective sigh of relief.

Why people ever settled on that island I couldn't guess. It was a barren rock that even grass had a hard time growing on. Fossils in the rock everywhere indicated that it must have only just emerged out of the sea. We all had a bath in a deep pool of fresh water up on the rocky ledge above our anchorage. There was a stream, but it was some way along the beach. There was no sign of houses from the shoreline, and to all intents and purposes the island looked and felt deserted from the sea. The village was in the middle, in a gully in the volcanic rock where soil had gathered and the villagers could grow vegetables. We intended to stay here for about three days for a good rest before the last and most difficult leg of our journey.

Going ashore on the afternoon we arrived we had a mini-shipwreck. We had all become very proficient in the dug-out – which took some skill to control – but on that occasion there were too many of us on board for comfort; the waves turned us side on to the beach as we were landing and toppled us into the waist-deep water. It was a faint imitation of what could have happened earlier that day. As I staggered ashore, dripping and laughing, I thought how fortunate it was that I had emptied my bag beforehand, and thus saved my cameras. But that narrow escape did mean that I hardly used them again on the journey – I was afraid of the damage the salt water might do to them and the films they carried. I missed a lot of pictures, but I kept my cameras.

On the first afternoon I took our sailing papers to the Kepala Desa – the headman – in the village. He was kind and welcoming. I was to treat him and his family as my family, he said, horrified when I admitted that I had not seen my parents for over a year and a half. I promised to drop in whenever I was passing. In the Chinese tokos (general shops) in the village square we bought enough vegetables to make our evening meal more pleasant. On the way back Alex refilled a couple of our water containers from the well, but managed to drop the bucket, rope and all, into the darkness below. I was busy sealing the containers some yards off, and only turned when my attention was drawn by strange scuffling and grunting noises coming from the well. As I neared the lip Alex's head and arms emerged slowly into the daylight, and the rest of him followed, cursing and fuming as he fell over the lip clutching the bucket. I rolled around in the track roaring with laughter, and fortunately he too saw the funny side of the episode. But after that I made no more excursions.

I have been unable to take up the Kepala Desa's invitation; a strange fever flattened me completely our first evening here. I am beginning to feel better now, thank God, but at times my temperature was up to 104. I just lie down here in the gloom of the cabin, listening to footsteps and voices on deck above my head. In the evenings one of the lads from the lambo (a type of Indonesian prahu) next door brings out his kecapi (local guitar) and plays and sings along with the rest of the crew. They are waiting for the weather to improve before taking a load of copra over to Dili. My legs feel stiff, and I have cramp. Perhaps I haven't been getting enough salt. Anyway, I'm glad it has happened here whilst we are anchored, and not out at sea.

Real excitement last night. I was lying on my bunk, groaning a bit, and staring at the hull where it was lit by the single hurricane lamp we keep in the cabin. As I was staring something slipped out of the shadows and glided down the curve of the hull. I watched it, petrified, until it had disappeared under my bunk, then raised the alarm. 'Snake – sea snake'. I had no idea if it really was a poisonous sea-snake, but I raced up on deck to make sure that I was well out of its reach nevertheless. Alex and Jamie hunted it with parangs, and pursued it into the pile of coconut logs that lay between the masts, but it was too dark and the logs were too heavy to move around with safety. Mindful of the Malay proverb "Don't stick your head into the crocodile's mouth to see if it has any teeth" we slept on deck.

The snake appeared again today, and Alex was at hand quickly enough to be able to chop it into small pieces at the foot of the cabin stairs, where it had come to find the sun. We are all mighty glad to see the back of it, as the idea of a poisonous snake loose in a small cabin is frightening. There are so many places that it can hide. No one has any idea how it came aboard: it could have come in one of the sacks of firewood that we have collected, or it may even have climbed up the anchor rope. I hope that there aren't any others lurking in the bilges.

We've exhausted all our money and bought enough food for the final part of the journey. In the morning we are to begin that last stretch. Beyond the point outside our bay it looks as if the sea is running high, so we will have to be careful and strong.

Then began the hardest time. At first we made good progress eastwards until we were close to the island of Leti by nightfall. We should ideally have gone south of Leti, to keep below the chain of islands in readiness for turning due south to Australia once the wind and our position allowed it. But we were moving reasonably with the tack that we had, so we just fell off from the wind slightly and slipped past the island to the north, telling ourselves that we would be able to pass through a gap in the chain at a later stage.

It was a testing night. A bowl between the twin peaks on Leti incubated squalls and threw them down on small passing boats. The sea whipped the sides of the *Chun Bhatera* and the rigging and sails creaked and groaned as we heeled into yet another breaking hill of water. But then everything would drop, the sails sag in heavy folds, the waves flatten into a deceptive calm, and our hopes for a quiet night be restored. On the shore of the island we could see the lights of a village, and their presence was comforting. But then the lights would disappear, and we would know that the mountain-tops had brewed us yet another test, and we strained our eyes for the shreds of cotton on the stays that would tell us which quarter to expect the next onslaught from. For the first time in many weeks I felt seasick again, but it was a time for aggression and not self-pity. As I pulled stays tight and lunged sheet-ropes around the reeling sails I found myself thinking again of those incongruous London buses. We had no sleep that night.

When daylight dawned it showed us that we were beyond Leti

and alongside the island of Moa, a long, flat and boring land mass that effectively blocked our passage south. The wind was strong and constant, but the swell had grown heavier and our progress was slow. We had to lay off from the wind enough to maintain sufficient speed to beat the waves: to get too close to the wind meant stopping dead every time we met a large wave head on, but falling off also meant that we made little progress in the direction that we wanted. That direction was right into the teeth of the wind. In the end the islands opened up to reveal a gap that we thought we could get through.

> I don't know what it is, but we just don't seem to be able to get close to this bloody channel. All afternoon we've been tacking around out here. On the northbound tack we go well, but lose that progress on the return run. The compass heading and the point of the bows is reasonable, but the wake belies all that: we are moving sideways across the sea. Jamie says the sails are all wrong, and we don't have enough ballast below. He says that we mustn't pump the bilges. But he's in a foul mood and has refused to do anything with the sails – says we must do it ourselves. He had another row with Largo this morning. We are just tacking backwards and forwards on an uninteresting patch of sea, and whenever we look to be coming close to the correct position to be able to take the channel, we are caught by a current that sweeps us sideways. I'm fed up. We have decided between us – Jamie has retreated to his cabin and left us to it – that we shall have to tack back and forth through the night and wait for daylight again before trying the channel once more. It's depressing to use time and energy on just staying in one place.

But it was not to be as simple as that. It was my watch first, as usual. The sea had suddenly got calmer and the wind lightened, but the crooked wake behind us showed that we were still crabbing across the sea. I stared at the sails, at the sea and at the cotton on the stays, but however much I adjusted them, the wake remained crooked. Exasperated, I left it all alone, and we just moved steadily sideways into the night. It was a night like no others I had seen.

> It is darker than it should be; quieter too. My watch is half-done, and I cannot wait for someone else to take responsibility. I know

> that something is wrong, something about to happen, the air smells different. Can't really describe it any more than that.

There were two others on deck – Alma and Riccardo – but I think that I was the first to see it. It was the stars, those hateful stars, that warned me. I always noted the position of the Southern Cross every night, as it proved a useful indication of our course without having to consult the compass, but this time it had disappeared. I had seen it half-an-hour before, but no longer. Even the stars above the masthead were being swallowed. Gradually my eyes could make out a line advancing across the sky, and once I knew where to look I could see the corresponding line across the sea ahead of us.

> There is a barrier across the sea, like a brick wall. It doesn't seem to be moving, but it seems to draw the sky and the sea into it. I can only see a few metres in any direction. We are motionless on a piece of sea like a dinnerplate. No land for bearings, no more stars for direction, a compass that tells nothing of where we are going, only where we are pointing. Not sure whether my shivering is nerves or cold. I have woken the others and we are all on deck, staring at this curtain stretched across the sea, wondering what stage of life we will have to play out on the other side of it. I wish that we could turn and run, but we are powerless. The sails are now hanging slack and lifeless, the 'sprit is pointing at that wall and nothing I can do with the tiller can turn it away. We all move about the more obvious tasks on deck. Both sails are reefed down two panels, the sheet ropes slack and in hand. Someone has dug out the oilskins, and we wait.

One moment we were on the outside of that wall, and then we were engulfed. There was no noise inside, just an intensifying of the darkness. Joseph Conrad describes just such a moment: "The immobility of things was perfect. If the air had turned black, the sea, for all I knew, might have turned solid." We could have been anywhere at any time; neither the future nor the past mattered, we were stuck in a timeless present.

We were not stuck for long. A hushed rushing sound came at us out of the darkness, and in moments the deck was drumming with rain. It sheeted into my eyes like sharp needles, and my hand was soon frozen to the tiller, but still the wind did not come. We sat on the deck, barely visible to each other, shrouded in oilskins like mourners at our own funeral, whilst the scuppers sobbed and gurgled with rain-water.

The sea grew steadily rougher, then the rain dropped and the wind started. It came from the same direction as it had always come, and it was manageable. With only three panels of both sails pulling, we could lie off from the wind enough to save the bowsprit and the bows from a hammering. The most disturbing thing was the compass reading – we were heading due north, in the opposite direction to the course that we wanted, and we were heading out into the open sea at some speed. There was no chance of tacking. The bowsprit was reeling wildly, stabbing at the waves, and it would have been highly dangerous to attempt to handle the jib in the darkness on the point. We plugged on, relieving each other on the tiller at intervals and staring up at the straining grey ghosts of the sails.

It was worse in the cabin than on deck. At least above there was some warning of the next wave, the next shock, and we could brace ourselves and concentrate on gluing ourselves to the retching deck beneath us. But the noise of the steep seas crashing into the bows filled the cabin below. I wedged myself between the coconut logs and the mainmast and tried to hold steady, listening to the cracks and groans of the timbers that protected me from the sea. Spray hammered into the deck above my head, and the water seeped through planks that had been cracked and dried by the long weeks of sun, dripping steadily on my face wherever I turned. The worst moments were those when the bowsprit took the water. The boat would stop suddenly as if its nose had been caught in a vice and there would follow a long, slow, juddering movement back upwards, accompanied by rending sounds from the bows as the 'sprit tore itself free. How long could it last, we asked ourselves, and what would happen if it actually got torn out of its mount? There was no chance of rest below, and it was harder lying down there and listening to the heart of the boat struggling than it was to sit on deck and be constantly drenched by the spray.

In the middle of the night we released the jib sheet and let the sail fly loose. It had been pulling the bows off-course, but as it was too dangerous to attempt to move out along the 'sprit to bundle it, we had to leave it. The triangular sail cracked and danced through the night like a demon, haunting us on the 'sprit. We were hypnotised by its grey shape flickering in the darkness up ahead. At one stage in the nightmare something gave way with a crack like a pistol-shot; we lurched around the deck, checking everything and found nothing. Only the daylight revealed that the top panel of the topan had gone, blown completely to shreds. The slotter – the rope that held the agung tight to the mast – also broke, but the sudden hammering of the sail battens against the wood of the mast warned of the danger, and a new rope was re-threaded before any real damage was done.

Daylight found us sitting huddled on deck tranced in our own private worlds. Visibility was not much better even in the daytime, but we could make out the shapes of the Damar islands ahead of us. According to the map we had come about eighty kilometres in completely the wrong direction during the night. We had to tack.

How we managed it I don't know, but we did. It took two attempts – the speed of the boat was not enough to bring her bows round through the wind and the waves the first time – but in the end the topan (or what remained of it) gripped the wind, and we came round agonisingly slowly. I nearly went overboard for the first and only time. The foredeck reared just as I was reaching out over the lashed dinghy to secure the starboard fore-stay, and I was thrown towards the sea. The anchor lying on the deck on the starboard side checked my headlong fall, and a spar cut me heavily just below the elbow. I found myself sitting on the deck, trembling. But we had got around, and safely.

We retraced our night-time course through the greys and whites of a storm-wracked day, taking it in turns to try to control the tiller, which thrashed wildly like a demented animal over the deck. We hadn't seen anything of Largo for some hours; he had curled up just below the forepeak the previous evening, and hadn't moved since.

In the evening the shape of Moa appeared once again on the horizon, and before night fell we were once more opposite the channel that had caused so many problems the previous day. The wind had relented a bit, but the sails were reefed and we did not have the speed, power or daylight to try to make it through the channel again. Defeated, we had a brief conference on the stern, grouped around the tiller, faces dented by the wind and skin drawn a thin white.

> We have decided to turn back for Leti [I recorded in my diary]. No one wanted to admit defeat, but we just cannot get through this cursed string of islands. We are shells of people, and the words sounded strange coming from our mouths. We haven't been doing much talking recently. Now that we have turned things seem a lot better, and we are fleeing with the wind at our tail, skimming the waves – suddenly they seem a lot smaller. Jamie managed to get out on the 'sprit in the smoother movement and rescue the demented jib. It's now bundled on the end platform. He says the sail itself is not too badly damaged, but the foundations of the 'sprit itself are splitting.
>
> We have just tried to eat our first meal for twenty-four hours. No one was very enthusiastic, but it seemed sensible to eat something if just to keep our energy-levels up. Also the deck was steady enough to be able to light a fire. Nevertheless most of us slipped the bulk of the food over the side. Largo has reappeared but no one has a word for him. Weakness is the worst thing that we want at this moment, we have to be able to depend on each others' strength, without that there would be no hope at all.

No one was pleased to see the familiar shape of Leti again, but the speed which we made with the wind behind us was reassuring, and the more comfortable ride had restored some of our confidence and allowed us to relax. Amazingly during the night the wind veered and came from the land, allowing us to follow the coast around and at last head southwards. Finally it looked as if we would get on to the course that we wanted and needed so badly. Every half-hour or so one or other of us would shout at the tiller to ask for a course-reading to check that we were really heading for home. It allowed us to hope.

During my watch that night I heard strange sounds on the foredeck, as if a lame bird had landed and was desperately trying to take off again. It was a flying-fish which had darted out of a wave-top straight into our sails, to flap down on to the deck below. Another soon followed it, and Alex and I put them on to the embers of the fire and ate them. The fresh meat tasted excellent, and seemed a sign that things were at last getting better.

But it was not to be so. As I lay on the floor of the cabin that night, trying to get some sleep after my watch, I could feel the motion of the boat starting to become more erratic again in heavier seas. A couple of hours before sunrise we were aroused, the boat shaking and shuddering once more. We had lost our course, and the coast of a small island off Timor was looming close and seemed to be pulling us in towards it. In the darkness it looked alarmingly close. We tacked; without the jib it was easier to go about, but the course on the new tack did not look good. Those of us not on watch returned to try to rest, but the motion of the boat was too violent for sleep and the sledge-hammering of the bows started afresh. At dawn we tacked again, vainly hoping that the other tack would be better.

By mid-morning the waves had grown to a momentous size, and they were driving us once again towards the coast of Timor. There was not enough wind to keep our speed up and our head into the waves, and the foredeck was washed and washed again by the surf. Whenever a particularly heavy wall of water hit the bows and the 'sprit quivered we would all turn to look accusingly at the helmsman. We sat in our own private thoughts, islands in the storm. Largo came up on deck again and sat in silence next to the tiller. Jamie turned on him.

"Scrub the deck."

"No."

"I said scrub the deck."

"And I said no."

The words themselves meant nothing – they were only an expression of hate. Alex and I quickly volunteered to scrub the deck ourselves to try to ease the tension. The absurdity of the idea did not even seem funny, and it was more than we could manage just to hold on. We had come out from Bali expecting and relishing the moment that we would be tested, and I was beginning to doubt that we could handle it any more. We were not strong enough. Conrad describes the root of this depression. "It was rather like a forced-on numbness of spirit. The long, long stress of a gale does it; the suspense of the interminably exhausting catastrophe; there is bodily fatigue in the mere holding on to existence within the excessive tumult; a searching and insidious fatigue that penetrates deep into a man's breast." No one liked one another any more; the whole world seemed pointless, and we only clung on to our lives from force of habit. There seemed to be no other reason.

In the middle of the day Jamie went to examine the base of the bowsprit. He came back without comment. Shortly afterwards a particularly heavy wave caught us nose on, and there was a loud rending sound. Jamie raced back to the bows.

"Go about," he yelled to the tiller. "Go about quickly – get the wind behind us, I don't give a fuck about the course." Within minutes we were flying with the motion of the waves towards the Timor coast, the sails spread wide.

The bowsprit had at last torn free from its moorings, and was only held in place by its stays. The stays were wire, and well-tightened, and as long as the bowsprit did not have to cope with the added weight of water or a pulling sail it would probably remain on board. We lashed it as best we could. We all knew what would happen if it went over: the stays would hold it against the wood of the hull, and with the strength of those waves behind it it would smash the bow-planking to splinters, and the *Chun Bhatera* would go down. Axes were brought on deck to chop the stays if need be, and we set course back for Kisar.

The return was a nightmarish journey, but somehow it was not as bad as it had been before. We had gone beyond the pale, and there were no more disasters possible. Strangely enough we started talking to each other again, as if the fact of our turning back had released some of the pressure. There was nothing more to be done that had not been done. The wind was in the right quarter to allow us to reach Kisar without tacking, and we pulled down the shattered topan to keep as much weight off the bows as possible. The bowsprit did not touch the water again – the speed of the boat kept us climbing the waves – but the waves themselves seemed if anything to grow in size. The motion of the boat was quite different, and if anything more alarming than before, but after we had all had our eyes glued to the bowsprit for long enough to establish that it was clear of immediate danger that motion seemed not to matter. In the mid-afternoon Alex and I were sitting by the tiller talking to Jamie, when Alex suddenly stopped in mid-sentence and stared over Jamie's head. We both froze. The boat was in a trough, and the crest of the wave stood five or six feet above our heads. I had read about such things in books, and I knew what usually happened next. Jamie turned and yelled to everyone to brace themselves and keep down – but the wave suddenly seemed to dissolve, as if it had achieved its purpose in making us face our own fates, and it slipped beneath the hull quite innocently. After that everything just became funny. Alex and I sat in the bows and pointed at the larger troughs that yawned beneath us and giggled.

We reached Kisar in the middle of the night, but the sky was clear and the moon full. The shelter of the little bay that we knew so well made all our fears and experiences seem unreal. Only the tatters of the sails proved to us that we had not been living in a dream. The agung came down, the anchor-chain rattled, and suddenly everything was quiet. A couple of other prahus bobbed gently at anchor in the moonlit bay; their crews slept on, unaware that we had returned.

We stayed a week on Kisar. It took that long to make the boat sea-worthy again. The agung was patched, the topan replaced (the wind had blown it into a cobweb). But most important of all we removed the bowsprit entirely, using the foremast and a series of ropes and pulleys to bring it on deck. There we chopped it in half, tailored the better half of it and reset it in a new mount at the foot of the mast. It looked absurd, that cocky little stub of wood jutting upwards from the foot of the mast from where there once had been a magnificent spear of wood, but at least it was safe, and a quick trial showed us that there was still room to manipulate the jib if ever we wanted to use it again.

There were few diversions in that week. Those not involved in the heavier jobs spent hours re-splicing the stays and scraping the hull. We worked, rested and argued – but we argued less than we had. We all knew that if we had to face that kind of weather again we had to be able to rely on each other more. We had finished all our money on the last visit to Kisar, assuming that we would not land in Indonesia again, so we bartered with what we felt we could spare: some tools, a length of anchor chain, cassettes, and even a small radio. In return we got more rice and dried fish, and three chickens which we kept on the foredeck. It was a limbo period of gradual healing of old confidence, and as we tended the boat we were at the same time re-building our own physical and moral strength. By the time that the boat was declared ready again, we too had been restored to something of our former selves.

The local sailors agreed that it was a good time to set sail. The moon had waned three or four days past the full, they said, and it was a good time for long sea-journeys. One of the prahus riding alongside us left in the afternoon for Leti: we decided to leave that evening. In the austere light of a beautiful May moon we once again hoisted sail and rounded the point into the open sea.

Again we reached Leti easily, but this time we managed to sail south of the island. The sea was not calm, but nor was it violent. Wind was in the right quarter to allow us to follow the south side of the chain of islands without risking being forced on to the rocks. For five days we followed those islands until we were well past Palau Babar and heading for Tanimbar, almost due north of Darwin. Then we turned and headed south into the open and unknown sea.

The crossing of the Arafura Sea was long and tedious, always into the wind and always quite rough. More flying fish flapped into the sails, but there was no other sign of marine life – nor were there any other boats on that deserted sea. It was a lonely and depressing time, but it was not as taxing as it had been, and at last we began to allow ourselves to think of what lay ahead; without the present to master the future became a possibility.

> We amuse ourselves by talking of the food we are going to eat on arrival, and laying bets on how many days it'll take. Lorraine has been talking of the food they serve in a vegetarian restaurant she used to run in Darwin, but while the rest of them seem to want to eat healthy food – quiches and things – all I can think of is a Mars bar and a bucket of chips. Yesterday Riccardo caught a large fish, but lost it just as he was hauling it in. It would have been welcome, as we are now on just pumpkin and rice again. We are keeping the frightened chickens for a special occasion, but by the time we get anywhere near Darwin they will probably have lost any of the flesh they might now have on their scrawny bodies. They are funny: they are tied by their legs, and they run around each other so much that this morning we found them in one tight-packed bundle of twine and feathers. The cock is getting

used to the boat faster than the hens, and yesterday evening he strutted out of the cover of the upturned dinghy as far as his string would allow him and stood on the edge of the forward hatch to crow at the sunset. Gave us quite a shock below decks. It's amazing what a source of amusement they are to us, those three stupid chickens.

Nobody showed their fears, but the most worrying thing about that period was our navigation. This hadn't been a problem before, as we had stuck close to land that we could recognise from our charts. But out on the open sea things were different. We had no sextant, only a compass and a chart, but neither were much good without land to take bearings. We navigated by 'dead reckoning', which involved fixing our last position in relation to the islands behind us and recording carefully in a log our estimated speed since that time, our compass bearing at that speed, and the length of time on the tack. Daily we would use these jottings to try to establish an approximate position on the map. The inaccuracies and unknowns (currents and side-slip) could have been huge, especially as we were tacking frequently, but the system was all that we had.

Or not quite all. What saved us in the end was our transistor radio. As we neared the Australian coast we picked up the Darwin radio station. The varying strength of the radio signal as we rotated the set told us where the beacon lay, and we headed for that spot. Excitement grew as the voice of the announcer grew stronger.

This morning the radio is much louder. We listen to it constantly and can repeat all the jingles and ads. Even the baby seems to listen to this strange voice that has invaded the boat. We all know exactly what is on in Darwin this weekend. Ads for soap powder, discos and restaurants can hardly have been listened to in a stranger environment and with such eagerness. Never has a radio DJ's inanities been so enjoyed. Alex shins up the mast at regular intervals: apparently the coast of the Northern Territory is flat, and can only be seen from three or four miles out. The sea seems to have changed during the last two days: it is no longer azure and clear, but cloudy and dull. There's even occasional litter. We are heartened this evening by what looks like a high cloud in the distance, but which apparently is smoke from bush-fires.

That night we saw the lights of the town reflected as a glow in the sky. We decided to eat the chickens in celebration, but we made a bad job of killing them until Alex went below for the axe. The birds had lost all their flesh, and the flavour of what little meat remained was swamped by pumpkin. But the meal was important symbolically, even though no one enjoyed it. In the morning a customs spotter-plane buzzed us and took pictures. I have never been so pleased to be photographed by the authorities. Somewhere, in some office in Australia, someone has a picture of seven burnt-out hippies cavorting and waving, quite naked, from the deck of a strange, hybrid, Chinese-style boat.

The low shape of the land was disappointing. As we rounded the entrance into the channel that led up to the harbour and town Jamie pointed out the chimney of the hospital and the water-tower, and gradually the rest of the town slipped up into view. Half-way in a modern yacht came alongside this curiosity entering their harbour. The crew of the yacht did not need to ask where we had come from; we stared at their ice-boxes and their cans of beer, their large-breasted and pink-fleshed women; they stared at our patched boat, at our bearded faces, and at the hungry looks in our eyes as we stared at them. It was a meeting between two tribes. Then they threw us cans of beer, sausages, pâté, and bread rolls and butter before tacking away. The beer – or was it the relief – went straight to our heads, and we danced on the foredeck, kissing the planks of the boat that had borne us.

If I had been in a frame of mind to keep harping on about Conrad then I might have felt some obscure satisfaction on arriving in Darwin. But I didn't even allow myself to think of the implications of our voyage. We had slowly emptied our personalities out on to the waters around us until only the dregs – or was it the foundation of what we were really like? – remained. There were many moments on board that we wanted to forget, but there are many which are a delight to recall. It was an experience that I will never match, but now as I sit in the suburbs of London the *Chun Bhatera* hardly seems a part of the real world at all. I have lost touch with the other crew members.

7 *Australian Interlude*

In fact I lost touch with the rest of the crew almost as soon as we touched dry land. Australian customs and immigration made us wait for twelve hours with a quarantine flag flying from our mast, whilst the sniffer dogs had a good whiff of our lives of the last two months. Then we were released.

I had never really wanted to go to Australia, but after two months deprived of all comforts it was superb to be in a developed, English-speaking country. Not that the Northern Territory of Australia is all that developed: it was a petrol-and-beer culture – petrol for the big gleaming cars that everyone seemed to have, and beer to sit on the front seat next to the driver, or the back seat if he had a girlfriend. The main event of Darwin's year is the beer-can regatta, where the results of a couple of weeks' drinking are lashed together to make boats of varying sizes and imaginations. As far as I could see it was impossible to buy a single 'tube' in an Aussie supermarket. Beer (no one bothers to notice which brand it is) comes either in cartons or half-cartons (one carton equals a dozen tubes), the former for partying and the latter for quiet TV suppers.

Once I had located my money and rediscovered the joys of buying things (largely ice-creams and chips) I went to ask for accommodation at a local squat, just as many other post-Asian travellers had done before me. The incumbents thought I was the police.

"I want somewhere to stay," I said to one of three German girls who stared at me down from the balcony. She looked uncertain.

"There are already many people, and some wait. We have no space," she said eventually.

"What about the shed in the garden?" I had noticed it on my prowl around.

She grudgingly admitted that no one was in residence at the time, presumably consoled by the thought that if I was the police at least I would be out of the house itself and having an uncomfortable time of it. So I made my home in a corrugated shed, together with the mosquitos and lizards. It was no palace, but at least it did not roll at night, and I could sleep undisturbed by the need to go about or to take my watch.

After a couple of days they accepted that I was not the police. They had some reason to be afraid, it seemed. Two of the girls had married Australians when they arrived from Asia just in order to get residency; they never saw their 'husbands'. We were all well-briefed on what to say should immigration ever appear on the doorsteps. The third German, although unmarried, was heavily pregnant by her Hungarian boyfriend. He was huge, leonine, passionate, and scared the rest of us to death. Besides these four there was a local, Darwin-born ex-hippie who lived downstairs with his dog; a remarkably dense but very kind New Zealander called Clyde, who made remarks like "don't turn the light out, it goes dark" which made most of us howl with laughter a lot of the time; and Steve, a self-styled musician and poet who would come and quote Bob Dylan and Eliot at me in the middle of the night once he learned that I had studied literature at university.

Less central to the community were two young and beefy Australians working on a local building site and an American who said he was a journalist, but who always avoided the subject whenever I brought it up. He was theoretically working on an aboriginal land rights story, and he had an aboriginal girlfriend. Sleeping with her was all the research he seemed to do.

In addition there was another couple, a very tense and silent Australian and his even more silent princess of a German girlfriend; Eva didn't even talk to the other German girls and hardly moved from her room, and when I did by chance come across her in the daylight she would smile incredibly sweetly and disappear behind the curtain that was their door before I could think of anything even remotely appropriate to say. Her boyfriend was the household's provider: he struck up acquaintances with the staff of local supermarkets, and they would put boxes of outdated or unsellable goods behind their stores for him to collect. The result was that we dined regally on endless quantities of rotten grapes, musty peanuts and purpling tomatoes.

The population of Darwin was a strange mixture. The town was still very much a frontier outpost, and seventy-five per cent of employment was in the administration machinery that kept it going. The employed section of the community was relatively small, however, and the civil servants were easily identifiable by their neatly pressed shorts and their white socks which never fell down. There was also a significant population of Asians, but these Asians did not stop and smile at white men. I had become so used to instant friendship on the road that I found the sophistication of the Asians in Darwin rather disappointing. I felt more affinity towards them than I did towards the official population, but they viewed me in the same way as the official population did: I was a hippy, a drop-out, one of the alternative element in the town. I grinned at them, but they hurried past, affecting not to notice.

There were few traces of the typhoon which had flattened the town some years before. On the contrary, Darwin seemed a sleepy backwater rather than an epicentre. It was like an eddy between two whirlpools. Out of the Australian whirlpool drifted a wide variety of young people who for some reason or other couldn't handle life in the mainstream, whilst out of the Asian whirlpool came odds and ends who were united by one factor – they had managed their paperwork cleverly enough to enable them to stay. This was not an easy thing to achieve: when a boatload of refugees turned up in the harbour in 1981 the Northern Territory sent them back to where they had come from.

All these peoples assembled, like pieces of driftwood, in the town. But whilst most of the white drifters were unemployed, the Asians were largely well set up in a variety of small businesses. Amongst all these the aborigines were in a class of their own. They were not driftwood by choice as the rest of us were, and as they waved their bottles and snored in the town centre we respected them as real Australians.

In Asia I was not a freak, but in Darwin I was pigeon-holed by the employed in their shorts and the Asians in their businesses as one of the burnt-out hippies. This was by no means such a bad thing, as the town was quite accustomed to its strange population and hardly discriminated against any elements. As a result I felt more at home in Darwin than I would have done in any other Australian city.

For a few days I hung around town trying to find my feet. I wrote letters, filed a couple of stories on aboriginal land rights for the *Straits Times*, and even had one published in the *Darwin Star*, which vastly increased my status in the squat. Thereafter I was accorded floor-space indoors.

More in touch with the life of the house, I was in on all the dramas. We had several nocturnal visitors. One in particular appeared very often, and he was virtually the only other Englishman I encountered in Australia. Robin was his real name, but everyone called him Kathmandu, largely because he had a shaven head and drifted around town in a sarong, telling people at bus-stops about Buddhism. He was slightly crazy but didn't always deserve the treatment meted out to him. The landlady of his hostel deprived him of everything and refused even to replace his only light-bulb when it fused. Kathmandu was forced to use a candle, and when he set his bedclothes alight one night she chucked him out. For a while he lived on the beach, and then he moved to a tree just around the corner from us, and we saw a lot more of him in more ways than one.

He would sit for hours cross-legged on the floor, laughing inexplicably or muttering something about Buddhism. It was evident from his responses to questions that he knew very little about the religion that he was following, and he had never been inside Asia. Sometimes he would throw off his sarong and sit there stark naked, staring at his penis and breaking into peals of laughter whenever it stiffened. Then one day, after an afternoon of this, he tried to assault one of the German girls. We put him out on the street and threw his sarong after him, but evidently he left it where it fell. The police picked him up for wandering around naked and he spun some story about how he had been robbed by us. A squad car came round to check, and for a while we were all on our best behaviour. Fortunately no one had been doing anything visibly illegal at the time, and they believed what we had to say. Kathmandu was well-known, and often spent a night in the local lock-up.

Then, fed up with the town, I 'went bush' with a bushie called Strider. His name had once been a nickname, derived from the curious loping half-run that he had developed in order to – as he claimed – move through the bush at speed with minimal effort; he had so liked it that he had changed from his old name and adopted just 'Strider' by deed-poll. He sounded the part and looked rugged; his movements were slow and deliberate and his speech quiet and thoughtful. He talked of spending days and weeks in one or other of his hide-outs in the bush. Fascinated, I asked to go along; flattered (I was wearing my journalist's hat) he agreed.

After twenty miles towards Alice Springs we got off the bus. A few tin houses stood on the blackened earth on either side of the road. Smoke from bush-fires belched into the skies all around the horizon. Strider's place – a corrugated shack, with the floor a simple continuation of the rough land outside together with all the associated insect life – was some three or four miles away from the road, but it was hardly remote: Strider's mum lived in a similar shack just next door, but she had all mod-cons (water, telly, solar power etc) in her place.

I was eagerly anticpating some arduous hunting expeditions off into the scrub, but I was to be disappointed. Strider happily showed me his gun and told me how often and how far he ranged in search of food, but he showed no desire to put his actions into words. Over the next couple of days he read books and wrote letters to the Territory's government. He was writing a book on the care that the earth needed, and as he himself had once been a civil servant (as he revealed to me on the second day in the bush) he felt it his duty to use his knowledge of the hierarchy to lobby against bush-fires and the like.

Disappointing though the lack of expeditions was, the wildlife around Strider's place was impressive. Flights of lorikeets skeeted across the skies; bright white cockatoos brought the otherwise dull eucalyptus trees alive. I climbed a skinny-bark tree some distance from the nearest house in order to take some pictures of the wildlife, and was amazed to see how many wallabies there were. I was disappointed to learn that these were not kangaroos at all. A pack of wild dogs led by one with three legs sniffed around the base of the tree, and then made off at high speed when they worked out where I was.

After a couple of days Strider went back into town. He said he had forgotten to do something or other, which didn't seem to marry with his claimed weeks of isolation. Imitating the Strider stride I loped back to the road and applied for work at the local chicken factory and battery. For two days I gutted chickens at a rate of eleven per minute, eight hours a day. It was not one of the most sociable jobs I have done, but it had its advantages: as I ravaged the birds with a steel hook the bile that squirted from them covered me from head to foot, and this potent layer kept all the mosquitos well away at night.

Strider's place gave me a taste for the bush and within a few days of returning to Darwin I was once again on the road to Alice, equipped with a mosquito net and a frying pan (technically known as a billy). This was to be my walkabout gear. I must have seemed a lunatic to the Kakadu National Park rangers, with my shoulder bag and my planned three-day route march across some of the wildest land. No Australian goes walkabout these days: they all have Toyota land-cruisers.

The rangers warned me of three things. The buffalo could be aggressive, water would be scarce away from the Arnhem Land escarpment, and finally I was to be careful not to start a bush-fire with my overnight camp fires. Nevertheless the latter were essential, they said, to keep the inquisitive wildlife away from my mozzie net.

I hitched a ride down to my starting point at Yellow Water and hooked my net up alongside the luxury tents and caravans of holidaying Australians. The guy who had given me the ride – at enormous speed to ride on the top of the bumps, he said – was a uranium-mine worker out for a fishing trip. He was very stoned, but despite being hypnotised by the stillness of the water he did manage to catch a fish, which he donated to me for my supper before disappearing in a cloud of dust back towards the mine, where he said an enormous steak would be ready and waiting his return.

And so, compass in hand, I wandered off into the bush. It was not hard to navigate once I had found the Arnhem escarpment, as the latter was the only non-flat land as far as the eye could see. Even though Arnhem land is aboriginal territory I met no one for three days; for companionship I had only the wildlife and the aboriginal paintings I found in some of the caves at the foot of the escarpment.

It was not particularly pleasant walking. At times the spear grass was chest-high; it tore my calves to shreds and left my shirt full of brittle barbs that stuck to my sweating skin and pricked me constantly. The worst thing about the height of the grass was that I could not see dangers close to me, and was unable to move silently. Many times my heart stopped at the noise of some beast crashing away through the undergrowth only feet away. Usually these were goannas or wallabies, and quite harmless, but the rangers' warning had set my nerves on edge. In the post bush-fire areas the going was much easier, although the burnt stumps covered my ankles in a thick layer of charcoal. Sometimes the fire would still be smouldering in tree-trunks or particularly hefty clumps of grass. It made an eerie, almost post-nuclear landscape, blackened, bare and smoking. It seemed appropriate that there was a massive uranium mine not so far away.

I ate and drank erratically. I boiled my billy whenever I came across a stagnant pool of water, and made myself cups of sweet tea. Sometimes this meant two long stops in half-an-hour; sometimes I walked for hours without seeing any water, but I never went short. For nourishment I survived on dampers, something I had learned to make from Strider. A damper is a flour and water pancake. Very basic, but quick and filling, and with jam in the bush it becomes a luxury food.

The nights were the worst time. The sun set at seven, by which time I had to have found a site to hang my net, sprayed it carefully with anti-mosquito (like everything else in Australia the mosquitos were enormous), made a fire and cooked my dampers. Then I sat as the light dwindled, intermittently talking to myself and listening to the crashing sounds coming from the undergrowth. When a particularly loud rustling came to a sudden stop I knew that eyes were on me, illuminated as I was in the light from my fire, and I prayed that either the fire was a suitable deterrent or the animal was not an aggressive one: even lizards can make a considerable noise in dry scrub on a still night. Once the smoke from the fire became too weak to protect me from the mozzies I retreated inside my net and listened to their angry buzzings at its walls. Both nights it took an age for sleep to come, however exhausted I was. On the second I discovered that I had pitched camp in the middle of an ants' trail, and that they were route-marching all over me as I tried to sleep. It took me an hour to move up on to a rock on the Arnhem escarpment, pick up all the disorientated ants out of my possessions, and rearrange everything for sleep again.

And so when the morning of the third day dawned I was quite pleased to think that I would be back in civilisation and comfort by the evening. The novelty of cave paintings, of hissing-matches with goannas, and of trying to out-stare tall and dignified grey kangaroos had worn off. But the wildlife had not finished with me.

After a couple of hours' walking in the period before it got really hot I reached the first perimeter fence of the uranium mine, as planned. It was a fairly flimsy barbed-wire job, but some distance beyond it I could see something much more impregnable that stood over ten feet high. There had been a fire in the area a few days before, but it hadn't been very hot. When a bush-fire gets really strong it reaches the tree-tops, igniting the oil in the eucalyptus leaves and starting a tree-top fire-ball. As it turned out, it was fortunate for me that that had not happened.

I had been walking the perimeter fence for a mile or so when I saw a herd of buffalo in the distance. As a precaution I nipped through the first fence. As I did so I was spotted by two large males, who were wandering a little apart from the herd. They came through the fence as if it didn't exist, and what had been a leisurely detour to avoid trouble became a blind panic. I was trapped against the main perimeter fence. Fortunately I had a clear lead, the bush-fire had allowed me that. I was still a good 70 yards clear when I chucked my bag into one tree and scrambled up into the other. Seconds later the beasts arrived at the base of my tree and stopped, and I was cursing my foolishness: I had put my bag in the big tree and climbed the small one. Judging by the way in which they flattened the fence these animals could flatten a tree as well. My tree was so small that my trembling made the scorched leaves rustle.

Luckily for me buffalo are rather dense, and these were no exception. They knew that I had disappeared, but they didn't know where to. Neither looked up, so neither spotted me. I remained in my tiny tree, quivering and terrified, whilst they circled beneath me.

The next twenty minutes seemed an age. Infinitessimally slowly the rest of the herd moved away, and the males' interest in my existence waned. After half-an-hour they were 20 yards away; an hour and that distance had increased by 200 yards. Fifteen minutes after they had finally disappeared from view I got down stiffly from my tree; every joint in my body seemed to have seized up. I picked my bag out of the other tree and made off as quickly as I could in the opposite direction to the herd.

I reached the uranium settlement three hours later than I had hoped. In my panic run I had dropped my compass, and in heading away from the buffalo I had also been effectively retracing my steps, so I had had to make a very wide circle. In the massive, modern and empty supermarket that catered for the tastes of the miners I bought two packets of biscuits and a couple of pints of milk, which I then ate at one sitting, watching a tap dribble clear water on to a ridiculously green and lush lawn, before hitching back to Darwin.

As the days that separated me from my return flight to Asia ebbed away I became more and more fed up. My girlfriend in England wrote to say that she had found another boyfriend, which was more of a blow than it should have been. In retrospect I realised that I should have been amazingly flattered by the length of time that she had persisted with my memory. I had often thought of her during the tougher or more tedious episodes of my travels, and her letter seemed to pull away a support from beneath me. I had been treated better than I deserved, for I had not been faithful for more than a couple of months.

There was no one I wanted to see in Darwin. The only members of the crew I could find still in town were the two Italians, and they were transformed. Glossily dressed and extremely popular, they were playing and singing on the club and restaurant circuit. It was ironic that they, who had been the most useless on the boat, should make the best start at life on land.

To while away the days less fruitlessly I worked behind a side-show at a weekend fair. The boss must have known he was on to a winner with me; he complained endlessly about how little money he made from the shows, whilst his Alsatian fixed me with a beady stare. I felt guilty asking him for my pay, but I was a sucker; several other people were taken on to attend the stalls for the busier nights, but I was the only one who turned up at pay time. The others had pocketed so much of the takings than the actual pay they were meant to receive was small enough to be irrelevant. The boss seemed to take it all in his stride, but he gave me no bonus for honesty. On the contrary, I think he thought me a fool.

I arrived back in Singapore on 25th July after an absence of four months, very glad to be back in Asia.

8 *International Express*

In the village of Chiang Khan, in the north-east of Thailand, there is a fabulous hotel. It is not fabulous in the way that the Bangkok Oriental is; this hotel is primitive, old, and cheap. There is no running water in the rooms, rips in the netting over the window let the mosquitos in at night, and the ceiling fans only operate at two speeds – very fast or off. The place is made of wood, and the whole building creaks with every footfall.

The hotel's good points far outweigh these minor problems. Its balcony hangs over the vast expanse of the Mekhong river, and the river water reflects the various moods of the seasons on to the ceilings of the hotel rooms and down its polished corridors. The people of north-eastern Thailand are particularly charming despite being the poorest in the country, and every night many of the villagers gather to listen to Lok Tham concerts in the dining hall downstairs.

I was in Chiang Khan for a more significant purpose than simply admiring the view. I spent my days in the refugee camp of Ban Vinai, interviewing and photographing the camp and its people. At night I returned to the hotel and stared at the massive area of water that slid past beneath the balcony (the Mekhong must have been over a kilometre wide) and marvelled at the feat of endurance that whole Lao families completed in swimming across it from one bank to the other. The other bank of the river was Laos, and the inmates of the Ban Vinai camp were predominantly Hmong Lao.

In the dark skies at night gunfire flashed periodically over Vientiane, the capital of Laos, which lay only a few miles inland. Further away real lightning spread a broader glow which momentarily transfixed the skyline. A village on the Lao bank opposite the hotel was plainly visible during the day, but at night it was marked by just two solitary lights. Was it because the village was largely deserted, or did they not have any powerful light source? I wondered what they made of the bright lights of Chiang Khan, over the water, and whether the music from the dining hall below me carried over the water to dozens of pairs of listening ears.

The Ban Vinai story was the pinnacle of the four months' knocking around Asia that followed my return from Australia. During this time I pursued various either self-originated or outside commissions. I interviewed a missionary in Indonesia and a planter in Malaysia; I wrote about Burmese pagodas, Indonesian trains, boat-building traditions and traditional architecture in a local hotel . . . in short, nothing earth-shattering, but at least it gave a purpose to my meanderings, and above all it was printed.

The Ban Vinai story was different; it earned a double-page spread in the *Straits Times*, and more importantly it pulled a trigger somewhere within me.

The Hmong are the Lao equivalent of the northern Thai hill-tribes, and like the latter they valued their independence from any government. They too had been cultivated by the forces of the West to resist the forces of the East – communism. Whilst the lowland Lao lived on happily enough in the new communist-dominated regime in their country, the Hmong were harassed as dissident elements, and many of them followed the Indo-Chinese trend of becoming refugees.

It made a sad story, epitomised for me by the scenes on Ban Vinai's holy hill, a little knoll of land that poked up from between the huts of the camp. The Hmong did not just climb the hill because the wind there was fresher than it was at hut level, but because the blue-grey ridge of their own mountains in Laos was visible through the surrounding hills to the north. Here a woman wailed publicly for a husband who had died away from his home; a father prayed for the life of his child, and a young man practised his gkang, the bamboo bagpipes that the Hmong use for their tribal music.

The Hmong were for the most part stuck in their camp. Many of them had suffered extensively from the hardship of the escape and the loss of whole families, and they could not envisage returning to their homeland unless the regime was to change; most did not want to move on to a third country, and indeed were quite unsuited to doing so, as the mysterious deaths amongst the Hmong community in America testify. The equivalent of a twelfth-century people does not blend easily into an urban American environment.

For various reasons onward settlement had dried up; settlement in Thailand was ruled out by an already hard-pressed Thai government (that season's harvest had been so bad in the area that I saw dead rats on sale as food in the Chiang Khan market), and repatriation was impossible for the majority. So they stayed. The men lost their sense of purpose more than the women, and the latter became the family earners with the small amounts of needlework they could sell outside the camp. Children were born and grew up in a camp environment. Only the leprosy victims, in a centre just outside the main camp, seemed happy. Back in the Lao hills they had been confined to a limited area anyway, but in the camp they had medicine, facilities to study and people to look after them, and they, more than anyone else, attended the camp's lessons with eagerness and enthusiasm.

Those few days of research had a strong and emotional effect on me. From some refugees I heard first-hand accounts of the impact of yellow rain on a tribal village, whilst I also met a few better educated Hmong who had left their country simply because they wanted to get to America. For the first time I was reporting something that had real human importance; my previous assignments had only been important to me to convince myself that I was working. Those days made me realise, too, that I had become increasingly insensitive to my surroundings. I came to view my own situation in a similar way to that of the Hmong, and I knew that if I stayed in Asia too long I too would be unable to go home. Finally, they made me realise that at last I had answered the question of what to do which had dogged me at university and after. I had forced my head and shoulders into journalism more by a self-conscious effort of will-power rather than a real show of talent, but here I was reporting a real journalist's story that was to be printed across a double-page spread in a major Asian daily: I had arrived; I had found a job.

All this did not come to me with a flash as I sat overlooking the Mekhong from that hotel balcony, but it began there. The rest dawned on me slowly as I returned to Singapore on the International Express. It was the third or fourth time that I had made the journey, transit days that allowed plenty of time for reflection and observation. It was a journey like many others that had preceded it, yet somehow it seemed to have greater significance. In the back of my mind an idea was taking shape – the idea that this might be the last journey I made in Asia.

The International Express left three times a week from Bangkok's Hualampong station. Departure time was four o'clock in the afternoon, one of the quietest times for station life. The dealers in children had long ago met the morning trains from the provinces and made their purchases. The night-time crowd of the poor and homeless had yet to gather, and pairs of pick-pockets were drifting aimlessly between the station benches, their hands plunged deep into their own pockets for once. Outside, in the shade of the station forecourt, the policeman who controlled the crowds at peak times had his feet up on his desk, alongside his silent megaphone. On platform seven a number of babies were being passed through the open windows of our train, like parcels to be stamped with a kiss and returned to sender.

The lady announcer was still announcing the train as we rolled out of the station. The list of our stops was so long that even as the last face and the last foot of platform slipped away I could hear her struggling with a number of what had become familiar names: Alor Star, Butterworth, Ipoh and Johore Bahru. I have always imagined announcers as Zeus-like and all seeing, up amongst the beams of station roofs, and I wondered whether this one could see the tail-light of our last coach as it bumped out over the points into the shimmering heat of the afternoon. But her voice gave no sign of faltering. Perhaps she was determined to master that list of names once and for all, or perhaps she was just a recording, and the real her was arguing the price of a silk panung in the market.

A hush fell over the travellers as we watched the vista of the city unroll like a stained carpet before us. 100,000 people come into Bangkok from the provinces in the years of bad harvests, and many of them make their homes alongside the railway tracks. If they are lucky they might have corrugated shacks that lean against the walls of the factories where they work, and their children grow up used to the rumble of the factory on one side and the rattle and threat of the trains on the other. A rejected sofa beneath an awning served as home for a samlor driver. The afternoon's sun, like a glass of white wine peering through the steam of the humid city, did little to dry the rags of clothes that were spread out on the tin roofs.

The train began to curve into the leafier, quieter and cooler parts of the city, for although we had started northwards (there is only one mainline station in Bangkok, and that points north) our journey was to be southwards, down through Thailand and Malaysia as far as the land goes. In the suburbs larger wooden houses backed on to the railway, duckboards leading from their doors over piles of rubbish and green slime-covered pools of water. In one of the standing pools a man stood chest-deep, casting and re-casting a drop-net, and in between casts he drew heavily on a cigarette to conquer the stench of the water. In the mornings the railway would be thronged with people using it to walk to work. Then we rattled over the breadth of the Chao Phya, the river that took the first missionaries to northern Thailand, but the main traffic on the swirling carpet of water was a string of barges on their steady way down to the sea. I dived forwards in search of the dining-car and a cup of coffee.

Thai dining-cars are a delight, and this was no exception. Fresh purple table-cloths and fresh purple orchids; cheap, quick, good food, and plenty to look at. Here were numbers of business-women with half-empty bottles of beer between them; beer-drinking women are a very rare sight in Asia, but in Thailand the women are a force to be reckoned with. Here too was a strong military presence – communists in the hills of southern Thailand have been known to attack the trains. The soldiers were drinking the Thai whisky, Mekhong, with relish. The Thais once thought of exporting this spirit, but rumour has it that the German laboratory which tested it sent back a report which soon stopped that impetus: "Liquid not fit for human consumption – what is it?" The soldiers evidently set little store by this verdict, and even if the liquid did not improve their aim, it was certainly fortifying their spirits.

Walking back to my carriage was like travelling through a multi-national village, where even the air smelled different as different nationalities unwrapped their suppers or took off their shoes and socks. It was the height of the durian season, and no Asian traveller with any sense ignored the profit-making possibilities of carrying durian down to Singapore, where the locals regard them as the king of fruits and will gladly pay extortionate prices for them. Durian have a very distinctive smell, and no airline will allow them on board. One wag once likened the experience of eating the fruit to eating an old raspberry yoghurt in a French urinal! One of these pungent objects rolled in the aisle in front of me, and knowing that to tread on the enormous spiky chestnut would be to explode a land-mine of stink around the carriage as well as antagonise its owner, I eyed it carefully and stepped over it as it rolled.

There was none of the newspapers-in-front-of-noses syndrome in my carriage, and everyone was busily getting to know each other, spreading out their possessions to stake out their territory within the village. In my immediate vicinity there was a stately negress from the Sudan, with a lively child who tottered up and down the aisle offering her milk-bottle to everyone. Then there were two fat Pakistani businessmen who smelt strongly of perfume and dealt in shirts. Two Frenchmen who found it very hot and looked very disgruntled. A young Singaporean with three Thais accompanying him to Singapore, and opposite me sat a quiet man who professed to be a Bangladeshi freedom-fighter doing a little business between cities and keeping other freedom-fighters in touch. We all swapped as much of our life histories as we thought necessary on our first meeting, and then fell to staring out over the evening settling on the padi fields on either side of the track.

I stayed a long time over my evening meal that night, thinking hard about my position and my ambitions. I was the last diner to leave the car. The head waiter had taken off his white jacket and was sitting at the end table adding up figures on a scrap of paper. The orchids had already begun to look a little sad under the electric light. On the longer bends I could see the headlight of the loco plunging into the darkness ahead of us. Occasionally the silhouette of a temple roof blotted out a few stars. Half the night came in through my open window, and the scents of the tropical night mixed with the smell of frying rice in the carriage. Mosquitos were an easy target at last, as they struggled to hold on to the table in the teeth of the wind from the window. Occasional flashes of lightning fringed the trees on the skyline.

Whilst I had been in the dining-car my carriage had been converted to its sleeping mode. I find continental-style sleeping cars – rows of berths behind curtains along the length of the central corridor – a little alarming. Whenever I pull the curtain on myself I find myself listening to every footstep in the corridor with a certain amount of trepidation, fearing that sooner or later a hand will tear back my curtain and reveal me to the world, foolish, half-naked and frightened. I thought, as I walked down the aisle of that morgue for the living, of each human body behind each of those curtains, some praying, some reading, some thinking, some crying. A breeze blew through an open window and revealed half a face, a pair of open eyes staring upwards, a nose, a white vest. Noises of coughing, scratching, snoring, sleep-muttering.

I would have walked straight past my own berth if it had not been for the Bangladeshi, sitting on the bunk opposite in his shirt-sleeves and drawing on an Indian beedee to keep it alight. I did not feel like talking, but evidently he had been waiting for me.

"You know, I cannot go back to my country," he whispered confidentially, leaning across the aisle. Apparently he had been blacklisted as a dangerous activist.

"My family, they are there. I have not seen them for two years."

I made sympathetic noises, but went through the motions of preparing my berth for sleep to show that I did not really want to talk, putting the most valuable things nearest to where my head would lie. He talked on.

"We need money and support from a foreign country. American peoples help many peoples in Asia to fight, so why not us? If we have American support then we will win. You are American, so you can help me."

I wearily pointed out that I was not American, but British, and that the sun had set over the British Empire many decades before. The images of the refugee camp were still very much in my mind's eye, and it wasn't the best of times to be talking of foreign interference. Anyway, I told him, I knew nothing whatsoever about Bangladesh, having only spent a few hours in the airport. I begged to be excused from the conversation and pulled the curtains across to cut out the light and a political discussion in which I knew I would come out worse.

The train emerged from the night into a flat sea of padi-fields punctuated by limestone outcrops that towered like volcanic islands. They were far from beautiful; occasional scars in the forestation of their sides revealed ugly cliffs of grey and black, but the stations we clattered through were freshly painted, neat, and planted with flowers. On the platform of each a uniformed officer bravely held out a green flag in the blast of the wind from the train, which threatened to blow his cap on to a neighbouring padi-field.

Wherever we stopped trays of food were thrust through the windows. Each station had its own speciality: at one it might be garlic chicken, at another quails' eggs, and at a third oranges and guavas.

Then we reached Had Yai, the burgeoning crossroads town of southern Thailand. I had been to Had Yai many times, but like most people I had just passed through. Only sex and missed rail connections delayed travellers in Had Yai; even if you happen to be a Thai factory worker in Singapore on your monthly visa-run you need only stay for a matter of hours.

In Bangkok sex is presented as public entertainment; in Had Yai it is more discreet. Customers here are of two sorts. There are the Muslim Malaysians who can escape the constraints of their faith by nipping over the border for a few days into the shrouding veil of a foreign country. Nipples are visible on the covers of popular Thai magazines, whilst fifty miles away across the border you would be lucky to even see ankles. Then there are the oilies – the offshore oil-rig workers – with many Europeans amongst them. In Had Yai they release the frustrations which pile up through life spent on board a hundred-square-yard platform with a hundred men in the middle of an empty ocean. These frustrations are exacerbated by the regular screening of sex-films, constant talk of women, and the threat of homosexuality, which is a terrifyingly close possibility for the sort of men who despise it most.

During the only night that I had ever spent in Had Yai the hotel floor-manager must have offered me women on at least four occasions, and the more I protested that I was not really interested, the more his eyebrows went up and his price went down. He could get me girls that had been boys, he said, he could get me Malays, Filipinos, or Chinese (though he did not personally recommend the latter). Or even girls under twelve years old? Surely I would like some 'steam and cream', a more personalised form of sauna. I gave up answering the knocks on my door after discovering a girl who couldn't have been much more than fifteen years old shivering half-naked in the corridor.

But on this occasion the train only stopped briefly at Had Yai, and there was no question of being tempted by the delicacies of the town. The locomotive shunted extra coaches on to the rear, and I stayed firmly in my seat for fear of losing it whilst around me the guards argued and wrangled with new and old passengers who had booked the same seats. An old man and his barefoot boy assistant wheeled a barrow repeatedly past the window. It was laden with magazines, papers, Krungthip, Samit and Gold City cigarettes, the man yelling '*rawn phleng, rawn phleng*' – newspapers, newspapers – whilst the boy chipped in with '*booree, booree*'. As he passed my face at the window he would vary his call to 'cigalet, cigalet', for my benefit. There was never any news worth reading in the Thai papers; they were full of scandal about Thai singers, the latest news in Thai boxing, and the newest love-stories. Most of the magazines carried a monthly story about the Thai royal family, and often a photo of one of them would stare out from the cover over the station platform. One cover, in a rare concession to foreign interest, had a picture of Princess Diana and her new baby.

The corridors of the train were rapidly filling with fruit and sacks of rice as we neared the border. Such things sell well in Malaysia, where the prices are higher and the rice-crop is harvested later. At the first stop on the other side of the frontier a fleet of trishaws would be waiting by the side of the track, ready to take the weight of the rice-sacks that spewed out of the train windows. Of course this was illegal, but most people were carrying something across the border to make their trip worthwhile.

On a previous journey across the same border I had been caught out by a lady with a couple of heavy sacks; I had helped her to heave both up on to the luggage rack, but she had then plumped herself down in the seat opposite, leaving me to sit beneath her 'luggage'. She seemed happy with the situation and nodded and smiled at me. I took this to mean that she was confident that the rack would not give way and dump sixty kilos of rice on my head. Then, as we approached the border and several uniformed customs officers started working through the train, she suddenly fell into a deep sleep. I was left sitting beneath two sacks which were not mine, with the officials eyeing me with some suspicion. Evidently the phenomenon of a rice-smuggling white man was not one they had met before, and they seemed flummoxed by it. One of them attracted my attention – which wasn't hard to do, as I was only too aware of my situation – and pointed to the sacks and then to me, enquiringly. I shrugged my shoulders. I was just a foreigner and I didn't understand. In the end they moved on and I breathed a sigh of relief. The lady woke up instantly and was smiling at me again, but

I turned my face to the window and watched the landscape clatter by. Between that journey and this one I had travelled enough to have become substantially wiser, but maybe my life was a little less full of surprises as a result.

Walking down the train beyond the dining-car I found myself in a different atmosphere, in a carriage that was full of peace. It was of a different vintage to the rest of the train, the walls panelled with some light-coloured wood and the corridor passing down one side of a series of compartments rather than through the middle of an open-plan coach. Through the doors of one of the compartments I saw two monks in their saffron robes. The older one was sitting cross-legged on the top bunk running his finger slowly down the page of an ancient volume, whilst the other – who couldn't have been more than thirteen – was staring raptly out of the window at his homeland flying past.

I returned to my seat in the wake of a brusque man in purple pyjamas who looked carefully at every girl that he passed. He stopped at one point to stare at a couple of European girls in one of the first-class carriages as they went through the process of putting on their make-up for the day.

At the border the freedom-fighter borrowed a few dollars to place across an appropriate palm (he said that it was getting increasingly expensive every time), but the two Pakistanis did not have enough ready money on them to be allowed into Malaysia, despite their opulent appearance. The Sudanese lady could not continue because she was travelling on a joint passport but without her husband, and immigration did not approve. The two Frenchmen suddenly reported that their money had been stolen whilst they were asleep; it was the first we had heard of it. The border official also did not believe them, and no doubt he would have stamped SHIT (Suspected Hippy In Transit) into their passports if that particular stamp had not been withdrawn once the authorities had discovered that many travellers were proud to qualify for it. I was given two weeks to get to Singapore, which seemed unduly pessimitic, but perhaps immigration knew something that I didn't.

So we trundled along into Malaysia, and suddenly the landscape became more organised and less interesting. The orange and gold curved roofs of the Thai temples were replaced by ramshackle corrugated-iron minarets and mosques, and concrete houses replaced the bamboo huts. A road ran alongside the railway, where before there had only been padi and pinang trees. Small motor-cycles overtook the train with a high-pitched whine. In the dining car the waiter whipped the tablecloths off the tables and the orchids wilted away from their homeland.

At Butterworth we had to change trains. Those of us who had thought that our International Express status was enough to ensure us of berths on the next leg were very much mistaken, and by the time that I had sauntered down the platform to the booking office all the berths had gone. A German lady in front of me in the queue was furious. The ticketing clerk was so in awe of her that he retreated several metres from the counter, as if the latter was not sufficient protection. She later reported triumphantly that she had blasted her way into the station-master's office and terrified him into showing her his secret reservations list. She got her sleeper.

On the train that night the man in the purple pyjamas (still) marched through our carriage with a posse of ticket-inspectors at his heels. Obviously he'd lost something important – his bed, his ticket, or his toothbrush? Opposite me a handsome Malay lady nudged her two twins together and jammed a pillow between their heads, which they succeeded in propping up all night. I didn't feel much like sleep; I had the beginnings of the Ban Vinai story sketched out on notes on my knee, but it had become too dark to work. We rattled over numerous level-crossings with their solitary attendants standing holding green lamps outside their huts, where presumably their wives and families slept soundly on. I watched the tornadoes of mosquitos beneath the station lights flash by, and a glass of beer sloshed around inside me as we bumped and swayed towards Kuala Lumpur.

In the end I slept, but my sleep was not sound enough to carry me through a rather disturbing incident that took place in the middle of the night and that had that nightmarish quality about it of events unfocused between sleeping and waking.

I woke to find the train silent and still. I wasn't aware of what had woken me, but the scent of jungle and earth after a heavy shower of rain was invigorating and I stuck my head out of the window to enjoy it.

Judging by the parallel lines of tree-trunks that disappeared into the darkness we had stopped in the middle of a rubber plantation, at a tiny station which was unlikely to be used by express trains. In another hour little flickering lights would be weaving slowly through those trees as the tappers collected the residue of the night's bleeding in the little coconut bowls tied under each incision, before it dried with the daylight.

At first the only sound I could hear was the quiet ticking of the diesel in the darkness ahead, but then a match flared in the darkness near me, momentarily illuminating the faces of two men on the platform, staring back past me down towards the rear of the train. Every now and then one of them would whisper to the other, who just nodded and continued to concentrate on the darkness. They started to walk slowly down past me, and the station light silhouetted the peaked station-master's cap on the head of one of them.

"*Boleh berchukup bahasa Ingerris?*" I called out softly as they passed.

"Yes sir," said the one with the cap.

"Why are we stopped for so long? This is not Ipoh."

"No sir. This is Padang Bawah. Ipoh is thirty kilometres from here." Judging by the accuracy of his language he must have been an Indian.

"Is anything the matter with the train?"

"No sir, nothing with the train. We are looking for someone on the rails." The station-master went on to say that the man standing next to him was better qualified to tell me what had happened. "This man is the driver," he explained, "and he saw the young people standing on the rails."

The driver's English was poor. "Have two persons," he said. "One man-one, one woman-one. Stand together same-same on railway. I think maybe boyfriend-girlfriend. I . . ." He couldn't think of the word, so he gestured with his hand to simulate the pulling of a cord and imitated the sound of a horn. "But they standing still," he continued, "they no move." This was all he had to say, and the station-master hastened to fill in the details. "This is a big train sir," he said. "It cannot stop quickly. It is not this man's fault."

It had been a suicide, that much was clear. I gathered that suicides were a common feature on the railways. Romances that cannot live publicly, pregnancies that would bring shame, bankruptcy . . . all have caused young and old to throw themselves under the wheels of the night expresses. Only the driver is witness to the last living moment of these suicides as they come into the range of the locomotive's headlight. This driver had seen three such deaths in the year already, the station-master was saying.

"You are English?" he asked. "In England you have so many ways of killing yourself." He sounded almost envious. "You have high buildings, guns, medicines and cars. For us guns are forbidden, medicines and cars are expensive and we don't know how, and we don't have high buildings. But we do have express trains. This way it is quick, but maybe a little inconvenient for the passengers." He added the latter as an afterthought, as if afraid that I would be angry over the delay.

At that moment there was some movement at the other end of the platform, and several men with torches emerged from the darkness. They were carrying something. The station-master and driver moved away towards the new arrivals, but I had no wish to see anything more so I slammed the window shut and turned my face back into the coach. In front of me the twins were sleeping quietly, and the electric fans whirred gently from their sockets in the ceiling. I could not help but visualise what the driver had seen momentarily in his headlight, and that image followed me into my dreams when the motion of the train once more lulled me into sleep.

In Kuala Lumpur's Moorish mausoleum of a station we again had to change trains. I breakfasted on dry toast, with the crusts removed in very genteel fashion. An attractive Australian girl asked me which way I was going, and then said that she was going in the opposite direction, which she did only moments later. The important-looking man, still resplendent in his purple pyjamas, was sitting on a newspaper on one of the benches staring glumly at Mohammed Ali on the station TV.

For the final leg of the journey we boarded a rather ramshackle train that struggled gamely from station to station. The landscape alternated between rubber and oil-palm plantations, and most of the passengers were poor Tamil workers moving between one station and the next. If in Butterworth the gloss of the International Express had thinned somewhat, here it had vanished altogether, and we had no more status than the battered parcels in the luggage van.

I had finished the Ban Vinai piece, so the freedom-fighter taught me a few useful phrases in Bengali (he had given up trying to enlist my political sympathies). He taught me 'I love you' and 'what time shall we eat?' Was there necessity in that order? I shall never know. I went to have a cup of coffee in the dining-car – now renamed the canteen – to think it over. Here I found a few ancient plastic flowers that were a poor reminder of the orchids we had started out with, rice wrapped in newspapers, and a solitary gentleman getting red-eyed over a bottle of stout.

The arrival of the International Express in Singapore made no more impact on the metropolis than did a piece of seaweed drifting into the eastern anchorage. Very few of those of us who struggled down the platform had come through from Bangkok, and those of us who had were too travel-worn and weary to feel anything but relief. The customs lady wisely decided to keep her hands out of my squalid bag, and the police dog took a disdainful sniff in my direction and decided that I needed a bath. Maybe I did.

In the back of the taxi that took me through the glass and concrete of the city, a thought that had been travelling upwards through my mind for some days finally broke through on to the surface; it was about time I started to head for home.

9 *Beyond the Shadow Line*

But far from being an occasion for rejoicing, going home increasingly became a journey of disillusion. A straight flight home from Singapore seemed a waste – there were so many countries on the homeward route I had not seen – so I planned a route that took me back via Thailand, Burma, Nepal, India, Russia and London. In the event it was I who wasted the places because I had lost the ability to extract the best from them. I was like a dripping sponge, supersaturated with experiences and little capable of really enjoying anything new unless it was testing in some way that I hadn't yet been tested. Progress for me was no longer just travel, it was breaking the travelling mould. My arrogance amongst other travellers was on the increase. Most of them seemed so naïve, and a few had been in Asia for even one-quarter of the time that I had. The inconvenience of cheap accommodation began to irritate me, but at the same time I became increasingly and perversely obsessed with spending no money, and accordingly stayed in increasingly basic hotels.

Six weeks through my return journey and I was in Nepal, telling myself that I would really enjoy this country. I had heard many good reports of Nepal, and I could see that Kathmandu was fabulous as soon as I stepped off the plane. But still it wasn't what I wanted. There were so many white faces in the crowds – faces similar to mine – that I feared I might meet a university or school friend come out for a trekking holiday who would remember me as I had been. I was disappointed to find that even the infamous Freak Street seemed to have become little more than a tourist boutique, although the whispers of 'marijuana, hashish, smack' still rustled down through the crowds like a breeze through a wheatfield. You could see the heads turning as the tourists tried to locate the sources of the whispers.

But I wasn't in Nepal to eat chocolate cake (very good in Kathmandu) or lie in the sun. Dismissing the city life as too soft, I set off into the Himalayas.

Like countless others I started my trek from Pokhara, and like many of them I decided that I didn't need a guide. But my twenty-two-day circuit of the Annapurnas was to be different in one respect – I would complete it in the direction that was not recommended, starting at the finish and finishing at the start. The climb over the highest pass on the trek was very steep from the side I had chosen, and most people went the other way in order to more readily acclimatise themselves to the altitude and thus lessen the danger of altitude sickness. What most people did was not good enough.

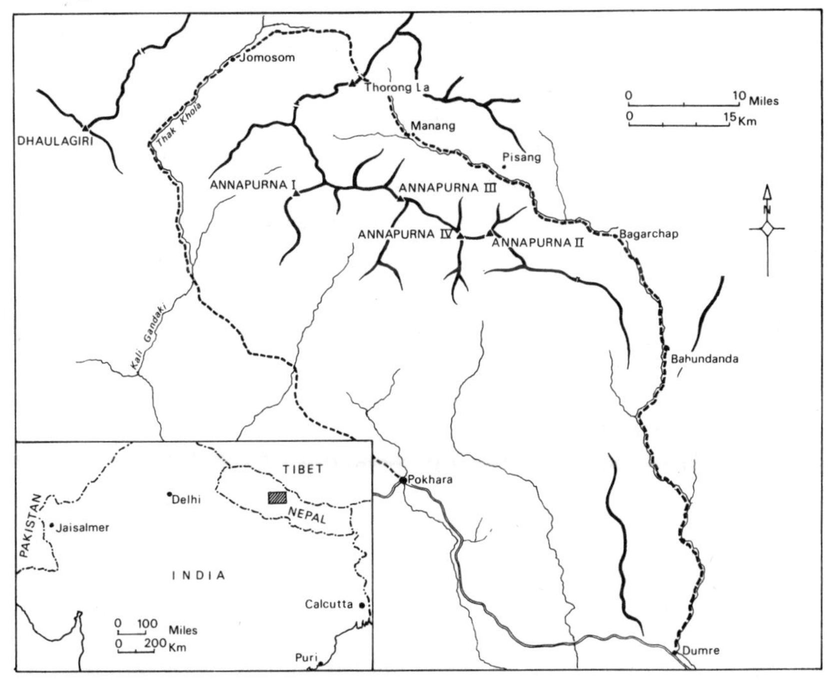

The trail turned out to be a veritable motorway amongst Himalayan routes, not only because it was the height of the trekking season. From Pokhara it leads up the valley of the Kali Gandaki river to the border with Tibet, at Mustang, 5,500 metres up in the mountains. Despite the fact that at times the Kali Gandaki is the deepest river gorge in the world and the path is narrow and treacherous, the route is still the steadiest ascent from the countries of the south of Tibet, and large numbers of mule trains and porters move along its length.

I covered the miles and the metres quickly, overtaking farting and jangling mule trains every day, although they would in return often overtake me either while I was lying half-awake in the early morning in a roadside bhatti (inn) or while I was sitting down over an evening meal of dahl baht – rice and lentils. In the higher and narrower sections of the gorge a notorious wind made walking both difficult and dangerous. Between ten in the morning and three in the afternoon during the dry season the wind funnels down the gorge, tugging at the porters and their loads struggling along its sides and threatening to hurl them down to their deaths. It brings with it a suffocating and blinding dust that turns faces raw, but no trekker or porter can afford to close his eyes, as the path in these steeper parts is often treacherous and damaged by landslides. The porters plodded slowly and miserably into the wind, stopping wherever they could for a cup of chay. I did the same.

The price of the chay was an altimeter – the higher the price, the greater the altitude. This was understandable, as every ingredient excepting the water had come up the trail from Pokhara on the back of a man or a mule. The price increased on average by ten paise every two days, and by the time that it reached Rp 1.50 I was well into the territory of the Tibeto-Mongoloid tribes. In the villages at this altitude the wind whistled down the deserted main streets and tore at the mantra flags on the roof-tops. In the courtyards the villagers packed the topsoil from their fields into sacks, for storage out of the reach of the wind. The sun appeared late from behind the mountains and disappeared early, and any dog unlucky enough to find itself spending the night outside curled up in the last light and did not move for hours if it wanted to preserve any warmth.

I bought a pair of socks from an old lady in Jomosom, eight days' walking out from Pokhara. I had hired a good down jacket before I started, but the rest of me was beginning to get rather cold. Two days after Jomosom I reached my most expensive cup of chay – Rp 2.50 – in the last bhatti before the pass, the 17,760 ft Thorong La. I had been monitoring the state of my head and stomach fairly carefully during those last two days in the thin air, and had found no signs of any mountain sickness. I could see no difficulty in attempting to go over the pass the following morning.

The bhatti was wild, inhospitable and dirty, a mud-hut clinging like a limpet to an outcrop of rock on the edge of the snow line. The building itself was not equipped to accommodate any overnight stayers apart from the family themselves, but there was a tent which had been left behind by a previous expedition, and it was in this that I placed my rucksack. I was surprised to find another Englishman staying in the same place; he too intended going over the pass the next day, he said, and we agreed to go together. During the remainder of the day we quizzed the trekkers who came down from the other side of the pass and stopped for some of the bhatti's tea. They reported the path to be clear, and weather fine, although they warned of ice. Encouraged, we went to bed early to prepare for what was going to be a hard day.

We set off the following morning well before daylight, but when the grey dawn finally came it revealed that the fine weather of the previous day's reports had not held. Clouds overtook us like express trains as we struggled up the slope. It was not warm enough for the path to thaw from the overnight freeze, and each step was a step of uncertainty: would there be a slide of ice hidden beneath the thin crust of snow? I felt strong and confident, but became increasingly frustrated with my companion who found every step a torment. As the thin fall of snow grew heavier he began to go more and more slowly, finding difficulty in breathing in the scant air. Finally, when we were already half-way up the side of the pass, he decided that the weather was too risky and turned back. Even though I knew that it was foolish to go on alone I did not want to waste the height we had gained, and without the irritation of a slow partner I thought I would forge over the top.

We did not part the best of friends, he and I. He thought I was foolish and arrogant, and I thought him weak and unfit. I was exhilarated to be alone again, and determined to prove his caution unnecessary.

The first hint that I could have been wrong came from the first people that I met on the path coming from the other side. The snow was getting heavy, they said. They whizzed past me down the slope, thankful to have conquered the worst, but they seemed bright enough, so I assumed that the situation couldn't really be that serious. Near the top I rounded a shoulder of rock and stepped quickly to one side of the path. A European girl supported on both sides by porters was being half-carried down the slope, her legs moving feebly in an attempt to take her weight. She did not look up as they moved past, and the porters were concentrating hard on avoiding the ice that lay beneath the snow. A little behind them came more porters and ponies, the ponies carrying two middle-aged women, whilst their husbands supported themselves down the slope with the aid of ski-sticks. They did not look as if they wanted to talk, so I let them by in silence.

I reviewed the situation only briefly. I suppose that I did not want the shame of turning back after having treated my former companion with scorn for having done just that. Anyway, I told myself, if people considerably older than me could make it over the top then I could too. The snow could stay blocking the pass for days, I reasoned, and I did not want to return to Pokhara the same way as I had come, meeting all the bright and confident trekkers coming up and telling them that I had flunked it. I was a seasoned traveller. So I continued.

The top was not far, but when I reached it there was no question of enjoying the view. The snow was heavier here than it had been during the climb, largely because it was coming from the other side, and I had been climbing in the lee of the mountainside. I spoke briefly to another group of trekkers sheltering behind a rock. The path was quite a good one, they said, and it should not take me more than three hours of reasonable walking to reach the first hut on the other side. They were more interested in the path that I had just covered. So I plunged down towards Manang and the Marsyangdi valley, full of confidence that I would be sitting huddled over a cup of tea within a matter of a couple of hours. Twenty minutes later I had lost the path completely.

Snow had followed the trekkers up the valley and whilst they had benefited from the fresh trail of those just ahead, by the time I had travelled a few hundred feet down the pass all trace of any footsteps had disappeared. I peered in vain into the gloom and the whirling snow for the reassuring sight of a struggling figure, black against the snow, but I saw none. Once I stumbled on to a piece of path that emerged from a drift, and I broke into a run to try to beat the falling snow that was beginning to hide it. But the path and my relief was short-lived; within metres the path was gone again, and my legs sank deeper and deeper into fresh snow, which made running difficult and dangerous. For a while I tried searching the ground for cigarette packets or orange peel, for broken sticks or even the yellow stains of urine, but the snow piled steadily deeper and stared blankly back at me.

I stopped and gazed back up the pass, talking myself slowly through the situation. "I could go back," I said aloud, and then repeated it more loudly at the snow, "I could still go back." But this hint of submission made no difference to the steady fall around me, and my words fell dead on the air. "Let's see, must be calm." I tried another tack. "It's only" – I looked at my watch – "twelve o'clock, so I have – um – about five or six hours of daylight left. Those people said three hours to the hut, and they came uphill, so it can't be more than an hour or so from here." I pulled my map from my pack and my compass from my pocket, and continued to talk to myself. "Down below – erm – somewhere over there," (the compass pointed a few feet out into the falling snow and I could see nothing) "is a stream, and further down, that stream is crossed by a path. Where the path crosses the stream there must be a bridge, or at least some sign of the passing of people." So I packed my map and compass away, checked the tiredness of my legs and thumped my hands together to try and get some of the feeling back into my fingertips, before setting off in the direction that the compass had indicated.

Half-an-hour later I was feeling very pleased with myself. What had at first been just a flat, snow-covered expanse had changed quite suddenly into a downward slope that led in the direction that I wanted to go, and I thought that I could hear the sound of running water in the distance. I was right. I came out below the cloud – or the clouds parted and lifted – and there below me I could see the stream winding along a narrow valley bottom, some 300 feet down. "No problem," I said to myself, "easy job. There, you see," as if a side of me had been panicking – which it had, subconsciously.

But it was not an easy job. The stream and the valley bed looked tantalisingly close and safe from above, but the side of the valley got increasingly steeper and more awkward. Then, as I stepped carefully down through the snow my foot hit something hard and before I could think I was sliding quicker than I had intended, flat on my back, towards the stream. I dug my heels in hard and flailed around in the snow, reaching out for passing bumps but failing to grip. After what seemed an age – but which must have been only a few seconds and a slide of only 20 metres or so – I saw ahead of me what could only be a collection of rocks breaking up out of the smooth flow of the glacier – for that was what I had stumbled on to. I dug in my heels again and again and steered myself into the rocks, coming to a grinding, sickening, halt. The loud rushing noise in my ears ceased abruptly and I could hear the blood pounding in my ear-drums. Snow dropped gently on my nose as I lay on my back and gathered my senses. When I stood up gingerly, fearing that I would again lose my footing or even start an avalanche that would take me down with it, I was pleased to discover that somehow I had broken no bones, and that somehow my pack had survived, although one of the shoulder straps had broken. My cameras too were intact, and I blessed Pentax for making them so robust.

Back up the glacier above me I could see the track that I had gouged out from the hillside. There was no way I could have climbed back up there even if I wanted to. Below me the snow looked much as it always does, but I knew now that its innocent white surface concealed a rock-hard sheet of ice. It seemed for a moment as if I was stuck clinging to this outcrop of rocks like a shipwreck in the middle of a sea of ice. But the stream was so much closer, I told myself, and all I had to do was reach it. I had survived the last slide, and I could survive another. I had no choice.

To my right the slope looked less severe, and the surface of the snow more uneven and broken, as if there were rocks beneath that would give me some grip, so I edged right and hoped. When I look back on that descent I realise how lucky I was, because although I had most certainly stumbled on a glacier, I had only found the tip of it, and in going to my right I reached the edge.

I covered most of the rest of the journey down on my rear; walking was impossible. However, the ground beneath the snow was a mixture of ice and loose stones and earth, and I was able to control the speed and direction of my descent to some extent, steering myself into rougher snow when necessary. If it hadn't been a fairly desperate experience it might even have been exhilarating.

At the bottom I took stock of the situation. It must have taken me only fifteen minutes or so to come down to the stream, but it had seemed an age, and ugly scars in the snow marked my passage down, as if my heels had wounded the earth and made it bleed. But I was unhurt, and my pack had not deteriorated any further. My legs felt strong (this I kept checking, as if the first sign of tiredness was a vital one. In fact I was without doubt very tired, but the adrenalin was coursing through my veins and I was not going to notice it for many hours). Above all I had reached the stream which would lead me to safety.

It was incredibly peaceful in that valley. I had dropped out of the wind, and the snow fell steeply and steadily. I tested my voice, but the words seemed to stop dead in front of my face and I was ashamed at the unnatural sounds they made; in trying to control my physical movements I seemed to have lost the ability to control my voice. A small stream coming down the hillside opposite me had frozen in mid-flow, the waterfalls standing like organ-pipes in the hall of the mountains.

"This is all very beautiful," I said to myself, "and I must remember this when I tell other people about this little episode." It was almost an academic decision, as if I was watching a film of myself in that situation, but was not actually there. In fact my body did feel rather distant from the rest of me, rather as my voice was disembodied and unrecognisable in the snow. I forced myself to check it over rather as doctors teach lepers to do to make sure that they haven't damaged themselves without noticing. My check told me that I had lost the feeling in my hands, and also to a lesser extent in my feet. My cheeks felt raw and red where they had rubbed along through the snow. When I was satisfied that I had revived my hands sufficiently I moved on towards the stream, my broken pack slung over my shoulder.

Then began a host of new problems quite different from the ones I had just survived, and all the confidence that I had just gained from that survival was soon knocked from me with my breath, as I lurched from rock to rock, tripping and stumbling over hidden obstacles under the snow. So slow was my progress along the side of the stream that it took me the same time to travel one-tenth of the distance that I had travelled on my bottom down the hillside. Thus it was quite some time before I looked up from concentrating on where my feet should go to discover that the valley had narrowed and steepened, and the stream was dropping down fast into what amounted to a ravine.

I reached the shelter of a tall, flat-sided rock at the mouth of the ravine and looked back. The scars of my descent were still visible, and they reminded me forcefully that there was no way back up there. Under my feet the snow was thin, the ground sheltered by the overhang of the rock, and somehow the rock's brown colour was reassuring amidst all that white. For a while I considered giving up and settling down to spend the night there, in the shelter, and hope that the snow would have cleared by the following day. But I knew that I would only survive a night out in those conditions with difficulty, and would be too demoralised by the awful night to be able to do much the following day. There was little chance of the snow clearing for a long time. The often-repeated cautionary tale of mountaineers who felt tired and lay down in the snow to rest, never to wake again, banished any thought of stopping. I had only one choice: to continue to follow the stream. If necessary I would have to walk in it, hoping that there were no sheer waterfalls. "Legs OK, time, yuh, still a couple of hours of some light left" (that was optimistic – the snow was making it grow darker already). I went through my check. What about my pack? It was broken, an encumbrance, should I leave it? What if I did have to spend the night out? Just for a moment these questions pulled the trigger of panic in my brain.

"Help." It was my voice again. "Help, help!" But the cries sounded foolish and futile in the middle of all that indifferent vastness, and the thin edge of my voice made me blush with shame even though there was no one to hear or see me. The shame renewed my determination. I had been stupid enough to get myself into the situation, and I had to get myself out of it. I would not call for help, I would help myself or pay for my stupidity.

This new resolve carried me way down into the ravine, and I hardly noticed the icy water as I fell into pool after pool. What looked like rocks were often just fragile, snow-covered ice bridges, and it was impossible to estimate what would and would not take my weight; I stumbled and splashed and staggered, the water coming up at first to my knees and then later to my groin. By some miracle I managed to keep my pack clear of it. I had removed my gloves some time before in order to be able to grip the rocks, and my hands had suffered in consequence. Every now and then I stopped to rub my hands, hitting them hard against a rock to try to feel the pain that would indicate the return of feeling. As soon as I felt at least some of the sensation returning I would turn back to the stream: the state of feeling in my hands seemed unimportant compared to the task before me.

I'm not sure how long that descent lasted. It was not long, perhaps three-quarters of an hour, but there was never any sign of the going getting easier. I became unwilling to look ahead of me because I never seemed to make any progress, and I concentrated only on the step ahead and where my feet would go next. Perhaps it was this concentration and this unwillingness to see what awaited me further down that prevented me from noticing it sooner, but all I remember is that suddenly the ravine had opened up into a valley again, leaving me as a small black figure beside a stream that flowed down between gentle white slopes. Moreover the sheer and ugly walls of the ravine had fallen away to reveal a squat black shape in the distance that was too square to be natural. A hut.

I fell many times as I struggled towards the hut, and I seemed to have lost all control over my limbs. Strange how the grip of fear had kept me together and goaded me on, and its release had spread me all over the snow like jelly in my eagerness to reach a visible sanctuary. I noted with relief as I got closer that a couple of ponies were hobbled in the lee of the hut, their heads against the wall out of the wind; somebody was at home. I stood still for a moment with the ponies trying to compose myself, suddenly nervous at who I should meet. I did not want to come staggering in dramatically out of the snow, and thus reveal my desperation and my stupidity in one fell swoop; I wanted to give the impression, as I loomed out of the snow and darkened the doorway of the hut, that I had just been out for a quiet stroll in the evening and it had inconveniently begun to snow. I tried to clear my face of all signs of fear or relief and to appear almost nonchalant.

The faces that turned to meet the shadow that blotted out what little light was coming in through the doorway were not unfriendly ones, and they showed no surprise at my appearance. But the three Tibetans must have appreciated the state I was in, and soon I was sitting in the prime position over the fire, where it smouldered and emanated little heat from a gutter in the hut floor. The main resident gathered a pan of snow to melt in order to make me some tea. I said very little for a long time, but I smiled continuously, partly from gratitude and partly to control my face, which was contorted with constant sneezing and shivering. After an hour or so I could feel most of the palms of my hands and all of my feet, and most of me was steaming gently. The fact that my feet had recovered their feeling whilst my fingers had not was surprising, because my feet had spent much of the time in icy water. I told myself not to worry about my fingers and that their feeling would return, and I was more surprised by the fact that the water in my waterbottle had turned to ice. The paroxysms of sneezing and shivering went on and on, long after I had stopped feeling cold. After a couple of hours of just sitting I stirred enough to remove my shoes and socks, and the old resident who had sat opposite me in silence, arranged them for me around the fire.

Gradually over those hours I had started to talk. I gathered from one of the two young porters in the hut that I had stumbled across the first hut on the path down to the Manang valley, and that my planning with the map had been quite right: the path did cross the stream only another half-a-mile downstream and there was a bridge. "Many snows," said the porter, "many snows," and he looked at me. They asked no questions about where I had come from or where the remainder of my party had disappeared to (it was rare for trekkers to move singly); I would tell them if I wanted to. "Many snows," the other porter repeated, and they looked out of the doorway into the darkness where the firelight picked out the larger snowflakes as they fell. In the end I gave them a brief account of my day's walk, facts only, no feelings. One translated my story into Tibetan for the benefit of the others, and they all three looked at me appraisingly. It was impossible to tell whether they thought that I had been lucky, stupid, brave or foolish, or whether I had just done something that they themselves did every day.

When I had recovered enough to be able to ask questions I asked the English-speaking porter what they were all doing there – did they live there? No, he said, but the old man ran the hut as a teashop when the weather allowed, which was for about four months in the year. He said that he and his friend had come up with the first signs of bad weather from Manang to see if they could guide any trekkers over the pass, and take the weaker ones on horseback. And had they? Yes, they had been to the top and back and earned good money. Furthermore it seemed that the quiet one, who looked little more than sixteen years old, had bodily carried a Tibetan porter down to that same hut that morning, after the porter's legs had seized up with the cold and lack of clothing (the majority of the eight deaths on the pass that year had been from the same cause – most of the porters were barefoot and they wore ragged shorts that gave them no protection at all). Once the frozen man had been handed over to someone with a horse who had taken him back to Manang, the porter had then gone back up to the top and recovered the load of eggs he had had to abandon, and brought it down to where it now lay in the corner of the hut. It took no great calculation on my part to appreciate that that sixteen-year-old had covered the same pass-side that I had had such difficulty with, not once, but four times in the same day.

It had been dark for quite a while when the two young Tibetans left, saying that they must lead their horses back to Manang: even for the horses a night out in that weather was potentially fatal. I could not have admired men more as I wished them a safe journey. They had done much more than me; they had been just as cold and tired, and they had known that they had to go out again into the snow for a further four hours in pitch darkness, and yet they still had given me the prime position in front of the fire.

The old man and I sat opposite each other over the smouldering wood, stirring it occasionally to try to provoke a flame, and turning my shoes and socks over and over to let them dry evenly. We did not speak, and it was a delight not to feel that pressure, but just to sit. Then he stood up and pulled a piece of corrugated iron out of the darkness to cover up the yawning hole of the doorway and indicated that he was going to sleep.

I hardly slept that night. I hadn't removed any of my clothes; I was in my sleeping-bag in a hut where there was a fire, and yet I was still cold. I concentrated on stopping myself physically from shivering to such a point that the effort of self-control became painful. I covered all of my face except my mouth, but still I could feel the sharp touch of the wind as it blew straight through the gaps in the rough stone walls of the hut. But as I lay there waiting for the dawn and the hope of some daylight warmth, desperate to urinate but not desperate enough to get out of my sleeping-bag, I thought that at least all the discomfort of the night meant one thing: I was alive, and feeling it.

When I got down to civilisation some time later I learned that

President Brezhnev had died whilst I was out in the snow, and I felt a certain sympathy towards him for it, as if our two completely separate lives had touched just for a brief moment that day, and as I went one way he had gone the other . . .

The beauty of the day after my escapade in the snow completely belied the dangers of the previous one. The sun shone clearly and steadily through a cloudless sky, which was so blue that it was almost black against the sheer brilliance of the snow. It was one of those days like the day after passing one's driving test or falling in love that makes one feel an immense amount of gratitude that things are as they are. I could only channel my gratitude in the direction of the old Tibetan keeping the hut, and even that was hard to communicate. I shook his hand hard, which act I think he found surprising, and wished him '*Namaste*' several times. For me the meaning of that word ('I salute you') could never have been more potent.

The snow must have stopped just before the two young men of the previous night had set out again for Manang, for their tracks were quite visible, indicating where the path lay. I made good progress in their footsteps, but I could see from the sliding marks left by some of the horses' hooves that they had had an arduous descent of it. Two hours down I came across a second tea-house. Here there was no sign of life, but a set of tracks from the main house to a secondary one showed where other trekkers were waiting for the snows to clear before continuing their journey, like salmon waiting for the floods to subside before trying to jump the waterfalls. I roused the owner of the house for a cup of tea, and found myself speaking Malay with him. He was one of the Manang people who had taken advantage of the special trading dispensation that a previous Nepali king had granted to the Manangba, and had spent some time in Singapore and Kuala Lumpur. It was a strange feeling, sitting there over a cup of tea in the Himalayas and speaking with a Tibetan in Malay about the city of Singapore.

As the days wore on I had to cover my face with a scarf: the brilliance of the sunlight on the snow was beginning to burn my skin. Some trekkers who were walking up experimentally from Manang to test the snow smiled at the strange apparition they met on the path, and I was stopped many times to answer questions on the state of the snow up ahead and whether I thought it possible to go over the pass the following day. I refused to commit myself to any opinion.

I had considered the sleeping-hut at the second teashop a waiting-pool full of salmon, but Manang was infinitely more so. The place was jammed with Europeans taking advantage of the sun, sprawled out on the roofs. They were waiting for the snow to melt out of the bottleneck of the pass. Over several glasses of hot rakshi (rice whisky) in the kitchen of the house that I had finally found accommodation in I found myself a hero. Someone had discovered that I had come over the pass in the blizzard, and soon I was being questioned from all sides about what it was like. Everyone in the town was talking of the pass; it was a threat to all of them that they had to conquer. I had conquered it in hard conditions, and I was a hero, and each time I told the story of my narrow escape I forgot a little more of how stupid and how lucky I had been. I cut a lot of ice in Manang, and I shouldn't have done. Then someone had some hashish and we all got stoned; I slept, sleeping all of the sleep that I should have had the previous night.

I spent the day in the village, basking in my own reflected glory. However the numbness of my fingers, which had at first been a useful testament to the extreme dangers I had survived, began to worry me. I was directed down to see an American doctor living in an outpost of the Himalayan Rescue Association three kilometres from Manang. A board advertising a free cup of tea along with advice to any callers stood on the track near the outpost. Dr Steven Boyer was not impressed by the tale of my descent, as I suspected he wouldn't be. He had come across the likes of me many times before. He said that he spent half his time warning trekkers who dropped in to see him of the dangers of the mountains, and trying to beat down their arrogance.

He listed the options for rescuing trekkers who get into difficulties. "An SOS message could be sent out for a helicopter, but news travels slowly in this neck of the woods, and by the time the helicopter is primed to take off in Kathmandu anyone stuck on a mountainside up here would be an icicle. Even if there is time to make a rescue attempt the helicopter will not leave the ground until someone has guaranteed payment for the job, at £400 per flying hour. You'd do better to hire a mule – that is, as long as you were well enough to survive a ten-day jolting down to the road at Dumre."

Dr Boyer had been on one attempt to climb Everest and was to go on another the following year. He was primarily up at Manang researching into the effect of altitude on the thickness of the Tibetans' blood, but mountain rescue was also part of his brief. He had led one attempt up the neighbouring Pisang peak the preceding month, to look for one of a party of Yugoslavian climbers who had fallen on the mountain. "We found nothing," he said. "I'm not surprised. We were too late and we did not have the right men or equipment. From my window here I can see the exact spot where I know that body is, and I know that we cannot get it down by climbing. So we'll leave it there." Although he did not say as much I could see that the doctor considered it fitting to leave the body where it was as a tribute to the mountain, rather than to waste unnecessary time and lives in further search attempts. It was a salutary story.

As I left, Dr Boyer pointed out to me the high path that he recommended I took down to Pisang, the next township down the valley, a path where he said he went jogging every morning. I wondered what the Tibetans, bent double beneath their loads, made of their jogging doctor.

Going down was a pleasure, and the days passed quickly. In Pisang I stayed with an old man and his wife, and together we watched the sun go down behind Annapurna II. They gave me aloos (potatoes) and chang (fermented barley beer) for my evening meal, the tiny potatoes cooked in garlic and chilli. Chips were never better. Later, at Chame, I had my first real wash for three weeks in the luxury of the hot springs, and lay back absorbing heat from the sun above me and the rocks beneath. I had left the snows far behind by the time I reached Bagarchap, and both villages and hillsides had begun to resume some of their previous colour. In Bagarchap it was the day of the cow, and the beasts' horns were garlanded with flowers. I wondered if the animals realised their importance on that day as they went about their daily business.

In the corner of the bhatti that I stayed in at Bagarchap an old lama was intoning steadily from a collection of handwritten leaves of paper, rocking gently backwards and forwards as he read. The papers, which were yellowed with age, were tied together with a ribbon to form a book. The lama wore a maroon hat and cloak and sat in a shaft of light that came down through a skylight above him, giving him an ethereal presence in the darkened room. He looked like a Rembrandt cardinal. I thought him much too majestic and mysterious to dare to take a photograph of him, but life seemed to go on much as usual around him and he was largely ignored except when someone took him some refreshment – which they did at regular intervals.

But when the lama put away his holy words and joined us round the fire that night, he surprised and disappointed me by drinking as much rakshi as the next man, and making what I understood to be bawdy jokes. He must have been a ngag-pa – one who takes up the priesthood as anyone does any job – and not a tulku, a reincarnated priest who is therefore accorded much more respect. Some villages in Tibet itself are under contract to provide a certain number of priests to the neighbourhood temple every decade, and in such a context I was not surprised to hear the story of two young lamas in the Manang district who deserted their monastery to work as porters on trekking expeditions. Apparently the Tibetans only visit their temples on special festival days, and the rest of the time a lama's life is spent in touring the villages and houses doing various small services and rituals for a fee. This particular ngag-pa obviously combined his spiritual powers with healing, and later on in the evening a young girl was brought before him with an ache in her neck, which he set about curing by a combination of blowing and recitation.

I dawdled more and more as the sun grew stronger and the grass grew greener. I did not want to reach the road. There was always someone beneath the banyan trees in the village squares to smile at and to smoke a cigarette with. I took to taking the more difficult and roundabout routes, even though someone told me a story of two trekkers who had been pushed to their deaths into the river-gorge off one of these quieter tracks. No one threatened me.

The mountains themselves no longer seemed threatening as I looked back from the hill at Bahundanda late one evening. I knew that I could not really justify delaying any more – Dumre and the main road were only two days' easy walking ahead, and the impersonal world of hotel rooms would soon swallow me up. From my vantage point on the hill I could see ladies of the Paharia

(Hindu hill-people) going visiting in the evening sun, while a father and son walked hand-in-hand back from school at the next town down. I could see a trekker coming up the path below me, and watched him stop beneath one of the pathside banyan trees, in front of a mother and her daughter who were taking it in turns to cry '*suntala, suntala*'. He dipped into his pocket and presented a handful of change to the woman, who took a few tangerines from the top of one of the pyramids of fruit stacked in front of her and handed them to the foreigner. As he turned away the woman smiled at her daughter, who was giggling at the strange-looking man.

I started down the hillside with mixed feelings. The trekker's down jacket was tied around his waist but mine was still zipped tight – the cold of the Himalayas seemed to have penetrated through to my bones. Nevertheless, as I moved down the path towards him, I felt strong and lean, better than I had felt for many years. But I was not looking forward to the days back in the restaurants and on the streets of Asia's cities; I was not looking forward to interminable and desultory conversations with fellow-travellers on subjects that should have died long ago, and I did not particularly want to speak to this one. Inevitably he would want to know what lay ahead of him up the track, but I did not want to stop. Thus it was that when he stopped and said good day I only nodded and smiled. The giant oaks were casting enormous shadows down the terraced rice-padi and clouds of crickets flew up from the soft grass beneath my feet, their wings rattling like locusts, and they made a noise like the crackling of a fast-burning tinder fire as they collided with the tall, brittle stalks of the ripe rice crop. As I passed the suntala seller I looked over my shoulder to see the trekker watching me from the top of the hill; moments later he had disappeared in the direction of the mountains. I was stopped by a man selling hashish just beyond the suntala sellers, and I bought some of the best quality he had. I had a feeling I would need it for India.

The sun never seemed to shine in Calcutta. It was always there if you wanted to look at it, but its warmth did not seem to reach the streets. Rather it was the thick and heavy haze that communicated the heat, sticking and clinging and dragging tempers down with it into the gutter. The piles of rotting garbage on the pavements seemed to emanate their own heat along with their stench, and a similar smell-laden warmth came from the walls covered with drying pats of cow shit.

The contrast to the peace and beauty of the foothills of the Himalayas was hard to take. Amongst all this detritus, life on the streets of Calcutta was lived to its utmost limits. I saw a bear, an elephant, several monkeys and scores of snake-charmers on the pavements, all working to attract the attention of some of the passing crowd for long enough to be able to wheedle a few paise or even a rupee out of them. The elephant seemed bored and most of the snakes were feigning sleep, tired of being poked with sticks. The bear was patently miserable and conveyed as much to all onlookers as it clattered around in its chains, climbing perfunctorily up and down little wooden steps dressed in a tatty apron. But it was the human street performers who were the most depressing of all.

The most effective of these human entertainments was performed on a mat in the middle of the bus station by two hideously deformed men. It was some kind of romantic opera, with one man playing the boy-hero and the other, wearing a tattered tutu, playing the girl-heroine. They had only one distorted leg between them, but their grotesque parody of a grand love-scene drew a huge crowd, and the coins chinked and shimmered as they rained down on the mat beside the passionate one-legged pseudo-ballerina, as he clutched his heart with a fingerless hand. Even the legless men on trolleys who accosted passers-by by virtually tripping them up could never hope to match the income of those two stars, and no doubt their parents would have been proud of them if they had been present to watch. Perhaps too they would have been proud of their original decision to maim the children at birth, in order to give them more chance on the competitive streets of the city.

I found just walking in the streets in the daytime a nightmare of jostling and constant harassment. Every inch of the pavement seemed to be someone-or-other's territory, and once I had stepped unknowingly on to it then I was ready prey to people who wanted to buy, to sell, or just to have money. At night the street wanderers lay down where they stood, and the pavements were littered with the sleeping forms of the harijanna, shrouded with the only piece of linen they had, more to keep the dirt off than to keep warm. They looked like corpses. Many of them were country labourers who had come into the city when their harvests failed, and who had never managed to leave again.

Even the transport was depressing. Where Burma had horse-carts and Thailand had trishaws, the rickshaw-wallahs in Calcutta just used their own two feet. For me this epitomised the lack of humanity in the city – and even in the nation. There was no question of using even the mechanical assistance of a bicycle to earn their daily bread. The passenger mounted the cart (he was usually very fat and opulent), the rickshaw-wallah lifted the traces (he was lean and sweating), and off they went at a trot, the handbell jangling all the while. Even though I found the principle offensive I had to admit, as I leapt out of the way of yet another red-faced rickshaw-wallah hurtling down the street with all the blood vessels in his neck looking fit to burst, they were effective, and the rickshaw-wallahs were better off than many of the outcasts who picked through the piles of rubbish on the pavements.

There was a traffic jam in every street and it was usually better to walk. The city fathers had been building a metro system for several years, but had only made tiny progress. All the labour on the scheme was manual, of course, for who could justify using machines when there was so much reserve manpower lying unused in the streets? The city was pock-marked with shallow pits where men clawed handfuls of earth out of the ground and dumped it into shallow baskets. The baskets then passed up the human chain out of the pit and ended up on the heads of women who spent their days walking backwards and forwards between the nearby tip and the lip of the pit. Balanced on almost every female hip was a child, earth-covered face streaked with recent tears as the earth crumbled through the basket above and fell in a light, gritty rain. The children appreciated the misery and the futility of the work just as their mothers did, and every year the monsoon rains turned the earth back into mud, and every year the tips slid back into the pits. The best that can be said of it is that it makes work for some of the city-dwellers.

Between all this chaos flows the Hooghly river, its water sizzling with insect life as it moves sluggishly towards the sea. Instead of cleaning up and carrying away the effluent of the city the Hooghly spreads disease up through the bustee villages built on its banks.

I stayed in the Sally Army Red Shield guest-house in Sudder

Street, right opposite the discreet Fairlawn hotel, which had been run by an English couple since colonial days, and where all the Sally Army residents went for their afternoon tea. Like the hotel, the guest-house was also run by an English couple. Their private quarters were full of horse brasses and flying ducks tacked to the wall alongside winter fox-hunting prints. On the polished table-tops stood black-and-white photographs of grandchildren on summer lawns in Sussex. The husband spent much of his time in this inner sanctuary, and we saw more of his matronly lady-wife. She must have thought her guests a strange bunch, for the Sally Army seemed to attract the most down-and-out of the Europeans in the same way as the streets outside seemed to attract the most down-and-out of the harijanna. There was smoking in the dorms after lights out, just as in school days, though in this case the hot air was heavy with the sweet scent of hashish, and the conversation did not dwell on football and gold stars, but on hits, deals and stashes. Of course this was strictly against the rules of the Sally Army, but the only rule that seemed relevant in Calcutta was that of survival, for Indians and Europeans alike.

The Sally Army noticeboard made sad reading. It was covered in pleas for help or information that might lead to the tracing of long-lost children. The forlorn parents had pinned photographs of their Robins and Carolines alongside the notices. Some of the pleas dated back several years, and many of them were reproduced at other similar guest-houses throughout India, but few of them could have been effective in helping to find the missing persons: the new Robin or Caroline would be far removed from his or her photographic image. Those faces were fresh and innocent, as their parents liked to remember them – just out of school, on holiday in France with the family, or even a studio portrait of the newly gowned and hooded graduate. How different the reality would be now.

I found Calcutta hard to take, partly because it is the fate of every traveller to focus his attention on the streets, and those streets were full of tiredness, tragedy and filth, and partly because the Indian culture was too large and too new for me to want to attempt to assimilate it at this late stage in my travels. Men here had retreated to their basic forms. Even the outcasts had a part to play in the city life, and they didn't attempt to change it – no one did. This was their fate, and it was largely stark and unattractive. After ten days in

Calcutta I left for Puri, one of India's four holy towns – though I don't think I set out actually looking for some proof of hope and faith in life; I just wanted to get out of the city, and Puri had a fine beach.

We get our word juggernaut from Puri; it derives from the annual festival of the Jaggarnath temple which dominates the town physically (it is 58 metres tall) and symbolically. Puri only comes alive once a year when the image of the god (a carved log from a nearby forest) is hauled round the streets on an enormous cart, over 14 metres high and 10 metres square. It takes 4,000 professional cart-pullers to haul all the carts in the procession, and once moving they are virtually unstoppable. Extreme devotees have been known to throw themselves under the wheels of these juggernauts carrying their Jaggarnath in order to be able to acquire merit for their next incarnation by dying in his sight.

Although the Jaggarnath festival was long since over when I arrived many of the city dwellers from inland areas had come to Puri for the festival of Durga Puja, to bathe in the sea for purification. The town's promenade was lined with guest-houses, and a constant stream of families moved over the sands between the sun and the shade. The act of bathing itself had little dignity or ceremony, as the sea was rough on that part of the coast and the surf rolled the giggling, fully-clothed women around in the shallows like barrels. Further out to sea the more daring and less clothed of the menfolk jiggled their bellies as they jumped the waves and kicked water at each other.

The Europeans also bathed on the beach in their own colony a short distance up the beach. We were considerably more scantily clad and considerably more seaworthy than the Indians; we thought them crazy to wear all their best clothes both on the sand and in the water, and they thought us obscene in the way that we flaunted our bodies in daylight in full view of the town. But whilst the grandmothers in the family group pursed their lips into a thin line of disapproval that matched the tightness of their grey buns of hair, calling to their grandchildren to stay close to them, the grandfathers were lured away along the beach. In their black jackets and beneath their black umbrellas they looked like predatory crows as they trailed slowly over the sand, their eyes fixed on the spots where we were deploying our flesh to the sight of the sun.

To walk out from the promenading and religious bathing part of the town was to pass through a collection of differing scenes. First came the bulk of the bathers, the reasonably well-to-do families with their best silks and their sand-shovelling children. Next came a stretch of sand backed by a strange collection of shuttered and silent grand houses that seemed to sprout from the sand. These were holiday homes of the very rich, and the architecture varied enormously from the very colonial to the very Moghul. In front of these few houses that were open were the more elaborate family parties. Striped canvas awnings were rigged over the parents as they dozed on the beach, and a couple of fishermen in conical straw hats looked after the children and made sure they didn't venture too far into the surf. A day's work as a lifeguard to the children of one of these families is a godsend to the fisherman, who can earn good money for doing what to him is not work at all.

Beyond these richer beach-bums come the real beach-bums – the Europeans – and behind them hover the men in black. But the old gentlemen go no further than here, for a little further along the beach is the fishermen's village, and even the constant attentions of the sea and the sand cannot keep that clean.

Fish are notorious for smelling quickly and evilly in hot climates, so it is hardly surprising that the piece of beach where several hundred fishermen work, breed, eat and sleep – all in a few hundred yards – smells strongly whichever way the wind is blowing. The fishermen were not Orissan people, but came from the neighbouring state of Andara Pradesch, but I was never sure whether it was this, or the fact that they spent all of their lives either on or beside the sea, that made their skins considerably darker than those of the locals. Certainly they kept clear of the locals, and the only movement towards the town from the village was that of the women and children who made a regular journey to the nearest well for their supply of fresh water.

When I first arrived I assumed that the encampment on the beach was just another bustee village like those I had seen in Calcutta, and I didn't relate the great wedges of wood lying on the sand between the huts to boats at all. I took little notice of the women sitting sewing sail-cloth outside their huts and boys playing with their kites, nor did I realise that the village was empty of men. Then, one afternoon, I rounded the corner from where I was staying to have an evening's walk along the beach and was confronted by a changed seascape. The water was covered with small brown and khaki triangular sails, all coming from roughly the same spot on the horizon, and all aiming for the bustee village. Despite the fact that the sails were quite plainly straining to master the weight of the wind, they hardly seemed to be moving at all. But moving they were, albeit slowly, and some of the first had already arrived in the now-animated village, and I soon realised the reason for the slowness of their progress towards the beach.

All the way along the coast the surf was considerable, and surf that was rough enough to roll fat Indian ladies around in the shallows was rough enough to capsize any normal boat several times over before it had reached those shallows. Thus the wooden hulls of these boats were enormously heavy, and the landing process was an exhilarating one, watched by wives and children with a keen appreciation of their menfolk's skill. Where the open water ended and the surf began in earnest the fishermen pulled down their sails and manoeuvred their boats with steerage oars into the correct position to ride the waves into the beach. A particularly lucky boat with a favourable wave could ride right into the shallows in one movement, but usually the weight of the boat or the strength of a cross-current was too much for the puny strength of the crewmen on the steering-oar, and the craft would slew out of control, broadside on to the waves. If the next approaching wave was some yards behind, the fishermen had time to get their boat at right angles once again to the beach and to brace themselves for the next ride. But if the next wave followed on too quickly most of the crew would be swept overboard like skittles and would have to fight hard to regain their places, their balance, and their control of the swinging boat. Over fifty per cent of the boats finally arrived on the beach with their crews floundering along in their wake, but no wave, however it might break on top of the hull, managed to overturn one.

I understood the phenomenon of the slow-moving and supremely stable boats when they were turned up like beached whales at the feet of the onlookers. The wood they were made from was massive. There was no attempt at planking or sealing the hulls. Like the carts that carried the images of Jaggarnath, these boats had been crudely sculpted out of the hardwood trees that grew inland, with perhaps two or three trunks contributing enough bulk and weight to make one hull. The finished product only remotely resembled a boat, but when the lashings that held it together were undone and the whole fell into two, three or even four parts, these enormous lumps of wood did not look like anything recognisable. This explained why I had not related the village to fishing or to boats, even though there had been lumps of boat lying all over the sand on my previous visit.

The boats needed to be heavy for the surf, but they needed to fall into bits to be carried, for what the surf could not toss or lift, man certainly could not. As it was, it took eight or ten men to shift the larger of the pieces up to the shore once the lashings had been undone, and they only achieved that with a good deal of grimacing.

The fishermen apparently went to sea for a few days at a time, during which they must have been constantly awash. Such crudely fashioned boats were not built to be watertight. Nor did they have any shelter from the sun apart from their sails and their conical hats. In these conditions they aged fast, their faces were lined and wrinkled and their hair thin. Only the shape of their bodies showed their true age, and most of them must have been in their twenties or thirties: the sea was too hard a taskmaster to allow men to survive it to a grand old age.

The men's share of the work ended once their boats had been conveyed (in bits) up to rest alongside their huts. Whilst at sea they had travelled as a fleet and returned as a fleet, once onshore they negotiated over the price of their fish as individuals – or rather, their wives did. The stretch of sand between the sea and the village was chaos as the womenfolk spread their husbands' catches around their feet and squatted opposite the buyers who had flocked from the town once the first sail had appeared on the horizon.

When I finally moved away from the fishermen's village that evening, carrying a fish that I had not intended to buy and which the other dealers had obviously refused to touch because it had been in the sun too long (as I found out when I asked my hotel-keeper to cook it for me), the last of the boats was ashore and the last of the loaded baskets was on its way to the waiting town and the lorries for Calcutta. Behind me the fishermen had come back on to the beach after their meal, but they had not come down to view the sunset. "Thank God for the sea," I murmured to myself as I turned my back on dozens of figures squatting in the shallows almost on their own doorsteps.

Beside the temple and the beach there was not much to see in Puri but, as with the other three holy cities of India, the place attracted its fair share of weird foreigners, and the inevitable traveller's tales. Demonstrate a knowledge of Buddhism, tell the story of a stay in a Thai temple, show the scars of a motorcycle crash on Bali, and you scored points. Half the time I tried to restrain myself from being sucked into the competition, but when someone made what I considered a crass remark about a place or a people I thought I knew well, I found it difficult not to put them right. Most people became aware that I had been around a long time and they avoided me.

The exception was Mireille, a French girl who had ended up in that ramshackle hotel in Puri against her will. Whenever I came in or went out she would be sitting at the long communal table, sometimes reading a book and sometimes sleeping with her head on her arms. She had been a secretary in Paris with no plans or ambitions until the day that a friend had pressed her into accompanying her to India. The friend had then decided that India was just awful, borrowed Mireille's savings and flown home, promising to send the money back when she arrived. Mireille was waiting, as she had been for weeks. Puri was as good a place as any to wait, she would say. She accepted her fate with a wry sense of humour. "I am one of those people who never have luck," she used to say. "I went into school, sat there, and then came out the other side, and no one noticed. No one said, 'There goes Mireille.'" Ironically, being marooned and hopeless in Puri gave her a distinction she had never known before, and everyone knew and liked her. She was the only person I talked to on a regular basis, and she would describe her quiet Parisian life in some detail.

Left to myself I developed a fascination with Indian idiom laid upon English. This went beyond collectable joke teashop signs like 'Banana lassi, pineapple lassi, toilet paper, mango lassi . . .' After I left Puri I crossed India from one side to the other by train. I was asked by a fellow passenger if I had 'a match to my credit'. Another struck up a conversation about 'the hilly people' of Mizoram, presumably the hill-tribes, and every now and then he spiced his side of the conversation with, 'Let it be, that's no matter' which seemed to have come straight out of a minor character in

Shakespeare. Pronunciation was a separate pitfall. After an interminable wait in the middle of nowhere whilst the sweat poured and the peanut shells piled high on the floor, my friend declared that our predicament was 'Indian fellow'. I continued to nod stupidly while my brain rattled. Was the problem that the driver was one? Or was there one lying strapped to the rails in front of the locomotive? Or was it the Indian equivalent of '*C'est la vie*'? I was about to plump for the last when someone with less alcohol on his breath than my neighbour explained in my other ear that "the problem we are facing at this current moment is that of engine failure." Ah, *engine failure*!

But the best English of the lot that I collected on that journey was the series of roadsigns that greeted me when I had at last decamped from the train and was bumping along the road to my destination – the Rajasthani town of Jaisalmer – in the back of a jeep. 'Hunting is prohibited, sight-seeing is solicited', read the first sign. The poet of Chetak (the road-builders) was nothing if not persistent, and a few hundred yards later came the next: 'Chetak maintains road. You maintain speed.' And then, just before the city gates, the punch line: 'Chetak toils day and night. You drive like hell.' It was a great introduction to a city.

I was in Jaisalmer to kill time. In doing so I was blending with my surroundings, because all the locals were doing the same. I had a couple of weeks left to wait before my flight left Delhi for Moscow, and the desert town seemed a good enough place to sit them out. Besides, I had had enough of cities, of mountains, of seas and of forests. The desert was about all there was left to see.

The streets of Jaisalmer were quiet and the sand blew everything clean. The test match between India and Australia played on every radio in the town, and listening to it made the days pass more easily. I sat in the marketplace – Manak Chowk – and read about how it used to be a very important trading arena on the caravan route linking India with the Middle East. My hotel keeper told me that today's trade between Manak Chowk and the markets across the border in Pakistan was illegal. Trucks laden with electrical goods left Jaisalmer in the dead of night to cross the desert and exchange their goods for Pakistani heroin.

I hired a camel and a guide and went out into the desert on a couple of day-trips. The ride was fiendishly uncomfortable. Only when the camel-driver (who sat behind me) really got to work on the hindquarters of the beast with his stick did the animal ever quicken its step, and it usually vented its anger at being so goaded by biting the rear of the animal in front, with the result that the other would then go charging off ahead in a cloud of sand, with my guide clinging to the pommel of the saddle and swearing horribly. I was only too glad when ours actually did run, because the ride up top unaccountably smoothed out when it did, rather in the same way as a car will ride more smoothly over a bumpy road when it is driven fast. There are altogether too many separate movements to a camel's walk ('walk' seems hardly an adequate word) to get used to in one or two days. Just when I thought we were on the down-swing another hoof would hit the ground and another part of the beast's back beneath me would rise sharply with agonising effect.

In this way I saw what the deserts had to offer to the north and south. It was a landscape of sand and sandstone, broken by patches of thorn, cactus and the spiky bushes that my camel seemed to relish. On the skyline stood rows of royal cenotaphs dating from the time of Jaisalmer's trade importance, and occasionally the sand thinned to reveal a stretch of ancient paved road that unnacountably headed for the horizon only to disappear in a matter of metres, like a glimpse of unexplained history.

The desert dwellers (goanwallas) are nomadic people and whole villages of thatched beehive huts were deserted. My camel-driver pointed out a rare Great Indian Bustard wheeling in the sky. "Its eyes shine like the eyes of a deer. Its voice is very sweet. When it is in flight its wings produce a sound pleasing to the ear," writes the flowery author of the Indian guide to Jaisalmer. To me it just looked like a big bird flying in the distance. A woman with a copper bowl under her arm in the middle of nowhere stood and watched us go past, whilst her daughter tottered in pursuit of a goat with a twig, fully intending to thwack the animal when she reached it, but never quite reaching it. The goat was part of the family and knew the family's habits.

The Thar desert stretches for 75,000 square miles around Jaisalmer. In 1974 India staged its first nuclear test there, and it is certainly an inhospitable place. In the months of May and June a hot wind blows across the sands and makes it impossible to travel at more than fifteen kilometres per hour on a motor-bike along the desert tracks, but in January the night-time temperatures drop below freezing point. As with the wastes in the Himalayas, it is the kind of place that made me wonder what it was that caused people to choose to live in such difficult conditions. The Thar desert has a population of fourteen million, making it one of the most densely populated arid zones in the world.

On the second afternoon on camel-back we arrived at the beginning of the dharna, the shifting sands that covered all pathways. "This is Sam," said my guide. "We can go no further." When I asked him who Sam was and why this person would not let us go any further he grinned, and pointed to a sign. "There Sam." The sign declared that no person was allowed to go beyond the confines of Sam in the direction of the border, by order, but the only thing that marked the place itself was a teashop on the edge of the rolling expanse of dunes. It was the simplest teashop I had ever seen. A woman sat behind a cactus, which protected her paraffin stove from the wind. The only other equipment was a bucket of water, a copper pot of milk, and what looked like an old school tuck-box, but this was enough. She used the sand for her washing-up, and the open lid of the box was the shop window where she displayed half-a-dozen packs of glucose biscuits and a similar number of packets of beedees. It was impossible not to have a cup of tea at Sam.

Given the surroundings she did brisk business. I could just imagine her husband bringing her to work with her tuck-box on the back of the family camel every morning, and returning to pick her up in the evening after office hours . . . Whilst we sat there sipping our chay as slowly as possible – every activity was eked out in the consciousness that once it was finished there would be nothing else to do – customers came and went in a steady trickle. We could see them coming for miles. The desert was flat away from the dunes themselves, and out of it came camels in twos and threes, all making a beeline through the mirage towards the teashop in the sand. The riders dismounted with few words, and sat cross-legged between their animals as they sipped their tea. When they had drained their glasses and finished any conversation that they thought worth waiting for, they would mount again and disappear to some other point of the compass into the shimmering distance. I wondered whether they really had something to do, or whether they were just wasting time, like me.

No one seemed particularly surprised to see me at Sam. One man was keen that I should buy his camel. "My camel good – taking?" He tugged at my sleeve as he asked the question and pointed at one of the chewing beasts. I tried to make it clear that I had no real use for a camel, and that he would do better trying to sell it to someone who needed it. I thought that I had finally got my message over when one of the more aloof tea-drinkers seemed to intervene on my behalf. He was a tall and handsome Rajasthani, with the typical bright orange turban and strong upward-curling moustache, and although he said nothing he nodded as if he understood my every word. He beckoned the would-be camel seller over and whispered something into his ear. The seller seemed enlightened by what he had been told, and came back to me with new purpose and hope in his eyes. "My camel *very* good – taking?" he said. It was a pity to have to disappoint him again after he really thought he had got the formula right, but I indicated to my guide that I thought it was time we left Sam.

10 *Delhi to Devon*

I couldn't decide what I felt about going home. The last month of travel was dwarfed by a piece of paper in my wallet – my ticket. I was to arrive in time for Christmas. The concept of a family Christmas seemed remote. I had spent the last two in Asia, the first on a beach in Thailand and the second on the *Barlian*. Nevertheless, go home I must, I knew. I hadn't planned to do anything else, and the whole of my travel had revolved around my self-imposed two-year limit, which I had already exceeded.

And so when the date on my ticket drew near I dug myself out of the pocket of India that I had hidden myself in and dragged my slow length to Delhi for the last time. There I joined the throng of the hollow-eyed whites on Paharganj, the cheap quarter of New Delhi. I kicked my heels for two days, finished the last of my books and sold it, wrote incongruous things in my diary on the grounds that they were great literature, calculated how much more money I could spend without having to break into another 50 dollar bill, and smoked the rest of my dope.

I never allowed myself seriously to consider what I would do with myself once I got home, and yet when I dropped my thongs, T-shirt and second pair of trousers by the head of one of the homeless sleeping on the street I was aware that I was doing something mighty symbolic, marking the end of an era. And then events intervened, as they had done so often in the past.

I had a sleepless final night in a stiflingly hot room. At first I thought that I was just over-excited, but as the night wore on I began to appreciate that something was not quite right within me. This feeling was confirmed when I hailed a taxi in the early hours of daylight and sat inside it on the way to the airport shivering uncontrollably. Just my luck to get a cold on my way home, I muttered to myself.

The departure of my Aeroflot flight was delayed for four hours, and as I sat for those interminable hours in the airport lounge my shivering fits got worse.

The contrast between the heat of India and the cold of Moscow in mid-December would have been hard to take at the best of times, but for me as I staggered off the aircraft the sight of a heavy snowfall was more than a depressant – it was a physical barrier. There were no taxis at the airport, and the nearest hotel was a quarter of a mile down the road. A quarter of a mile! A month previously I had been doing twenty miles and a few thousand feet in a day, and here I was baulking at a few hundred yards! But standing was hard enough for me in that state, let alone walking.

I managed the trek across the snow in short stages, and it was less difficult than I had feared. The hotel receptionist seemed not to notice anything wrong with me, and gave me a room which I was to share with a Syrian businessman. The latter must have been surprised at how much time I spent flat out in bed as a result of my 'cold'.

After thirty-six hours of lying prone I decided that my cold was improving. I went downstairs and forced most of a meal down my throat before sitting in the foyer to wait for a bus to town. The bus arrived, bleak-faced passengers staring out into the snow. I staggered up the steps, pushed a few kopecks into the ticket machine and watched the suburbs roll.

After half a dozen stops I had to get out. I was ready to vomit and could hardly stand. There was a railway line behind the bus-stop, and beyond that a few tall blocks of flats. A dribble of people came steadily out of the flats to stand at the bus-stop, and only a few of them looked at the foreigner sitting on the bench with his head in his hands. When I felt strong enough I crossed the road and caught a bus back in the opposite direction. Three stops along I was jerked out of my daze by a fearsome-looking lady in uniform who wanted to check my ticket. I hadn't bought one. A torrent of abuse in Russian rained on my head and shoulders as I fished into my pockets and proffered a handful of change, flushing red with illness and embarrassment. The bus discarded me at the airport, where I sat in the warmth and collected my thoughts.

I'd often said in jest whilst on the road that there were only two ways of arriving home in style – haggard and emaciated or thoroughly tanned and healthy. I had so nearly made it the second way, but the pendulum had swung, and I realised that I was badly ill with some kind of oriental disease.

I went to the enquiries desk in the terminal and asked for a doctor, and was directed to a modern surgery. The woman doctor spoke no English and I no Russian, so the only symptoms that I could mime were the shivering and the sickness. She took my temperature with a gracious smile and was suitably impressed by the reading to order an ambulance to take me the quarter-mile back to my hotel. In the foyer I booked myself on to that evening's flight to London and sent a telegram to warn my parents that I was coming.

Ten hours later I was in Heathrow, negotiating the narrow lanes of the arrivals lounge and staring at the toy policemen with their funny hats and lopsided Christmas grins. I felt a true foreigner, and was so taken aback by the fact that the girl behind the information desk spoke English as well as – if not better than – me, that I was completely at a loss for words. To fill the embarrassed silence whilst I ransacked my brain to find my own language and marshal it into a sophisticated form she asked me which country I was from, sir.

The words I eventually found were 'medical centre', and not long afterwards I found myself outside the place itself, having first established that there was no one waiting for me and no messages. I had beaten my telegram back, not realising telegrams had become first class post in my absence. The satisfaction of having achieved one of my two ways of coming home in style seemed hollow when I realised that that style was to have no audience. In the doctor's waiting room I decided that I felt a lot better, and began to fear that I would be denied the little glory that remained – that of relating weakly from my hospital bed how I had staggered gasping across the continents to breathe my last in Tooting.

When the doctor finally arrived he took a look at my eyes and my urine and told me flatly that I had hepatitis. Somewhere out there I must have eaten a chappati that someone had cleaned the toilet with.

By the time that I was safely cocooned in the family home and the dog had conceded that it was me, despite the funny smell, jaundice had set in. In the blurred and wobbly weeks that followed I could not decide which were the more remote – the scenes of English life that swam past me or my more recent life abroad. Sitting in the old armchair, watching the same old faces come and go on the TV screen and treating myself to the luxury of BBC 2, which had finally reached the village, I knew what it was like to be one of those squidgy sleeping-bags squeezed back into its container bag. The villagers did not know what to make of the stranger with the careful English, the hard stare (a hangover from the old 'don't-you-dare-try-to-get-your-hands-on-my-travellers'-cheques' look) and the yellow-tinged face, who took increasingly frequent constitutionals down the main street dressed in a huge black coat.

My remedy was something that doctors could not prescribe. I needed to reabsorb my Englishness through a fair tonnage of Yorkshire puddings, apple pies and Sunday roasts. I needed the newspapers, walks in the woods, summer holidays in the Lake District and plenty of pints of bitter. Only once I had learned to accept all these things once again would I cease to be a stranger in my own country.